ARCHAEOLOGY AND THE REVELATION OF JOHN

A VISUAL GUIDE

David A. deSilva

Baker Academic
a division of Baker Publishing Group
Grand Rapids, Michigan

Published by Baker Academic
a division of Baker Publishing Group
Grand Rapids, Michigan
BakerAcademic.com

Printed in the United States of America

Library of Congress Cataloging-in-Publication Data
Names: deSilva, David A., 1967– author
Title: Archaeology and the Revelation of John : a visual guide / David A. deSilva.
Description: Grand Rapids, Michigan : Baker Academic, a division of Baker Publishing Group, [2026] | Series: Archaeology and the New Testament | Includes bibliographical references and index
Identifiers: LCCN 2025054099 | ISBN 9781540969231 paperback | ISBN 9781493455881 ebook | ISBN 9781493455898 pdf
Subjects: LCSH: Bible. Revelation—Antiquities
Classification: LCC BS2825.55 .D47 2026
LC record available at https://lccn.loc.gov/2025054099

Unless otherwise indicated, Scripture translations are the author's own.

Unless otherwise credited, photos are the author's.

Cover design by Paula Gibson
Cover photo © David deSilva

Baker Publishing Group publications use paper produced from sustainable forestry practices and postconsumer waste whenever possible.

26 27 28 29 30 31 32 7 6 5 4 3 2 1

To Donna Jean,
my favorite traveling companion,
in honor of our thirty-fifth wedding anniversary

CONTENTS

Introduction ix
Abbreviations xv

1. The Roman Province of Asia 1
2. Patmos 19
3. Ephesus 29
4. Smyrna 66
5. Pergamum 83
6. Thyatira 113
7. Sardis 121
8. Philadelphia 138
9. Laodicea 145
10. Rome 165
11. Reading Revelation in Roman Asia 193

Bibliography 207
Author Index 219
Scripture and Ancient Writings Index 223
Subject Index 227

INTRODUCTION

The popularity of tours of "The Seven Churches of Revelation"—an itinerary offered by almost all tour companies that cater especially to a Christian clientele—shows that many readers of Revelation intuitively sense that immersing themselves in what remains of the lived spaces of John's congregations will bring them closer to understanding this text. What such travelers intuit aligns with the approach that almost all biblical scholars would encourage as the surest path to interpreting Revelation in the manner most in keeping with the nature of the text and the purposes of its author.

It is easy to forget, in the midst of its array of visions, that Revelation is written as a letter. After an introduction in the third person reminiscent of the opening of several books of the Hebrew prophets (compare Rev. 1:1–3 with Isa. 1:1; Jer. 1:1–3; Hosea 1:1; Amos 1:1), John writes: "John to the seven congregations in Asia: grace to you and peace" (Rev. 1:4). This is a signal to readers in every age that John has a particular audience in mind as he gives shape to and sends out his text, an audience that he will further specify as consisting of the Christian groups "in Ephesus, Smyrna, Pergamum, Thyatira, Sardis, Philadelphia, and Laodicea" (1:11). As the German scholar Johann Jakob Wettstein affirmed as early as 1752: "The Apocalypse was written specifically for the benefit of certain people who were living at that time, and for the purpose of being understood by them."[1]

Another signal appears when we set Revelation alongside the canonical book that most resembles it—namely, Daniel. The contents of the book of Daniel are presented as visions pertaining to "what things must necessarily

1. Wettstein, *Novum Testamentum*, 2:893, translation from Wainwright, *Mysterious Apocalypse*, 133.

happen in the last days" (Dan. 2:28). Daniel is instructed to "seal up" the contents for a much later time (8:26; 12:4, 9), indicating that the relevance of these contents would not be perceived by an audience living in the sixth-century BC setting of the narrative frame of the visions. John, by contrast, presents his material as concerned with "what things must happen quickly" (Rev. 1:1; 22:6) and is explicitly commanded *not* to seal up his book "because the time is near" (22:10). Craig Koester rightly concludes from this that "from its inception, Revelation was designed to be an open book that addressed issues facing its earliest readers," and, thus, reading Revelation alongside those late first-century Christians in Roman Asia becomes a reliable approach to understanding its message and significance.[2]

Revelation was meant to shape these first-century Christians' perceptions of *their* everyday realities and to motivate particular responses to *their* circumstances. A grounded reading of Revelation that takes its author's purposes seriously approaches this book as we would naturally approach Paul's letters to the Christians in Galatia or Corinth—namely, as a piece of communication that reveals its meaning and message to us most fully when we immerse ourselves in the contexts and conversations of its intended first-century audiences and discipline ourselves to hear it as a pastoral intervention in the midst of *their* circumstances and concerns.[3]

The chief obstacle to understanding Revelation is not that John writes in a mysterious code but that modern readers are far removed from the ideologies, landmarks, and practices with which John and his audiences were deeply familiar. The first word in the Greek original of John's book is *apokalypsis*. It means "unveiling," not "mysterious, coded message." John did not send his book to his circle of congregations as a mysterious text needing to be interpreted. Rather, John sent Revelation to interpret the world and the lived experiences of those congregations. Many modern interpreters claim to have found the hidden key that finally unlocks the meaning of Revelation after these many centuries. On the contrary, Revelation *was* the key by means of which John's audiences could unlock the spiritual significance of what was going on around them in their world so that they could respond to those experiences and challenges in a manner that aligned with "keeping the commandments of God and the testimony of Jesus" (Rev. 12:17; cf. 14:12). Revelation "lifted the veil" from prominent landmarks in their landscape and familiar practices in their environment so that they could see these things "as they really were" in

2. C. Koester, *Revelation*, 852.

3. This book adopts the view that John, an early Christian prophet, composed and sent Revelation to his congregations at some point during the reign of Domitian. For a fuller discussion, see deSilva, *Discovering Revelation*, 29–32, 35–39.

light of the bigger picture of God's purposes for his creation and the cosmic rebellion against those good purposes that God would ultimately defeat. More importantly, John lifts the veil obscuring the spiritual significance and the larger consequences of the challenges and choices before them so that they might choose wisely in the light of God's eternity. The Christ-followers addressed by John would not need to look beyond their own settings to understand John's message and to hear therein a radical unmasking of the ideologies and realities of their world, along with its challenges and temptations.

The primary goal of this book is to help the reader cross over more fully in his or her informed imagination into the world that John's audiences occupied, to see what was ever before their eyes, to hear the propaganda with which they were perpetually bombarded, to understand the social pressures and economic incentives (and disincentives) to which they were regularly subjected. This book invites you, its readers, to immerse yourselves in the context of Revelation's target audience so that, as you further immerse yourselves in the text of Revelation, you may hear it alongside the Christ-followers in Ephesus or Smyrna or Pergamum and understand more fully how Revelation worked on their perceptions and their assessments of how to live amid the challenges, tensions, and enticements they faced, given the past and future interventions of God and his Anointed in their world.

The next chapter presents an overview of the Roman province of Asia, the shared political context of all seven congregations. A short history of the territory will provide a touchstone for references to specific rulers and periods connected to particular archaeological remains in the chapters treating individual sites. An introduction to how Roman power was perceived and celebrated throughout the province will also provide important background for particular manifestations of imperial ideology in each city.

Chapters 2 through 10 allow readers, in effect, to tour each site. We begin with Patmos as the physical context in which John himself had his visionary experiences, reflected on them, and gave shape to their literary expression. We proceed through each of the seven cities in the order John presents them both in the initial listing in Revelation 1:11 and in the order of the seven oracles that the glorified Lord speaks to each assembly in Revelation 2:1–3:22. This is also the order in which an itinerant prophet like John might have visited each of the congregations when he was present among them on the mainland, traveling along well-built and maintained roads in order to exercise his ministry of encouragement and admonition. The tour concludes, perhaps unexpectedly, in the city of Rome itself. Even though the Christians in Rome were not among John's addressees, no earthly city is more in view in Revelation than the city at the heart of the empire—the city represented throughout the province of

Asia as a goddess to be worshiped alongside her emperors but given a most extreme makeover at John's hands.

The discussions of each city draw not only on archaeological remains, though these always have pride of place, but also on the witnesses that literary texts, inscriptions, and coins bear to the physical structures that existed in the early Roman period to be seen by John's audiences. In many instances these latter witnesses are of great importance, given the fact that ongoing occupation has allowed for only the most selective archaeological excavation in several sites—for example, Smyrna, the site of the bustling modern city of İzmir. Also, while I have foregrounded structures known to have constituted part of the lived landscape of a late first-century audience, I also discuss second- and even third-century structures as well, particularly when these represent later iterations of institutions that would have existed earlier in the city's history or when they represent later stages of trajectories that were already emerging in the first century. To some extent, this is a concession to the state and priorities of archaeological work on several of these sites. If we were to limit the discussion strictly to the remains of structures that were extant by the late first century AD, there would be nothing to say here concerning Philadelphia and almost nothing to say concerning Smyrna and Thyatira. In part, however, it also stems from a desire that this book should serve travelers visiting each of these sites as well as those who engage it in the classroom or the study.

As with *Archaeology and the Ministry of Paul* and *Archaeology and the World of Jesus*, an indispensable part of my own preparation for writing this book, not to mention providing most of its photographic illustrations, was repeated travel to each of the sites discussed between its covers. I undertook such a trip for the first time in 2011 as a solo traveler, spending a little more than a week divided between the sites at Ephesus, İzmir (Smyrna), and Bergama (Pergamum). I am profoundly grateful to Abdullah Gur of Meander Travel for arranging the logistics of that trip on my behalf and for lending me an exceptional guide, Mehmet Tanriverdi, to accompany me on the first walk through each site. I traveled to some or all of the sites covered in this book in the course of trips undertaken in 2014, 2015, 2017, and 2022 courtesy of James Ridgway and Educational Opportunities Tours, a leader in archaeological tourism who has thereby contributed immensely to my own knowledge and experience of sites throughout the eastern half of the Mediterranean. More recently, Levent Oral of Tutku Educational Travel afforded me multiple opportunities to travel to the sites of all seven churches addressed by John, first in conjunction with the Second Global Smyrna Conference in 2023, then as part of two splendidly organized tours in 2025 (experiences greatly enhanced by our guides, Macit Saszade and Tulu Gokkadar). Mr. Oral also generously allowed me to incorporate the excellent site maps designed for his tour company into the present volume, significantly increasing its value for readers. I will always remain grateful to these leaders in educational travel. I undertook solo trips to Rome in 2015 and Türkiye (once again) in 2019 in conjunction with study leaves from Ashland Theological Seminary, which also provided financial support for these trips. If I have been productive in my scholarly career, it is in large measure because the administration and trustees of Ashland have been supportive of its faculty contributing not only to Ashland's own classrooms but also to classrooms, research libraries, and lives throughout the world through scholarship and publication. Finally, I wish to extend my thanks to Mr. Brad Nelson of Classical Numismatic Group, LLC (www.cngcoins.com), and my various correspondents at Numismatica Ars Classica, AG (www.arsclassicacoins.com), for their generosity in allowing me to incorporate their images of coins that provide indispensable witnesses to the architecture and ideology of the Hellenistic and Roman periods.

ABBREVIATIONS

GENERAL

cf.	*confer*, compare	l(l).	line(s)
e.g.	*exempli gratia*, for example	v(v).	verse(s)
i.e.	*id est*, that is		

OLD TESTAMENT

Gen.	Genesis	Eccles.	Ecclesiastes
Exod.	Exodus	Song	Song of Songs
Lev.	Leviticus	Isa.	Isaiah
Num.	Numbers	Jer.	Jeremiah
Deut.	Deuteronomy	Lam.	Lamentations
Josh.	Joshua	Ezek.	Ezekiel
Judg.	Judges	Dan.	Daniel
Ruth	Ruth	Hosea	Hosea
1 Sam.	1 Samuel	Joel	Joel
2 Sam.	2 Samuel	Amos	Amos
1 Kings	1 Kings	Obad.	Obadiah
2 Kings	2 Kings	Jon.	Jonah
1 Chron.	1 Chronicles	Mic.	Micah
2 Chron.	2 Chronicles	Nah.	Nahum
Ezra	Ezra	Hab.	Habakkuk
Neh.	Nehemiah	Zeph.	Zephaniah
Esther	Esther	Hag.	Haggai
Job	Job	Zech.	Zechariah
Ps(s).	Psalm(s)	Mal.	Malachi
Prov.	Proverbs		

NEW TESTAMENT

Matt.	Matthew	1 Tim.	1 Timothy
Mark	Mark	2 Tim.	2 Timothy
Luke	Luke	Titus	Titus
John	John	Philem.	Philemon
Acts	Acts	Heb.	Hebrews
Rom.	Romans	James	James
1 Cor.	1 Corinthians	1 Pet.	1 Peter
2 Cor.	2 Corinthians	2 Pet.	2 Peter
Gal.	Galatians	1 John	1 John
Eph.	Ephesians	2 John	2 John
Phil.	Philippians	3 John	3 John
Col.	Colossians	Jude	Jude
1 Thess.	1 Thessalonians	Rev.	Revelation
2 Thess.	2 Thessalonians		

OLD TESTAMENT APOCRYPHA

Bar.	Baruch

JOSEPHUS

Ag. Ap.	*Against Apion*
Ant.	*Jewish Antiquities*
J.W.	*Jewish War*

CLASSICAL AUTHORS

Aelius Aristides

Or. *Orationes (Orations)*

Anonymous

Sib. Or. *Sibylline Oracles*

Dio Cassius

Hist. rom. *Historiae romanae (Roman History)*

Dio Chrysostom

Or. *Orationes (Orations)*

Eusebius

Chron. *Chronicon (Chronicle)*
Hist. eccl. *Historia ecclesiastica (Ecclesiastical History)*

Herodotus

Hist. *Histories*

Ignatius

Eph. *To the Ephesians*

Irenaeus

Haer. *Against Heresies*

Jerome

Vir. ill. *De viris illustribus (On Illustrious Persons)*

Martial

Spec. *Spectacles*

Orosius

Adv. pag. — *Adversus paganos* (*Against the Pagans*)

Pausanias

Descr. — *Description of Greece*

Pliny the Elder

Nat. — *Natural History*

Pliny the Younger

Ep. — *Epistulae* (*Letters*)

Polybius

Hist. — *The Histories*

Polycarp

Phil. — *To the Philippians*

Strabo

Geogr. — *Geography*

Suetonius

Aug. — *Divus Augustus*
Nero — *Nero*
Tib. — *Tiberius*

Tacitus

Agr. — *Agricola*
Ann. — *Annales* (*Annals*)
Hist. — *Historiae* (*Histories*)

Tertullian

Praescr. — *De praescriptione haereticorum* (*Prescription Against Heretics*)

Virgil

Aen. — *Aeneid*

Vitruvius

De arch. — *De architectura* (*On Architecture*)

DEAD SEA SCROLLS

1QH — *Hodayoth* (Thanksgiving Scroll)
1QM — *Milchamah* (War Scroll)

INSCRIPTIONS AND PAPYRI

IEph — *Die Inschriften von Ephesos*. 8 vols. Edited by H. Wankel et al. Bonn: Habelt, 1979–84
ILaod — *Die Inschriften von Laodikeia am Lykos*. Edited by T. Corsten. Bonn: Habelt, 1997
IPhil — Inscriptions from Philadelphia, in G. Petzl, *Philadelphia et Ager Philadelphenus / Tituli Lydiae* 5/3. Titula Asiae Minoris. Vienna: Österreichischen Akademie der Wissenschaften, 2007
ISmyrna — *Die Inschriften von Smyrna*. 2 vols. Edited by G. Petzl. Bonn: Habelt, 1982–90

1

THE ROMAN PROVINCE OF ASIA

While most of the chapters that follow are also windows into "the Roman province of Asia," the view through each of those apertures may be better appreciated after acquiring a broader view of the landscape. This chapter, therefore, provides first a historical overview of the territory that would come to be incorporated into the empire as the province of Asia and, thereby, a fuller framework into which to fit the stories of the individual cities to follow. It also introduces the origins and general conditions of the Jewish communities that took root throughout the province and that proved to be both important seedbeds for and spirited antagonists of the emerging Christian movement. Finally, it immerses the reader in one of the defining features of the "spirit" that animated the province as a whole—namely, its embrace of and support for the ideology of Rome and its emperors, who presented their rule as the means by which the beneficent gods exercised their watchful care over the known world.

An Overview of the History and Administration of the Province

All seven of the cities whose Christian residents John addressed (see fig. 1.1) were essentially *Greek* cities. The majority of surviving inscriptions from the region are written in Greek. Each city had the physical structures basic to Greek cities (council halls, theaters, stadiums, gymnasiums, temples to identifiably Greek deities). Along with ten other cities in Ionia, Ephesus and

Figure 1.1. The seven cities addressed by Revelation.

Smyrna were already founded as Greek cities before the sixth century BC. These cities, along with the entirety of Asia Minor, were absorbed into the Persian Empire but "liberated" in 334 BC by the forces of Alexander the Great. After his death, they became the disputed holdings of one or another of the so-called successors to Alexander's empire.

Roman interest in this territory coincides with the expansionist urges of Antiochus III, king of the Seleucid Empire from 223 to 187 BC, an empire founded by Seleucus I, one of the major players in the initial division of Alexander's empire. Rome's leaders regarded Asia Minor as the buffer zone between their sphere of interest (which, for them, extended throughout all of Greece and marginally into the Balkans) and the powers to the east, including the Seleucid and Parthian Empires. Antiochus, on the other hand, viewed Greece and the Balkans as a more appropriate buffer zone between Rome and the east and pushed westward to take hold of the majority of Asia Minor.[1] Eumenes II, ruler of the small but wealthy kingdom of Pergamum and an ally of Rome, recognized the threat posed by Antiochus and thus sought to persuade Rome that war against Antiochus was necessary to safeguard Rome's interests in Greece and western Asia.[2]

Rome might have allowed Antiochus to retain control of the territories he seized in Asia Minor, but when Antiochus crossed into Europe, he came to

1. Errington, "Rome Against Philip," 282.
2. Errington, "Rome Against Philip," 279–80.

be seen as too great a threat to Rome's interests to tolerate. In the war that followed, Antiochus was beaten back into Asia and eventually surrendered after a defeat in Magnesia ad Sipylum (a site related to the modern city of Manisa). He was forced to withdraw completely from all areas west and north of the Taurus Mountains and to pay an enormous war indemnity of 15,000 silver talents over the course of twelve years, thus repaying the Romans and their allies for all the expenses of the war. This put an end to his aspirations for western expansion and economically crippled his capacity for expansion otherwise.[3]

As a result, Rome's loyal ally Eumenes II received additional territories in westernmost Asia Minor north of the Meander River, including all the territory that would include the cities later addressed by John, and he would show his appreciation by continuing to look after Rome's interests on his side of the Aegean Sea.[4] Upon his death in 158 BC, the kingdom passed to his younger brother, Attalus II Philadelphus, who earned his moniker—"devoted to his brother"—through his genuine, lifelong loyalty to Eumenes, which Rome at one point sorely tested.[5] When Attalus II died in 138 BC, kingship passed to Attalus III, Eumenes II's son and Attalus II's nephew. He died only six years later and, having no heirs, left his kingdom to the Roman people in his will. A certain Aristonicus, who claimed to have been an illegitimate son of Eumenes II, rallied sufficient support to resist Rome's claim to the territory for four years. By 129 BC, however, the kingdom of Pergamum had been transformed into the Roman province of Asia.[6] Presaging the shape of things to come (notably the cult of the Roman emperors), a priesthood and cult of Marcus Aquilius, the Roman general who finally defeated Aristonicus, existed in the new province by 126 BC.[7]

The produce and profits from the cultivation of "royal lands"—the immense agricultural estates owned by the Attalid family—went to the Roman state, which leased these lands to others (including Roman citizens who moved abroad to take advantage of the new opportunities there).[8] Roman rule meant a significantly greater tax burden for the inhabitants of the new province. During the period of the Roman Republic, taxes were to be collected by financial cooperatives composed of agents called *publicani* (hence the "publicans" mentioned in the King James Version of the Gospels). These

3. Errington, "Rome Against Philip," 286–87.
4. Errington, "Rome Against Philip," 288.
5. Habicht, "Seleucids," 373, 376.
6. Habicht, "Seleucids," 379–80.
7. Lintott, "Roman Empire," 34.
8. Worth, *Seven Cities of the Apocalypse and Roman Culture*, 51.

associations of financiers would pay up front to the Roman treasury the import taxes, export taxes, and agricultural taxes that were estimated to be due from the province and then be authorized and empowered to collect that sum—and a good deal more—from the province itself. This arrangement allowed Rome to enjoy its funds immediately and saved the state the trouble of creating, staffing, funding, and monitoring its own bureaucratic structures for collecting both direct and indirect taxes throughout its vast territories.[9] It also created opportunities for the *publicani* and their agents to oppress and exploit provincials. This method of extracting taxes was predatory as far as the provinces were concerned.[10]

There was sufficient dissatisfaction with the new conditions under Roman rule that Mithridates VI of Pontus was able to rally widespread support throughout the former kingdom of Pergamum when he launched a rebellion against the Roman presence.[11] Mithridates ruled over the kingdom of Pontus on the Black Sea (what is now north central Türkiye) from 120 to 63 BC. The first Mithridates had carved out a kingdom for himself in the wake of the battle between Lysimachus and Seleucus I, two of Alexander the Great's "successors," in 281 BC.[12] Eventually it came to include almost all the lands surrounding the Black Sea.[13]

Rome became concerned about the sixth Mithridates's expansionist policies and tried to dissuade him from continuing. A Roman envoy was reputed, with typical Roman tact, to have told the king "either to be greater than the Romans or to obey them" (Plutarch, *Marius* 312–13).[14] Mithridates decided that he would aim for the former, at least on the Anatolian Peninsula. In 89–88 BC, he launched a campaign and established control over Bithynia and a portion of Asia to the west and southwest of the kingdom of Pontus, defeating several armies raised by the Roman generals dispatched to contain him.[15]

In 88 BC, Rome declared war on Mithridates, appointing Lucius Cornelius Sulla to lead the campaign. In response, perhaps as a preventative measure to remove a potentially hostile presence in his newly acquired territory, Mithridates ordered the slaughter of Italians living in the cities of his expanded realm. Ephesus and Pergamum were among the cities that enthusiastically obeyed. Mithridates also launched his own preemptive campaigns into Thrace

9. Van Nijf, "Social World," 285–86.
10. Richardson, "Administration," 584–85.
11. Lintott, "Roman Empire," 34.
12. Hind, "Mithridates," 130–31.
13. Hind, "Mithridates," 139–40.
14. Quoted in Hind, "Mithridates," 142.
15. Hind, "Mithridates," 144–45.

and Greece to establish a foothold on the European continent and to hold off the Roman forces there. This led, however, to the loss of significant portions of his army. Sulla eventually weakened Mithridates sufficiently for the latter to agree to terms in 85 BC. Mithridates relinquished all his newly conquered territory and retired to the old borders of the kingdom of Pontus, handing over much of his navy to Sulla and paying a hefty fine.[16] The relative leniency of this settlement was due to brewing civil unrest in Italy that required a speedy settlement of the problems in Asia Minor. The cities that had resisted Mithridates were rewarded with the status of "free cities" (Aphrodisias was one of these); those that had massacred their Italian residents, however, faced harsh reparations. Ephesus, for example, was made to pay Rome five years in back taxes it had withheld (despite the fact that it had already paid tribute to Mithridates for those years), resulting in severe economic hardship for decades.

During the period of the Republic, Roman governors enjoyed extraordinary freedom from oversight in their provinces. This grant of *imperium* was intended to give them wide latitude in the exercise of their duties.[17] It was possible, however, for people in the provinces to bring complaints against a *former* governor to a special court in Rome.[18] The governor had a small staff at his disposal—a quaestor in charge of financial matters, a number of senatorial advisers (*legati*), a cadre of personal advisers of his own choosing, and attendants and scribes.[19] Rome placed a great deal of responsibility on local civic governments for the functioning of the provinces. It was, of course, to Rome's advantage to have the provincial elite that made up local governments shoulder as many of the local tasks of the administration and judiciary as possible so that Rome would not have to develop and staff an extensive infrastructure. Aediles (junior officials in city government) and *agoranomoi* (market regulators) were important local offices for ensuring that there would be enough grain available for a given city's population, providing a check for weights and measures used by merchants in the forums, tending to street repair, maintaining public buildings, and overseeing private construction projects.[20] Local elites individually funded a great deal of a city's public works, religious activities, and public entertainment, all for the love of the recognition and honor that accrued to them for their generous underwriting. Roman

16. Hind, "Mithridates," 158; Worth, *Seven Cities of the Apocalypse and Roman Culture*, 44–46.

17. Richardson, "Administration," 575.

18. Richardson, "Administration," 578, 594–95.

19. Richardson, "Administration," 580–82.

20. Galsterer, "Local and Provincial Institutions," 352–53.

administration also made no provisions for public transport, cultural activities, education, research, health services, or social welfare.[21] Roman bureaucracy was, therefore, significantly leaner than modern people might expect.

The Roman governor was responsible for hearing judicial cases throughout his province, generally cycling through the cities that had been chosen as centers for that purpose. While cities and villages maintained their own local courts, those dissatisfied with the outcomes of cases—or cases involving disputes between parties in different local jurisdictions—might come before the governor or one of his delegates.[22] The governor also heard cases that might result in the imposition of capital punishment, as this generally fell within his sole purview.[23] To this end, Asia was divided into thirteen districts (*conventus*) for judicial and administrative purposes, with particular cities being selected as locations for the governor's judicial activities in his annual itineration. Ephesus, Smyrna, Pergamum, and Sardis were all seats of their respective districts.[24] Perhaps most importantly, governors had command of any legions stationed in their particular provinces. Governors were often tasked with policing and keeping the peace, and they might draw upon the soldiery and, especially, their officers for other administrative and civil tasks.

Under Julius Caesar, the purview of the *publicani* was restricted to indirect taxes, such as duties on imports and exports, while local city governments in cooperation with Rome-appointed officials took over the collection of direct taxes.[25] During Augustus's reign, as reliable estimates became more difficult to make, the associations of *publicani* also ceased to pay a fixed sum up front and were rather obligated to pay a fixed (and very high) percentage of the sums their agents and networks had collected through indirect taxes.[26] There remained, nevertheless, opportunity at multiple levels for the *publicani* and their staff to squeeze extra profits for themselves out of the people with whom they trafficked.

The province suffered significant economic hardship during the Roman civil wars of 48–31 BC: first between Caesar and Pompey, then between the assassins of Caesar (Brutus and Cassius) and Caesar's avengers (Octavian and Marc Antony), and then, finally, between Octavian and Marc Antony after their falling out. Brutus and Cassius were particularly vicious in their extortion of money from the eastern provinces, demanding the payment of

21. Galsterer, "Local and Provincial Institutions," 345.
22. Richardson, "Administration," 589–91.
23. Bowman, "Provincial Administration," 366.
24. Worth, *Seven Cities of the Apocalypse and Roman Culture*, 51.
25. Magie, *Roman Rule*, 1:407.
26. Van Nijf, "Social World," 295.

ten years' worth of tribute in advance in order to fund their war efforts against Caesar's partisans. After their defeat, Marc Antony attempted to extract the same amount from the already-impoverished province.[27] Asia was milked dry.

The emergence of Octavian (soon to be granted the honorific moniker "Augustus" by the Roman Senate) as the sole leader in 31 BC ushered in a new era of stability and restored prosperity for Roman Asia. The century between 31 BC and AD 69 would be one of almost unbroken peace for Asia, during which the region could prosper and for which its elites might indeed offer genuine thanks—though increased prosperity for the province also meant increased taxes due to Rome.[28] Asia produced a wide variety of raw materials and goods for export, including pottery, perfume, dyes, draperies, clothing, wines, grain, salted fish, dried fruits, hides, wool, parchment, metals, timber, sculptures, and a great deal of the marble that would be used in the facades of countless buildings in the capital city.[29] Its cities flourished through trade under the "Augustan Peace."

Augustus reorganized the system for provincial government, retaining for himself (through senatorial governors that he would select) the *imperium* for certain provinces and allowing the Senate to select its own governors for other provinces. Augustus and his successors tended to retain direct control over provinces in which the majority of the legions were stationed. Provinces might be transferred from one pool to the other as circumstances changed.[30] The Senate's appointees continued to serve for one-year terms; the imperial appointees might find themselves serving for longer periods. Asia remained a senatorial province.

Under Augustus, the provincial council, called the *Koinon Asias*, came to play an increasingly important role. It was a convenient body through which emperors and their agents could disseminate instructions to the provincial elite; it also provided a venue through which to channel the ambitions of local elites in directions that rewarded loyalty to the emperor.[31] The members of the provincial council, and especially their presiders, were also the primary diplomats of the province.[32] They would staff and underwrite the cost of

27. Magie, *Roman Rule*, 1:427–28; Worth, *Seven Cities of the Apocalypse and Roman Culture*, 46.

28. Levick, "Greece (Including Crete and Cyprus)," 672.

29. Worth, *Seven Cities of the Apocalypse and Roman Culture*, 70–71.

30. Magie, *Roman Rule*, 1:445–46; Bowman, "Provincial Administration," 345–46.

31. Levick, "Greece (Including Crete and Cyprus)," 669.

32. The *Koinon* was composed of 150 members in 4 BC (Magie, *Roman Rule*, 1:448). The "Asiarchs" are often assumed to have been leading figures in the *Koinon* as well as the high priests of the provincial imperial cults (as in Worth, *Seven Cities of the Apocalypse and Roman Culture*, 118–19), but a growing consensus asserts that these were separate roles, even though the same small circle of provincial elites would often rotate through and acquire several or all

embassies to the emperor, whether to convey birthday greetings, petition for financial support, or request judicial intervention.[33] They would increasingly promote the cult of Rome and the emperors throughout the province and finance many of the activities related to the same. The landscape of the province would also increasingly reflect acknowledgment of imperial favors (undoubtedly in the hope of continued favor), as in Ephesus's civic forum (see below in chap. 3).[34] For the sake of speedier communication, Augustus also moved the capital of the province from Pergamum, which lacked a seaport, to Ephesus, probably in 29 BC.[35]

If the relationship between the province and the center of empire was rocky and oppressive in the period before Augustus, it took a swift and dramatic turn toward the mutually beneficial and cordial under Augustus and his successors. By the last third of the first century AD, several members of the Asian elite were inducted into the Roman Senate, including T. Julius Celsus Polemaeanus of Sardis and C. Antius Quadratus and C. Julius Bassus of Pergamum.[36] Celsus and Bassus would both later return for stints as governors of the province of Asia. The *publicani* appear to have disappeared from the scene entirely between the accessions of Vespasian (AD 69) and Hadrian (AD 117) in favor of entrusting the collection of all taxes to Roman officers, which removed a long-standing source of abuse.[37] The proliferation of imperial cult temples, especially under Trajan and Hadrian, can be understood as a measure of both the mood and the prosperity of the cities of Asia under the emperors of the late first and early second centuries.[38] This is not to say that there were never dissenting voices. For example, the anonymous Jewish author of the fourth *Sibylline Oracle* wrote, probably during the reign of Titus, "Great wealth will come to Asia, which Rome itself once plundered and deposited in her house of many possessions. She will then pay back twice as much and more to Asia, and then there will be a surfeit of war" (4.145–48).[39] John is himself the best-known dissenter. Nevertheless, for many in Asia, the rule of Rome under the emperors brought the conditions for significant prosperity and the comfort of a great safety net.

---

of these titles in the course of their public service. Magie, *Roman Rule*, 1:449–50; Horsley, "Inscriptions," 138; Friesen, *Imperial Cults*, 30.

33. Eck, "Provincial Administration," 268–69.

34. Tacitus, *Ann.* 3.66–68; 14.15; Levick, "Greece (Including Crete and Cyprus)," 658.

35. Friesen, *Twice Neokoros*, 158. Marianne Coudry and François Kirbihler argue that the transition happened much earlier, around 85 BC in the wake of the Mithradtic Wars. Coudry and Kirbihler, "La lex Cornelia."

36. Levick, "Greece and Asia Minor," 610.

37. Magie, *Roman Rule*, 1:567.

38. Levick, "Greece and Asia Minor," 612.

39. Collins, "Sybilline Oracles," 387–88.

Jews in Roman Asia

Many Jewish communities in the province of Asia would have had deep roots by the late first century. Flavius Josephus, the Jewish historian and propagandist from the late first century AD, preserves the text of a letter from the last decade of the third century BC in which Antiochus III gives instructions to Zeuxis, governor of the western province and stationed in Sardis, concerning the strategic resettlement of two thousand Jewish families (an estimated eight thousand to ten thousand people) that Antiochus was relocating from the Seleucid heartland in Babylonia to the territories of Lydia and Phrygia. These Jews clearly enjoyed Antiochus's confidence, for the goal of their resettlement was to increase the stability of these newly acquired territories, which had been susceptible to rebellion (Josephus, *Ant.* 12.148–53).[40] Intrinsic to this resettlement were grants of land, start-up supplies, and tax exemptions, all of which was bound to cement their loyalty to the crown, as well as permission to order their lives in keeping with their ancestral laws and customs and to enjoy some measure of self-regulation along those lines.[41]

The privileges accorded the Jewish communities were often challenged by local parties or recently arrived authorities and, thus, stood in frequent need of being reaffirmed. Josephus is particularly interested in this history, establishing as it does important and pervasive imperial precedents for these communities' ongoing enjoyment of the necessary toleration and leeway that allowed them to remain faithful to their ancestral law and thus preserve their distinctive identity. Shortly after the assassination of Julius Caesar in 44 BC, Hyrcanus II, high priest and ethnarch of Judea, successfully petitioned the Roman governor of Asia to grant Jews exemption from military service and permission to observe their ancestral customs, which compulsory military service would jeopardize (Josephus, *Ant.* 14.223–30). Ephesus and Sardis issued decrees during the late Republican period confirming Jews' rights to observe their laws, exercise a measure of self-regulation, and be allowed to gather together in a regular place for such matters (14.235, 256–64).

Following the precedent set by Julius Caesar, Augustus confirmed the right of Jews living in cities throughout the empire "to assemble, to engage in cultic activity in the synagogue, and to collect the tribute for the Jerusalem temple."[42] Of particular importance is the record of Augustus's edicts concerning the Jewish communities in the province of Asia:

40. Trebilco, *Jewish Communities*, 5–6.

41. Trebilco, *Jewish Communities*, 6. Migration throughout the Roman period would continue to grow these diaspora communities.

42. Schnabel, "Jewish Opposition," 244; Josephus, *Ant.* 14.196–222.

> The Jews may follow their own customs in accordance with the law of their fathers, just as they followed them in the time of Hyrcanus [II] . . . and that their sacred monies shall be inviolable and may be sent up to Jerusalem and delivered to the treasuries in Jerusalem, and that they need not give bond [to appear in court] on the Sabbath or on the day of preparation for it after the ninth hour. And if anyone is caught stealing their sacred books or their sacred monies from a synagogue or an ark [of the Law], he shall be regarded as sacrilegious, and his property shall be confiscated to the public treasury of the Romans.[43] (Josephus, *Ant.* 16.162–65)

Augustus's right-hand man, Marcus Vipsanius Agrippa, confirmed these rights in letters addressed to officials in Ephesus and Cyrene; several governors of Asia are also recorded as having affirmed them in letters to Sardis and Ephesus (Josephus, *Ant.* 16.167–73).

These various edicts incidentally reveal matters that appear to have been of particular importance to the Jewish communities making the petitions: the right to abstain from work on the Sabbath, reckoned from evening to evening; the right to assemble and exercise some level of intra-community discipline; the right to have access to foods allowable by their ancestral law; and the right to collect and send their annual contributions to the Jerusalem temple, by means of which they affirmed their connection with and investment in the sacrifices offered therein.[44] There was a very practical reason for the frequent local opposition to this last practice: Large amounts of money were leaving the city rather than being used to support public-works projects to enhance the life of the very city in which the Jewish community resided and, to some extent at least, prospered, enjoying special rights beyond those of ordinary, non-Jewish residents.[45]

The Ideological Context of Roman Asia

Equally important as the political and economic contexts of life in Roman Asia for understanding the situation of John's audiences is the *ideological* context in which they lived and were saturated. The manner in which Rome and its emperors were presented; the narratives about the benign, divine forces at work through Rome and its emperors; the exuberant assessments of the

43. From *Josephus in Ten Volumes*, 273, 275.

44. See Trebilco, *Jewish Communities*, 12–19, for a helpful discussion of each of these.

45. Barclay, *Jews in the Mediterranean Diaspora*, 268–69. For a richly documented discussion concerning the confirmation of, threats to, and reaffirmation of the rights of Jews living in the eastern Roman Empire to observe particular traditional customs and practices, see Schnabel, "Jewish Opposition," 243–59.

value of the imperial ordering of life in the province; and the claims made on the emperors' behalf all grated against John's sense of what was due the one God and what was genuinely due mortal authority figures and human empires. And these things all contributed, as far as John was concerned, to masking the substantial evils that the Roman Empire perpetrated (and would continue to perpetrate) against humankind in general and against the followers of the one God in particular.

One text that provides an important window into the picture of the emperor and his rule promoted by the provincial elite is known as the Priene Calendar Inscription. In 9 BC, the *Koinon Asias* held a contest offering a victor's wreath to the person who could devise the most appropriate honors for Augustus. The winner was Paullus Fabius Maximus, the proconsul of Asia for that year. Even though the winning proposal came from a member of Rome's senatorial class, the enthusiasm with which the *Koinon* embraced it shows the degree to which the proposal aligned with their own enthusiasm for the emperor.

Maximus recommended that the province adopt a new calendar with September 23, the emperor's birthday, serving as New Year's Day. Maximus described this as

> a date that we could probably without fear of contradiction equate with the beginning of all things, if not in terms of nature, certainly in terms of utility, seeing that he restored stability, when everything was collapsing and falling into disarray, and gave a new look to the entire world that would have been most happy to accept its own ruin had not the good and common fortune of all been born: Caesar.[46]

The *Koinon*'s response in support of Maximus's proposal is nothing short of messianic:

> Whereas Providence that orders all our lives has, in her display of concern and generosity in our behalf, adorned our lives with the highest good: Augustus, whom she has filled with virtue for the benefit of humanity, . . . who has made war to cease and who shall put everything in . . . order, . . . with the result that the birthday of our God signaled the beginning of Good News for the world because of him; . . . the Greeks in Asia Decreed that the New Year begin for all the cities on September 23, which is the birthday of Augustus.[47]

46. Translation from Danker, *Benefactor*, 216. The full text and an excellent explanation of the Priene Inscription can be found in Danker, *Benefactor*, 215–22; see also Friesen, *Imperial Cults*, 32–35.

47. Translation from Danker, *Benefactor*, 217, with minor modifications for clarity.

The first month of the new calendar year was, moreover, henceforth to be called *Kaiseros* ("Caesar's month"), rather than *Dios* ("Zeus's month"), its name in the Macedonian calendar. Copies of the decree were inscribed and set up in the provincial Temple of Rome and Augustus in Pergamum as well as in imperial shrines in district capitals and beyond. Substantial physical remains of the inscription were found at Priene, a city 25 miles south of Ephesus, giving the inscription its name.

The provincial elite embraced the notion of reordering time itself around the coming of Augustus (that is, his birth) as the provision of divine providence for the inauguration of a new age—a golden age (cf. Virgil, *Aen.* 6.792–93) in which hope, prosperity, and security had been restored after a period of want, hopelessness, and insecurity. In all fairness, the "before" and "after" images were rather accurate. But the ideological overlay was substantial. Augustus was hailed as the savior of the world itself, the person who renewed the world when it was spiraling into chaos.[48] Resetting New Year's Day would be a perpetual reminder to all the residents of the province of the "new beginning" that Augustus had brought to them all, indeed, to the whole world. The notion of a "golden age" appeals to a mythical view of time as a series of successively inferior periods—gold, silver, bronze, iron—followed by a return of the golden age. The age of Augustus was thus the renewal of "the best of all possible worlds," one that, according to imperial propaganda, would now last forever, world without end.[49] Aelius Aristides, a second-century elite orator from Smyrna, invoked this eschatology twice in the conclusion to his laudatory speech on Rome: "To compose the oration which would equal the majesty of your empire . . . would require just about as much time as time allotted to the empire, and that would be all eternity! . . . Let all the gods and the children of the gods be invoked to grant that this empire and this city flourish forever!" (*On Rome* 108–9).[50]

It will be of interest to students of early Christianity to observe the phrase "the beginning of Good News" in the Priene Calendar Inscription. The Greek word used here, *euangelia*, is a plural form of the word that was later used to speak of the Christian "gospel" or "good news" (*euangelion*). Josephus also used the word with reference to the spreading of the report of Vespasian's successful accession to the reins of empire: "Every city kept festival for the good news and offered sacrifices on his behalf" (*J.W.* 4.618).[51] It would not be going too far to call Roman imperial ideology a "gospel," since this

48. Friesen, *Imperial Cults*, 125.
49. See, further, the discussion in Friesen, *Twice Neokoros*, 122–31.
50. Translation from Oliver, *Ruling Power*, 907.
51. Translation from Josephus, *Jewish War*, 3:183.

language was indeed used in connection with the emperors and the order and stability—the "peace"—they brought to the world. When Luke later told his story of the birth of Jesus under the shadow of Augustus, speaking of the "good news" of the "birth" of a savior who would bring the blessings of peace and usher in a renewed kingdom, his audiences would be hard pressed to miss the implicit contrast with and criticism of imperial propaganda in this regard. And, of course, the early Christian proclamation of the return of this savior—at which time "the kingdom of this world" would "become the kingdom of our Lord and of his Anointed One" (Rev. 11:15)—would be heard very clearly as clashing with the eschatology of imperial propaganda that promised "Rome without end," without successor.

Despite their enthusiasm for Augustus and his successors, citizens of important cities like Ephesus, Smyrna, and Miletus were not persuaded to abandon the old, Macedonian calendar in the long run.[52] They were, however, fully committed to actualizing and promoting Roman imperial ideology by another, far more dramatic means—building temples, instituting priesthoods, and offering worship to Augustus, his successors, and members of the extended imperial families. This phenomenon, referred to as the "imperial cult," pervaded the cities of Roman Asia (and, indeed, other eastern provinces of the empire).

Nicolaus of Damascus, once an educator in Cleopatra's household and later a personal friend of Herod the Great, explained the logic of the imperial cult thus with particular reference to Augustus:

> Because mankind address him [as Augustus] in accordance with their estimation of his honor, they revere him with temples and sacrifices across islands and continents, organized in cities and provinces, matching the greatness of his virtue and repaying his benefactions toward them. (*Life of Augustus* 1)[53]

Because the emperor's gifts—given his seemingly limitless resources and his power to move them—were deemed to match the goods for which his subjects prayed to the gods, their expressions of gratitude took on proportional dimensions. In Asia, of course, the emperors were in this regard simply the heirs of the Persian kings, Alexander, Alexander's successors, and a long chain of other benefactors and authorities. Such expressions of gratitude and respect as were offered to the emperors in both provincial temples and local shrines presented the people of the province as a whole or its individual cities as loyal and worthy recipients of ongoing imperial favors. The cult also presented a strong, divinely empowered emperor as the surest safeguard

52. Magie, *Roman Rule*, 1:481, 481n40.
53. Translation from Price, *Rituals and Power*, 1.

against the disruptions (from within, from without, from nature) that could upend the fragile lives of the majority of people in the provinces. The other side of this popular devotion shown to the emperors was the suspicion and disapproval with which the devotees looked upon those who withdrew from such expressions of loyalty and gratitude toward the rulers upon whom the peace and well-being of the community was perceived to depend.

We will encounter multiple first-century imperial cult sites in the seven cities whose Christian inhabitants were addressed by John. In every case, it will be important to bear in mind that the imperial cult—like the cults of the traditional gods—did not merely involve lifeless, static marble images and structures but involved processions of priests, worshipers, and sacred images through the cities, sacrifices of incense and animals, hymns recited by trained choirs, public feasts, and athletic and artistic competitions.[54] Sacrifices made to the traditional gods were often accompanied by prayers on behalf of the emperors, who, though worshiped as divine themselves, were also honored as the benign agents of beings who had *always* been recognized and worshiped as gods. Steve Friesen explains their interrelationship with admirable clarity:

> It was appropriate for the inhabitants [of the province] to sacrifice to the emperors because the emperors functioned like gods in relationship to them. It was also correct for inhabitants of the empire to sacrifice to the gods on behalf of the emperors because the emperors were not independent of the gods. . . . The gods looked after the emperors, who in turn looked after the concerns of the gods on earth to the benefit of humanity. Imperial authority ordered human society, and divine authority protected the emperors. . . . The crucial issue was the role of imperial authority in creating the kind of society which pleased the gods.[55]

The goddess Roma, the divinized personification of the city and people of Rome, was worshiped in tandem with the emperors as she had, indeed, been worshiped in several of the cities of Asia during the earlier period of the Republic. Such worship reinforced the public discourse about Rome's role in the divine ordering of the world. The Latin poet Virgil, an evangelist of the gospel of Rome, gave expression to this at several points in his *Aeneid*, which became a sort of court epic in the age of Augustus. At one point, Jupiter promises Venus that the Romans would "rule the sea and all the lands around it" (*Aen.* 1.236–37). Later, Jupiter speaks to Mercury of Rome's destiny to "bring the whole world under law's dominion" (4.232). Both passages promise universal rule to the Roman people. Such universal rule would continue to be

54. Thompson, *Book of Revelation*, 162; Friesen, *Imperial Cults*, 104–13.
55. Friesen, *Twice Neokoros*, 150, 152.

ascribed to Rome despite the authors' awareness of tribes and nations existing beyond Rome's borders, often hostile to Rome. Thus even Minucius Felix, a Christian writer of the second century, would claim that Rome's "power and authority has occupied the circuit of the whole world" (*Octavius* 6).[56] His near-contemporary, Aelius Aristides, would claim that Rome "rules the whole world" and that its "possession is equal to what the sun can pass" (*On Rome* 9–10).[57] First-century readers presented with a beast and its "one-world empire" in a text like Revelation (cf. Rev. 13:3b, 7b–8) need have looked no further for a real-life counterpart than the images projected of the very empire under which they had been living. Similarly, they would have been immediately familiar with John's depiction of a local authority orchestrating the worship of the beast and the (demonic) powers behind it (as in 13:4, 11–18). John the Seer has a passionate interest in seeing God vindicate his own honor and that of his worshipers against both the cults of the traditional gods and the imperial cult.[58]

A stunning example of the *visual* expression of the ideology of Roman rule has come to light in the excavated remains of the Temple of Rome and Augustus (the Sebasteion) in the city of Aphrodisias, a city of Roman Asia located about 90 miles east-southeast of Ephesus and 40 miles west-southwest of Laodicea. Inscriptions indicate that the construction of this complex began during the reign of Tiberius and was completed during the reign of Nero, funded principally by two of the city's ultra-elite families.[59] A large inscription indicates that the whole was dedicated "To Aphrodite" (the patron goddess of the city), "the *Theoi Sebastoi*" (the Augustan gods), and "the *Dēmos*" (the people of Aphrodisias).[60]

The complex is distinctive among imperial cult sites in that the temple itself stands at the east end of a 250-foot-long corridor formed by two parallel, three-story porticoes built about 40 feet apart (see fig. 1.2). At the west end was a propylon with niches once featuring statues of members of the imperial family. This grand entrance to the complex was accessible from Aphrodisias's principal forum. The primary purpose of the long corridor appears to have been the display of an estimated 190 carved reliefs placed on the second and third stories of both the north and south porticoes.[61] A major theme of the northern portico was the expansion of the empire through conquest or

56. Translation from Roberts and Donaldson, *Ante-Nicene Fathers*, 4:176.
57. Translation from Oliver, *Ruling Power*, 896.
58. Biguzzi, "Ephesus," 276–77.
59. Smith, "Imperial Reliefs," 90; Friesen, *Imperial Cults*, 83–84.
60. Smith, "Imperial Reliefs," 90.
61. Friesen, *Imperial Cults*, 85.

Figure 1.2. The partially reconstructed Sebasteion, looking out from the temple into the long courtyard toward the propylon.

reception of a wide array of people groups, each represented in carved relief by a stylized personification of the nation or ethnic group with an identifying caption. The Egyptians, Judeans, Arabs, Dacians, Cretans, Sicilians, Cypriots, and many others are included among surviving figures or fragments.[62]

The south portico combined scenes from Greek mythology with scenes depicting various emperors and members of the imperial family in propagandistic ways that seemed to add them alongside the Olympian gods and their exploits to the cultural repertoire of myth.[63] A number of scenes reinforced the northern portico's theme of creating empire through conquest (see fig. 1.3). Reliefs of Claudius subduing Britannia and Nero subduing Armenia are among the surviving pieces. Imperial victory is celebrated also in a number of other scenes: the goddess Roma placing a wreath of victory on Augustus's head as Augustus himself decorates a trophy while a bound captive sits at its base; Agrippina placing a victor's wreath on the head of her son, Nero, in military attire with his helmet at his feet; Augustus and a winged Victory (*Nikē*) preparing a trophy, again with a bound captive beneath; the goddess

62. Smith, "Imperial Reliefs," 95–96; Friesen, *Imperial Cults*, 86.
63. Smith, "Imperial Reliefs," 137.

Figure 1.3. Left: Augustus and Roma beside a Roman trophy. Right: Claudius subduing Britannia.

Author photos, courtesy of the Aphrodisias Museum, Türkiye.

Roma in military dress with a captive beneath her. The whole was clearly calculated to make an impression that would make worshipers exclaim—to use John's unflattering idiom—"Who is like the beast? And who is able to make war against him?" (Rev. 13:4).

Other reliefs display scenes from the Greek myths—Leda and the Swan, Hercules liberating Prometheus, Achilles and Penthesilea, Ajax and Cassandra. As one approaches the imperial temple, the scenes connect the mythic past with the imperial house through the story of the Fall of Troy. These include a scene of the goddess Venus (Aphrodite) and the Trojan Anchises looking upon their infant child, Aeneas, and a later scene of the adult Aeneas leaving the burning city of Troy with his aged father and his son, Ascanius (also known as Iulus and, as such, the mythic ancestor of the Julian family line).[64] As if the scenes by themselves would be too subtle, an inscribed caption below a niche on the propylon of the Sebasteion indicates that the niche was once occupied by a statue of "Aphrodite, progenitor of the Augustan gods."[65]

The Priene Calendar Inscription, the phenomenon of the imperial cult, and the panoply of visual images at the Sebasteion of Aphrodisias are all reflections and expressions of an ideology in which religion and political arrangements are perfectly wedded to offer a profound degree of legitimation to Roman imperial rule. All of its manifestations that pervaded the seven cities

64. Photos of these two panels appear as figure 10.7 in chap. 10 below.
65. Friesen, *Imperial Cults*, 81.

Figure 1.4. Augustus (or possibly Claudius) standing in authority over land and sea, the personified land giving him a cornucopia (a symbol of fecundity) and the personified sea handing him a rudder (symbolizing its navigability and, therefore, the prosperity of trade under his aegis) (Smith, "Imperial Reliefs," 106). Was such an image part of the inspiration for John's vision of a fiery, radiant angel—a decidedly more awe-inspiring figure than an emperor—standing with one foot on land and the other on the sea, declaring that God was about to reclaim sovereignty over this realm (Rev. 10:1–2, 5–7)?

and the lives of the Christ-followers addressed by Revelation bore witness to a widely embraced gospel: The gods in their good will toward humanity gave the world Augustus and his successors (their divine agents) and raised up the power of Rome to safeguard the whole of the civilized world, sustain the conditions for stability and prosperity, and aid their loyal and grateful devotees when the latter fell into adversity. Thanks be to the gods!

The Christ-followers living in this environment would immediately recognize John's assaults on this ideology and its physical and ritual manifestations. A great deal of the material in Revelation is devoted to unveiling this alternative "gospel" for what it is, in John's view—another, more desperate attempt of Satan, the enemy of God's good order, to deceive the nations and lead them astray from the worship of the one, unique God and his genuine agent of deliverance, Jesus the Messiah.

2

PATMOS

"I was on the island called Patmos on account of the word of God and the testimony of Jesus" (Rev. 1:9). With these words, John begins his narrative of the sights and sounds that filled his mind as he prayed to God and considered the challenges facing his churches on the mainland. Though scholars have occasionally argued that John went to Patmos for the sake of preaching there or for the purpose of reflection and receiving a word from the Lord,[1] everything points instead to John's having been relegated to this island contrary to his own will as a result of some judicial action against him. This was the understanding of early Christian writers of the third through fifth centuries as well as the clear, contextual sense of the expression John employs.[2]

Many Greek and Latin authors of the Roman Republican and Imperial periods bear witness to the practice of emperors and governors exiling persons condemned of certain crimes to particular islands, with the size and conditions of the island corresponding to the perceived egregiousness of the crime.[3] For example, Juvenal, a Roman satirist active toward the end of the

1. See, e.g., Thompson, *Book of Revelation*, 173.

2. See Tertullian, *Praescr.* 36; Eusebius, *Hist. eccl.* 2.20; Jerome, *Vir. ill.* 9. Comparison with similar expressions concerning executions occurring "on account of [*dia*] the word of God and the testimony of Jesus" (Rev. 6:9) or "on account of [*dia*] the testimony of Jesus and the word of God" (20:4) strongly suggests that the preposition *dia* in the same expression in Rev. 1:9 also indicates the cause of some untoward consequence rather than purpose.

3. Dio Cassius, *Hist. rom.* 56.27.1–2; Philo, *Flaccus* 1.51, 157, 159; Tacitus, *Ann.* 3.69; 4.13, 30; 15.71. See the extensive study of the different types of exile and the particular cases of *relegation ad insulam* ("relegation to an island"), including discussion of these texts, in Rapske, "Exiles," 315–22, 325–30.

first century AD, describes several Greek islands that are near to Patmos as "rocks crowded with our noble exiles" (*Satires* 13.246).[4] Though these authors do not mention Patmos specifically, this smallish island would have served such a function well, a place to send largely elite undesirables, removing them from their places of influence where they might foment trouble or otherwise cause embarrassment for Rome and its leaders. Such relegation to a particular island was a sentence available to provincial governors and might have been particularly suited to John's case.[5]

Figure 2.1. The island of Patmos.

Patmos was thus the place of John's banishment, his removal from the mainland where he had no doubt been stirring up trouble with his virulently anti-Roman views and his promotion of an eastern cult that turned good, gods-fearing people into virtual atheists. It is a mystery that he was banished rather than simply executed, though banishment *from* a locale or exile *to* a locale was sometimes chosen as the remedy for peddlers of unwanted superstitions—and particularly for astrologers and prophets whose predictions undermined confidence in the present order of things.[6] It is tempting to consider, though impossible to demonstrate, that the sentence of exile (rather than execution) was applied to John because John enjoyed some claim to elite status, most likely connected to his status in Judea. Roman officials often mitigated a sentence out of consideration for the higher status of those found guilty of crimes. On the other hand, the diminutive size of Patmos argues for the seriousness with which his conduct was viewed.[7]

Patmos is an irregularly shaped island that stretches 7 miles from north to south (see fig. 2.1). At its widest, it is about 5 miles; at its narrowest, just

4. Quoted in Boxall, *Patmos*, 174.
5. Boxall, "Reading the Apocalypse," 30n29; Rapske, "Exiles," 319, 324–25.
6. Rapske, "Exiles," 320–21; C. Koester, *Revelation*, 243.
7. Rapske, "Exiles," 332.

Credit: James-Michael Smith

Figure 2.2. The landscape of the central portion of Patmos. The white buildings mark the modern port city of Skala at the western end of a long harbor.

a few hundred yards. Pliny describes it as having a circumference of about 30 miles (*Nat.* 4.23), but this figure masks the small size of the island. The irregularity of its coastline means that Patmos has an area of only 13 square miles. Patmos was one of several islands within the jurisdiction of the city of Miletus (28 miles south of Ephesus) during the Hellenistic period. Lying 42 miles west-southwest of Miletus, Patmos had been colonized and fortified to provide protection for Miletus (and its trading lanes) by sea.[8] The island continued to support a local population throughout the Roman period and remained a regular stop on maritime trade routes between Asia Minor or other eastern Mediterranean points of origin and Greece. The island itself, having a very uneven coast, offered many natural harbors to ships carrying goods back and forth across the Aegean (see fig. 2.2).

When John found himself on Patmos, then, he did not look out upon barren, rocky, deserted landscapes—the image of Patmos passed along in countless works of art and poorly researched study Bibles. It was inhabited by families (not just prisoners or exiles) throughout the Hellenistic and Roman periods, to judge from cemeteries (*nekropoleis*) and funerary inscriptions and monuments that have been discovered throughout the island.[9] There is no physical evidence of mines or a penal colony on Patmos, calling into question the traditional image of John having been exiled to Patmos in connection with being condemned to a mine or a particular prison.[10] Removal from his

8. Saffrey, "Relire L'Apocalypse," 386–87; Tibor, *Patmiaka*, 3; Wilson, "Social and Geographical World of Patmos," 620–21.

9. C. Koester, *Revelation*, 240.

10. Hemer, *Letters*, 27; Boxall, "Reading the Apocalypse," 24n3.

sphere of influence appears to have been deemed sufficient to neutralize the threat he presented.

Tradition paints a more eloquent picture than does the actual evidence concerning the conditions of John's stay on the island. A mosaic over an entrance to the traditional "Cave of the Apocalypse," a major tourist destination on Patmos, depicts John dictating his visions to his scribe and disciple, Prochorus, known in Scripture only as one of the seven deacons introduced in Acts 6:1–6. Prochorus sits inside the cave where John allegedly lived during his season on Patmos (see fig. 2.3). Such a scene comes to us not from Scripture, however, but from a fifth-century AD legend found in the "Acts of the Holy Apostle and Evangelist John the Theologian," written in the name of Prochorus.

Figure 2.3. A modern-era mosaic at the entrance to the so-called Cave of the Apocalypse depicting John receiving visions and Prochorus dutifully writing down what John says.

The landscape of Patmos is currently dominated by the Monastery of Saint John, founded in the eleventh century, set on a hill opposite Mount Kastelli. This monastery now stands on a site that had once been occupied by a temple dedicated to Artemis, which previously commanded the Patmos skyline as its Christian successor does now.[11] An inscription found on the island, variously dated to the second through the early fourth century AD,[12] bears witness to the presence of a cult and temple of Artemis Patmia, claiming the goddess for the island in a manner comparable to what we find in Ephesus (Artemis Ephesia). The inscription honors a priestess of Artemis named Bera (or Vera) and calls Patmos "the most noble island of Leto's daughter," Leto being the mother of both Artemis and Apollo (see fig. 2.4).[13] An inscription was also found on part of an altar under the monastery complex itself that names Artemis Patmia as the dedicatee of a temple there.[14]

11. Boxall, "Reading the Apocalypse," 25–26.
12. Tibor, *Patmiaka*, 3–4.
13. Saffrey, "Relire L'Apocalypse," 399–405.
14. Tibor, *Patmiaka*, 6–7.

Figure 2.4. The inscription honoring Vera, priestess of Artemis Patmia.

An acropolis once stood on the top of Mount Kastelli, which overlooks the modern port of Skala. Those who hike to its summit can still see the remains of significant fortifications from the Hellenistic period, particularly of the walls surrounding the acropolis (see fig. 2.5). These fortifications had been built and manned primarily to protect the shipping lanes from piracy. From this altitude, lookouts on the watchtowers could keep an eye on the ships coming in and out of the island's ports and intervene if any criminal activity threatened the flow of trade east and west.

Only the foundations and lowermost courses remain of buildings that would have stood proudly here during John's time of exile. These might represent the foundation of a military fortress, though a temple

Figure 2.5. Remnants of the fortification walls surrounding the Hellenistic-period citadel.

Figure 2.6. A portion of the remains of an unidentified Hellenistic-period building atop the citadel.

might also have stood here (see fig. 2.6). The fifth-century legendary Christian text *The Acts of John* speaks of a Temple of Apollo on the island. The hill opposite the one on which the Temple of Artemis once stood would have been an apt location for such a cult site of Artemis's twin brother.

The paucity of remains are the result of a practice that has ravaged archaeological sites across the Mediterranean over the centuries—recycling. Nothing is so attractive to the next century of builders as a pile of precut stones from a derelict building ready to be repurposed for some new construction. Unfortunately, there appear to be no plans for further excavations that might lead to greater certainty about the purpose or extent of the structures on the acropolis.

There were also major temples of Artemis on the mainland (as in Ephesus and Sardis); a temple to her brother, Apollo, in Miletus, of which Patmos had been a kind of satellite island; and a monumental temple to Apollo at Didyma, 10 miles south of Miletus and 38 miles south of Ephesus. Temples to the twin deities were not infrequently found together, as in Didyma, on the island of Rhodes, and in Rome itself (on hills facing each other across the Circus Maximus). The Temple of Apollo at Didyma—a structure almost as large as the Temple of Artemis at Ephesus—was home to a famous oracle of Apollo,

Figure 2.7. A statue from Miletus depicting Apollo holding his *kithara*.

the deity most closely linked with prophecy throughout the ancient world. Apollo's oracles at Didyma, Claros, and Delphi were consulted by elites and occasionally non-elites on matters of diplomacy, strategy, and policy as well as personal matters, and the oracle would give cryptic responses that were received as messages from the god himself.

Scholars of Revelation have suggested that John, as a prophet of the one true God, might have been particularly alert not only to the activity of rival *Christian* prophets like "Jezebel" in Thyatira (Rev. 2:20) but also to the pervasive belief in prophets of the Greco-Roman gods—those claiming inspiration by Apollo being by far the most prominent in Greek culture (see fig. 2.7). John would have regarded these as mouthpieces for demons, ultimately part of the web of deception spun over the inhabitants of the earth by Satan himself (12:9; 20:3, 7–10; see also 13:13–14).[15] The author of the fourth book of the *Sibylline Oracles*, another Jewish writer from the late first century AD, explicitly denounces the "prophecy" connected with Apollo (Phoebus) and promotes the prophets of the one God (including himself!) as the genuine spokespersons for the divine:

> I am not an oracle-utterer of false Phoebus, whom vain
> men called a god and falsely called a prophet,
> but of the great God, whom no hands of men made
> like speechless idols of polished stone. (*Sib. Or.* 4.4–7)[16]

Some have suggested that John's audiences would have made a connection between the rider armed with a bow who goes forth with the opening of the

15. On the association of the traditional gods and their idols with demons, see Ps. 106:37; Bar. 4:7; 1 Cor. 10:20–21; and Rev. 9:20.

16. As quoted in Stewart Lester, "Revealed History," 469.

first seal (Rev. 6:1–2) and Apollo. The bow is Apollo's weapon of choice (as also that of his sister, Artemis/Diana) and widely linked to him in Greco-Roman literature beginning with Homer, who uses epithets for Apollo involving a bow (e.g., "Apollo of the Silver Bow") throughout the *Odyssey* and the *Iliad*.[17] On this reading, the breaking of the first seal unleashes false prophecy—perhaps even specifically the prophecies concerning the divine role that Rome and her emperors played and Rome's destiny to rule forever.[18] Contrary to the public discourse about Rome, John claimed that its rise did not mean peace and prosperity for the world but rather rampant bloodshed, famine, and pestilence (6:3–8).

John may take another shot at Apollo in his depiction of the horrors that follow the sounding of the fifth trumpet (Rev. 9:1–12). One of the epithets applied to Apollo was Parnopius, which means "expeller of locusts" (cf. Pausanias, *Descr.* 1.24.8; Aeschylus, *Agammemnon* 1080–86). John's visions may recast the god elsewhere celebrated for ending plagues of locusts as the leader of a horde of demonic locusts, with *Apollyōn* ("Destroyer"), the name of this leader, offering a sinister play on Apollo's name (*Apollōn*, in Greek). Such a transformation would be in keeping with John's conviction that the gods worshiped throughout the Greco-Roman world are, in fact, demons (Rev. 9:20), with Satan as their chief.

Perhaps the most widely accepted point of resonance between the visions of Revelation and the background of Greek and Roman myths connected with Leto and her children was to be heard in John's depiction of the confrontation between a pregnant, celestial woman and a dragon or snake that wishes to devour her offspring to prevent his own demise—which he nevertheless fails to do (Rev. 12:1–6). John could be heard to reconfigure the popular myth concerning the births of Apollo and Artemis. According to this legend, the serpent Python, itself a prophetic spirit, received knowledge that it would be killed by a child born of the human woman, Leto. When Python learned that Zeus had visited and impregnated Leto, it sought her out to destroy her and, with her, the unborn threat to its own life. Leto was carried off by the north wind (named Aquilo—a name related to the word for "eagle," cf. Rev. 12:14) to the island of Delos, where she was hidden and could give birth safely. When her male child, Apollo, was four days old, he sought out Python and killed it in revenge for its attempt on his mother's life.[19]

17. See the many references in Kerkeslager, "Apollo," 118–19.

18. Boxall, "Reading the Apocalypse," 28–29.

19. The legend was, of course, told at different times with a number of variations. For more details, see Yarbro Collins, *Combat Myth*, 57–85; Edwards, "Rider on the White Horse," 529–33; Stewart Lester, "Revealed History," 464–69.

The likelihood that the residents of the cities of Roman Asia would have had knowledge of this story is demonstrated by the popularity of depictions of its scenes in household art and on coins as well as references to its characters in inscriptions—including the inscription honoring Vera, the priestess of Artemis, which identifies Artemis as "Leto's daughter."[20] They might have heard John *correcting* this myth, now casting Christ as the divine child and Satan, "the dragon, that ancient serpent" (Rev. 12:9), as the antagonist whose efforts ultimately fail in regard to the woman and to her male child. Thus Satan now turns his vengeful, destructive attention to "the rest of her children," among whom the members of John's audiences find themselves, before his own inescapable end (which will be narrated in 20:1–10). With the "true story" behind the familiar but twisted myth laid out in this fashion, the audience would further understand John to align Rome's emperors, who were often joined to the heroic Apollo in the public discourse about their rule,[21] with the dragon/serpent instead. In John's telling, the dragon would go on to summon these "heads" of state and enforce their worship as divine beings as part of his plan to harm the many brothers and sisters of Christ (12:17–13:18).

Figure 2.8. The inscription concerning the "torch runners" from the gymnasium.

Other archaeological finds testify to the relative liveliness of Patmos as an island. An inscription from the second century BC bears witness to the presence of a gymnasium (see fig. 2.8). A gymnasium provided a venue for the practice of Greek athletic games and keeping oneself in shape. But a gymnasium was also typically a place for the education of the young, training them in all the facets of the Greek curriculum, including grammar, logic, rhetoric, arithmetic, geometry, music, and astronomy. The presence of a gymnasium indicates the presence of

20. See, further, Yarbro Collins, *Combat Myth*, 117–19, 245–52; Aune, *Revelation 6–16*, 667–76; van Henten, "Dragon Myth"; Balch, "Woman Clothed."

21. Virgil hailed Augustus as Apollo (*Eclogue* 4.10), while Nero's chorus of "Augustiani" praised him as Apollo, Pythios, and Pythian Victor. Dio Cassius, *Hist. rom.* 62.20.5; Cuss, *Imperial Cult and Honorary Terms*, 77–80; van Henten, "Dragon Myth," 192.

a larger well-functioning society of families continuing to inculcate the next generation in the Greek way of life. The inscription in figure 2.8 speaks of an association of torch runners, a kind of club within the gymnasium, who participated in a sacred race to take fire to an altar of Hermes, the patron god of gymnasia, on the island. The location of both the gymnasium and the altar or shrine dedicated to Hermes remain unidentified.[22] A temple to Aphrodite is also believed to have once stood on a rocky promontory in Grikos Bay in the southeast area of the island.[23]

The bold landscape of Patmos well suits John's visions. Vistas to the sea on every side invite us to imagine the forces of evil rising from them like Hydra-headed monsters. We can imagine the twenty-five or so islands visible from Patmos's own shore shaking and falling before the coming wrath of God and God's Lamb. Active cult sites even here on the island of John's banishment—where the worship due the one God was, in his opinion, being offered to demons (Rev. 9:20–21)—serve as a reminder of how fully against the grain Christian practice went throughout the empire. Exile was the consequence of John's witness, but it did not silence his witness, and so he left to his own churches and the church in every age a vibrant call to witness to what was due the one God and to avoid compromising that witness at any cost.

22. Saffrey, "Relire L'Apocalypse," 393–97.
23. Wilson, "Social and Geographical World of Patmos," 622.

3

EPHESUS

Unlike the other six cities addressed by John, Ephesus was an early epicenter of the emerging Christian movement. Paul and his team had worked to plant congregations there over the course of several years (AD 53–55; see Acts 19:1–20:1). They apparently used it as a base from which to spread the message about Jesus to the many residents of the province whose business brought them to Ephesus (19:10, 26) and to plant congregations in at least several of the other cities of the province (see, e.g., Col. 1:7–8; 4:12–13, which speak of Epaphras's ministry in Colossae, Hierapolis, and Laodicea). Several writings that would come to be part of the New Testament were written from Ephesus (e.g., 1 Corinthians) or addressed to readers in Ephesus (e.g., Ephesians, 1 Timothy).[1] Ephesus may also have served as a hub for the Christians most directly nurtured by the Johannine literature of the New Testament. Tradition associates both the apostle John and "John" the Elder (the author of 1–3 John) with Ephesus.[2] If this is the case, then the drama of the rival church factions behind 1–3 John played out against the backdrop of this city as well.

Geography and Demographics

Roman Ephesus was located near the mouth of the Cayster River (the modern Küçük Menderes River; see fig. 3.2) on the shore of a harbor opening onto

1. Murphy-O'Connor, *St. Paul's Ephesus*, 201–2, 235–43. Paul Trebilco (*Early Christians*, 206–9) favors the view that both 1 and 2 Timothy were addressed to Christian communities in Ephesus (though as letters that were written in Paul's name between AD 80–100 and circulated after his death).

2. See discussion in Trebilco, *Early Christians*, 241–92.

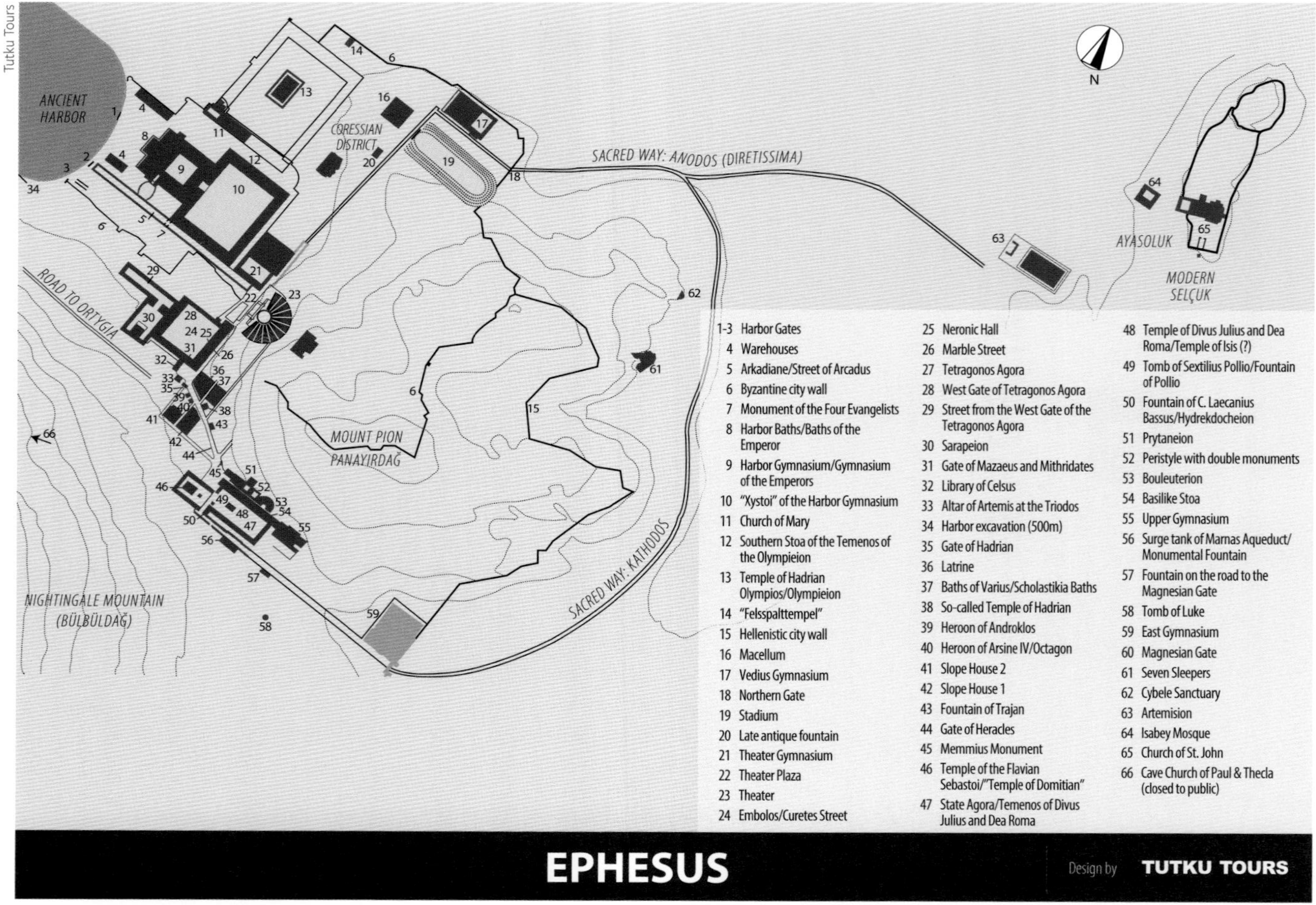

Figure 3.1 Map of the excavations at Ephesus

the Aegean Sea. The city stretched inland into the valley between Mount Pion (Panayır Dağ) and Mount Coressus (Bülbül Dağ) and up the lower slopes of both hills. The natural harbor, which had to be periodically dredged because of the silting caused by the Cayster River, made Ephesus a major node for shipping in trade between east and west (Strabo, *Geogr.* 14.1.24). The effects of the constant silting can be dramatically seen from the fact that the ruins of Roman Ephesus now sit 3 full miles inland from the Aegean shore, the ancient harbor having become a swamp.

The location of Roman Ephesus is the result of a decision made around 300 BC by Lysimachus, one of Alexander's successors. A settlement had been established in the eighth century BC on the north side of the base of Mount Pion.[3] During the Classical period, the settlement relocated to an area about a mile to the northeast, between the base of a third hill (the Ayasoluk) and the famous Temple of Artemis. Lysimachus chose the city's final location to make of Ephesus a major port city and fortified it with a perimeter wall of about 6 miles in circumference.[4] One frequently encounters the suggestion that the Ephesian Christians would have connected the glorified Christ's warning—"Otherwise I am coming to you swiftly and I will move your lampstand out of its place, unless you repent" (Rev. 2:5)—with this history of relocation.[5] I find it highly unlikely, however, that two relocations over the yawning space of eight centuries, the second of which lay almost four centuries in the past, would have been an association these Christians would have made. The threat, moreover, is not about the inconvenience of relocation but about something more substantive—

Figure 3.2. A statue of the Cayster, portrayed in the standard fashion of a river god.
Author photo, courtesy of the Ephesus Archaeological Museum, Türkiye.

3. Hemer, *Letters*, 35.
4. Wilson, *Biblical Turkey*, 199–200; Fairchild, *Christian Origins*, 23.
5. See, e.g., Hemer, *Letters*, 52–54.

not merely being sidelined and losing its status (something to which, as we will see, the people of these cities were highly sensitive) but being removed from the scene entirely.[6]

Ephesus was the westernmost point on a series of highways that led east as far as India, most of that route having originated as the "Royal Road" from the Persian period linking its western capital, Sardis, with the Persian heartland (Strabo, *Geogr.* 14.2.29; Herodotus, *Hist.* 5.53–54).[7] It was also a node on a major Roman-period road running from north to south along the coast of Roman Asia. Ephesus was thus well positioned to prosper from trade both by land and by sea.

The population of first-century Ephesus is estimated to have fallen between one hundred twenty-five thousand and two hundred thousand people, making Ephesus the fourth- or fifth-largest city in the empire.[8] Immigration was a huge factor in the growth of the city. The infant mortality rate was about 33 percent during the first year of life and 50 percent by the fifth year; the maintenance of the population suggests a steady flow of immigrants.[9]

There is no significant archaeological evidence for the presence of a Jewish community in Ephesus beyond a handful of inscriptions and other artifacts bearing common, iconic Jewish decorations (the menorah, shofar, lulav, and/or etrog).[10] There is, however, ample literary evidence, particularly in Josephus's *Jewish Antiquities*. Josephus documents the exemption from military service, first of the Jews in Ephesus who were Roman citizens (*Ant.* 14.228) and then, from 43 BC on, all Jews in the province of Asia (14.225–27).[11] He also records that Augustus affirmed the right of these Jewish communities to collect money and to transport it to Jerusalem for the maintenance of the Jewish temple and its sacrifices and personnel—a special exemption from the general prohibition of moving significant amounts of silver and gold across provincial lines for any but imperially sanctioned purposes (16.167–68).[12] Acts, of course, also bears witness to a Jewish community there, centered on a synagogue (Acts 19:8–10) but also sufficiently attached to the Jerusalem temple to make pilgrimages there and zealously guard it against perceived violation (21:27–29).

6. C. Koester, *Revelation*, 270; Aune, *Revelation 1–5*, 147.

7. Murphy-O'Connor, *St. Paul's Ephesus*, 36–37.

8. Murphy-O'Connor, *St. Paul's Ephesus*, 131–32; Wilson, *Biblical Turkey*, 200.

9. White, "Urban Development," 45.

10. Wilson, *Biblical Turkey*, 216.

11. Murphy-O'Connor, *St. Paul's Ephesus*, 80; Trebilco, *Early Christians*, 37–51. See the more extensive references in Josephus, *Ant.* 14.223–27, 228–29, 230, 234, 238–40, 262–64, 301–13, 314–17; 16.27–65; *Ag. Ap.* 2.39.

12. See, further, Trebilco, "Jewish Community."

The Landmarks of Downtown Ephesus

Many scholars consider John to have exercised an itinerant ministry among these seven congregations, for which he appears to have had a particular burden and with whom he appears to have been closely acquainted. As he did so, John might have had occasion to enter Ephesus from the road that leads west from Laodicea. If so, he would have entered Ephesus by the "Magnesian" Gate, the major opening in the fortification walls on the southeast side of the city. Magnesia on the Meander was the next major city along this road, lying about 15 miles to the east.[13] A short walk would have brought him into the civic forum, the center of the city's government. Here he would have seen a largely open courtyard of about 525 by 190 feet surrounded by columned porches, the most magnificent of which would have been the Basilica Stoa, constructed around 11 BC by Sextilius Pollio.[14] This two-story, three-aisled portico was 50 feet wide, stretching the entire length of the civic forum on its north side. Its covered area, supported by 67 Ionic columns, would have been a popular place for businessmen and city politicians to meet and conduct business out of the sun or rain. The stoa was dedicated "to Artemis of the Ephesians, Emperor Caesar Augustus, son of a god, Tiberius Caesar, son of Augustus, and to the Ephesian people" with larger-than-life statues of Augustus and his wife, Livia, in an alcove on its easternmost side (see fig. 3.3).[15]

Figure 3.3. The Basilica Stoa, together with the remains of the statues of Augustus and Livia that once graced its easternmost alcove.
Author photo, courtesy of the Ephesus Archaeological Museum, Türkiye.

13. Murphy-O'Connor, *St. Paul's Ephesus*, 35; Wilson, *Biblical Turkey*, 207.
14. Wilson, *Biblical Turkey*, 209; Murphy-O'Connor, *St. Paul's Ephesus*, 190.
15. Price, *Rituals and Power*, 140, 255; Friesen, *Imperial Cults*, 95–96; Wilson, *Biblical Turkey*, 209.

The city was well supplied with water, with significant amounts being brought in by aqueducts, one of which was also constructed as a gift to the city by the same Sextilius Pollio (see fig. 3.4). A major water-collection node, called a *castellum aquae* in Latin, was located on the south side of the civic forum. Water would be distributed throughout the city, through both stone and clay channels, to public fountains and private residences. Several veins of clay water pipes are now visible where the pavement of the civic forum has been cleared away. The water system also serviced several bathhouse installations throughout the city, one of which was located in the east corner of the civic forum, not yet sufficiently well excavated to reveal all the various elements of a Roman bath experience that it once offered—notably the warm bath, sauna and hot pools, and cold plunge pools.

Figure 3.4. A portion of the Pollio aqueduct visible to the south of the city. A Roman road once passed through the central arch.

Several public buildings dominated the first-century civic forum, three of which stood on the north side of the Basilica Stoa. The first of these was the Prytaneion, located in the northwest corner of the forum. This was the site of the city's sacred hearth, the symbolic fire kept perpetually burning, and as such was dedicated to Hestia, the goddess of the hearth (whether of a home or of the city as a whole). As a symbol of the city's hospitality, state dinners would have been held and foreign dignitaries entertained here. It appears also to have housed a cult of Demeter Karpophoros ("Fruit-Bearer"), celebrating Demeter as the goddess of an abundant harvest.[16] Inscriptions on the re-erected pillars record the names of the priests—the *kouretai* (Latinized as *curetai*; see fig. 3.5). These priests oversaw cultic rites to Hestia in this building and also oversaw the rites of the Ortygian mysteries of Artemis. The latter were celebrated not far from Ephesus in a sacred grove on Mount Solmissos,

16. Friesen, *Imperial Cults*, 63.

Figure 3.5. The remains of the Prytaneion with a close-up of one of the many column drums bearing the names of the priests who both served and subsidized the cults of Hestia and Artemis in the city.

near modern Şirince (Strabo, *Geogr.* 14.1.20). A fairly consistent record of these *kouretai*, along with the *prytanes* (the Prytaneion's chief officials), can be reconstructed from the reign of Tiberius through the mid-third century AD on the basis of these inscribed pillars.[17] Alongside the priests, the inscriptions list several other ritual offices: an "inspector of the victims," a "sacred herald," and a flute player at the drink offering.[18]

A small temple of Artemis, the city's patron goddess, stood next to the Prytaneion. By the turn of the era, part of this temple had been rededicated also to the worship of Julius Caesar (see fig. 3.6). It consisted of a courtyard of about 108 by 95 feet surrounded by colonnades on three of its sides; on the fourth side, a series of seven steps led up to twin shrines.[19] The blending of the imperial cult with the cult of Artemis was significant in Ephesus. Its elite was eager to demonstrate itself pious in regard to its devotion and duty toward both Artemis and the *Augusti* or the *Sebastoi* (the emperors, all of whom inherited the title "Augustus" or, in Greek, *Sebastos*). Sextilius

17. Rogers, "Ephesian Tale," 81.

18. On the "mysteries of Artemis" at Ephesus, see Llewelyn and Kearsley, *New Documents*, 6:196–202.

19. Price, *Rituals and Power*, 139, 254; Murphy-O'Connor, *St. Paul's Ephesus*, 190–91. See Dio Cassius, *Hist. rom.* 51.20.6–7, regarding Augustus's authorization of this shrine for the Roman citizens living in Ephesus.

Figure 3.8. The foundations and a sampling of architectural fragments from the Temple of Augustus and Roma (top left and bottom). In the first century, the edifice would have closely resembled the Temple of Augustus and Roma still standing in Nimes, France (top right).

God of Israel and his Messiah, Jesus, who would truly "reign into the ages of ages," rather than Rome's emperors (11:15).

John would have left the civic forum by a single, columned street beginning in its northwest corner and leading eventually to the commercial center of Ephesus (see fig. 3.9). Archaeologists have named this road "Curetes Street" because it begins at the Prytaneion where the *kouretai* carried out their duties. In antiquity it appears to have been known as the *Embolos* (the "Wedge") because it cut diagonally across the city's grid pattern.[24] The street was lined with shops built into recesses behind the colonnades as well as statues set atop bases that bore inscriptions honoring public benefactors of the city (and thus, incidentally, bearing witness to the cultural importance of honoring them as such). For example, a local physician was celebrated with a stone statue set upon a base bearing this inscription: "The council and the citizenry honor the physician Alexander, son of Alexander." Grander honorary monuments were also found along this street. One of these is a memorial built to Caius Memmius, a grandson of the dictator Lucius Cornelius Sulla, who had recaptured the territories taken by Mithridates VI of Pontus (Appian, *Mithridatic Wars* 12.4.22–23; Valerius Maximus, *Memorable Deeds and Sayings* 9.2.4).

24. Murphy-O'Connor, *St. Paul's Ephesus*, 191.

Figure 3.9. The view looking southeast down the Embolos, or "Curetes Street."

Figure 3.10. The remains of the monument honoring Caius Memmius. The reliefs represent members of his family as well as personifications of his virtues.

What made Memmius deserving of such recognition beyond having an illustrious, if controversial, grandfather is unknown. It is likely, however, that Memmius himself, being a member of the ultra-elite, also served as an important benefactor of Ephesus during his lifetime (see fig. 3.10). Another monument served as a tomb for local benefactor Sextilius Pollio, appropriately erected just beyond and below the west end of Pollio's Basilica Stoa. In this, Pollio was given special consideration, for burials almost always took place outside the city walls.

At the base of the Embolos stand two blocks of town houses, the second of which sits under a protective Kevlar roof, having undergone significant restoration. The houses in

Figure 3.11. Two views into the interior of one of the terrace houses, one showing the re-erected peristyle courtyard at the heart of one of these units, another showing their ornately frescoed walls and mosaic-adorned floors.

this block give visitors a glimpse into the colorfully decorated interior spaces of ancient homes (see fig. 3.11). The quality of their preservation approaches that of houses in Pompeii. Though the foundations of the houses date back to the first century BC, they remained occupied (and continued to be modified) at least through the fourth century AD and, thus, reflect a later period in the form in which they have been recovered. Nevertheless, there is little in them that would not also have been at home in the first century AD, as the residential blocks of Pompeii bear witness. This second block appears to contain six or perhaps seven individual units, most of which originally had a second story (given the presence of the bases of staircases).[25] Two of these individual units measure about 4,000 and 7,000 square feet, respectively—lavishly spacious even by modern standards, and all the more so by ancient standards. The size of these dwellings, the provisions for indoor plumbing (and even private bathhouses complete with saunas), and the elaborate decorations that adorn them in the way of frescoes and mosaics show these to be the houses of the rich and powerful citizens of Ephesus, the elites who most prospered under Roman administration of Asia.

More monuments were found at the base of Curetes Street. In front of the second block of town houses once sat the monument of Arsinoë IV, a half sister of Cleopatra VII of Egypt (see fig. 3.13). Toward the end of her failed run as a rival claimant to the throne, Arsinoë sought asylum in Ephesus's Artemision. She was dragged out from the sacred precinct and killed by Marc Antony's soldiers in 41 BC to advance Cleopatra's

Figure 3.12. Greek and Roman houses often had shrines (varying in size and ornamentation, depending on the economic status of the householder) equipped with small images of select deities and even small altars for offering incense.
Author photo, courtesy of the Ephesus Archaeological Museum, Türkiye.

25. For detailed discussion, see P. Scherrer, *Ephesus*, 100–113; Erdemgil et al., *Terrace Houses*.

Figure 3.13. Left: The base and some architectural fragments of the tomb monument of Arsinoë. Right: Architectural and decorative remnants re-creating one of the original eight faces of the monument.

interests in Egypt.[26] While little besides the base remains on site, a number of architectural fragments housed in the Ephesos Museum in Vienna give us some idea of the monument's stately grandeur. The impetus and the source of funding for the construction of the monument remain unknown, leading some to speculate that the monument was funded by Octavian himself after he and Antony began to fall out, as a means of memorializing the latter's act of sacrilege against the Temple of Artemis. A monument also once stood at this crossroads to honor Androclus, the legendary founder of Ephesus (Pausanias, *Descr.* 7.2.6–9; Strabo, *Geogr.* 14.1.3).

Figure 3.14. One of the public latrines in Ephesus. This installation, with seats lining three of the room's four sides, could accommodate forty-eight users. Note the channel in front of the seats, through which water constantly flowed. Sponges on sticks were provided for personal hygiene.

Opposite the terrace houses and adjacent to a bath complex that likely postdates the first century, there is an excellent example of an ancient latrine (see fig. 3.14). Modern visitors are always surprised at the lack of privacy and personal space that the ancients required for such functions. Latrines were frequently

26. Josephus, *Ant.* 15.89; cf. Dio Cassius, *Hist. rom.* 48.24.1–2; Appian, *Civil Wars* 5.1.9; Murphy-O'Connor, *St. Paul's Ephesus*, 45–46.

Figure 3.15. Above: The south gate to the commercial forum. Right: A close-up of the dedicatory inscription.

positioned near bathhouses so that, as the water in the latter was changed, the runoff could flush the latrines. Less expensive blocks of multistory apartments, or *insulae*, climbed Mount Pion on this side of the Embolos.[27]

The Embolos opens at its base into a public square that also affords one point of access to the commercial center of Ephesus—the *Tetragonos agora*, or the "Square Market." A magnificent gate built by Mazaeus and Mithridates, two freedmen (that is, former slaves) of the house of Augustus, gave access here to the southeast corner of the market (see fig. 3.15). An inscription in both Greek and Latin dedicates the gate, completed in 3 BC, to the honor of their former master and perpetual patron Augustus; his wife, Livia; Marcus Agrippa (at the time, Augustus's heir apparent); and Julia, daughter of Augustus and wife of Agrippa.[28] At the same time, it has brought recognition to Mazaeus and Mithridates for two millennia. The magnitude of the structure attests to the wealth that could be amassed by well-placed imperial freedmen during this period.

27. Murphy-O'Connor, *St. Paul's Ephesus*, 198.
28. Harrison, "Epigraphic Portrait," 32–35; Wilson, *Biblical Turkey*, 217.

Figure 3.16. The commercial forum and the street leading from the Embolos ("Curetes Street") to the theater, seen from the highest terrace houses.

As a sign of the city's growing economic importance, the commercial agora doubled in size during Augustus's reign, reaching dimensions of 370 by 370 feet (15,200 square yards).[29] Ephesus was indeed, as Strabo (*Geogr.* 14.1.24) called it near the turn of the era, the "largest emporium in Asia."[30] Columned porches on all four sides would have provided an ideal venue for buying, selling, or open-air preaching by promoters of a variety of philosophies and religious cults. These porticoes were impressive two-story structures with stairs at the corners giving access to the upper floor. The bottom floor of three of the porticoes gave access to sixty or so permanent workshops and stalls, like a great, ancient strip mall. A side street running north from Curetes Street alongside the agora and past the great theater also gave access to the upper story of the porticoes through a basilica, a great columned hall that was built during the early years of Nero's reign and dedicated to Artemis Ephesia, Nero, Agrippina, and the people of Ephesus (see fig. 3.16).[31] The vast open courtyard of the commercial forum would, of course, have also been filled with vendors' carts and tents (see fig. 3.17). Statues of public benefactors, including members of the imperial household, graced the complex. In AD 43, for example, an association of Roman merchants commissioned an equestrian statue of Claudius, who had recently risen to the throne.[32] As throughout the urban centers of Roman Asia, people sharing a common trade or craft formed associations in Ephesus. Inscriptions attest to associations of

29. Murphy-O'Connor, *St. Paul's Ephesus*, 197.
30. Quoted in Murphy-O'Connor, *St. Paul's Ephesus*, 26.
31. P. Scherrer, *Ephesus*, 142; Murphy-O'Connor, *St. Paul's Ephesus*, 198.
32. P. Scherrer, "City of Ephesos," 8; *Ephesus*, 142.

Figure 3.17. A view of the southeast area of the commercial forum.

"architects and fishermen, bankers and bakers, basket makers and bath workers, carpenters and cobblers, hemp-weavers and linen-weavers, silversmiths and slave dealers, wineskin-makers and wool dealers" in Ephesus, and the list is likely not exhaustive.[33]

From the commercial agora, John could have found his way to the harbor by two paths. One led through a gate in the west side of the agora that opened onto a street leading west to the harbor; another led through a gate on the north side that led eventually to a broad thoroughfare running between the great theater and the harbor (see fig. 3.18). This street was 36 feet wide and a third of a mile long.[34] It led past storehouses and more venues for vendors and merchants to conduct their business or inspect cargo and eventually to the harbor itself, which, in John's day, was one of the busiest seaports of the Roman Empire, a major node in the flow of goods from the east to Rome.

As such, it was also carefully regulated. A massive inscription was found on a slab that had been reused as construction material for a Byzantine-period

33. C. Koester, *Revelation*, 256; Harland, *Associations*, 39–40; Worth, *Seven Cities of the Apocalypse and Greco-Asian Culture*, 29.

34. Murphy-O'Connor, *St. Paul's Ephesus*, 27.

church (see fig. 3.18). The inscription, dated to the equivalent of July 9, AD 62, details the customs regulations of the harbor as well as penalties for smuggling and other infractions as laid out in 120 BC with updates in the form of a series of amendments extending to the principate of Nero. It prescribes the requirements for declaring cargo, the penalties for evasion (ll. 53–58), and classes of persons and properties that are exempt from having to pay customs duties (ll. 58–66).[35] The city of Pergamum, for example, petitioned Augustus for, and was granted, a special exemption on all customs dues for a thirty-day period surrounding the celebration of the quinquennial games in honor of Rome and Augustus, the *Romaia Sebasta* (ll. 128–33). A number of clauses protected merchants and shippers from the excesses of tax collectors and their agents. For example, while a tax collector who suspected a shipper of failing to declare all the goods liable to duty could order the shipper to unload his cargo for a closer inspection, failure to discover deception resulted in the tax collector having to pay the costs incurred in offloading and reloading the cargo.[36] Such a provision was likely instituted to stop tax collectors from *threatening* to have the cargo offloaded and searched as a way of prompting a payoff from the shipper to avoid the hassle and

Figure 3.18. Left: The broad street leading to the now silted and swampy harbor. Right: The inscription detailing the customs regulations for the port of Ephesus. The present shape of the slab resulted from the reuse of the massive stone in a later construction.

35. Line numbers are taken from Cottier et al., *Customs Law of Asia*.
36. Van Nijf, "Social World," 290.

expense. There is also mention of lawsuits against tax collectors (l. 150), though that line is too damaged to know the details.

There were several incentives for merchants and shipowners who were willing to put themselves in Rome's service. The harbor customs inscription stipulates that "no one is liable to pay tax for goods carried in service to the people of Rome, nor for goods conveyed for religious purposes."[37] The emperor Claudius provided insurance for ships dedicated to delivering grain to Rome, should they be lost at sea, which gave a major incentive in a risky industry. An inscription above the entrance to the somewhat pretentious tomb of one Flavius Zeuxis, a merchant and sea captain from Hierapolis, boasts of his making seventy-two successful trips around the southern coast of Greece to Italy (most likely using Ephesus as his port) in trade with Rome (see fig. 3.19). He was thus part of the enormous trade network that catered to the demands of the center of the empire, "by whom all those having boats in the sea grew rich" (Rev. 18:19). Zeuxis was the sort of person whom John would envision standing far off and lamenting Rome's demise and, with it, his source of income (18:15–19).

The Ephesian harbor indeed afforded a distinctive view into the Roman imperial economy, which directed a disproportionate percentage of the world's goods—both luxury items and staples—toward "the great city" (Rev. 17:18; see esp. 18:11–20). Much of the cargo listed in Revelation 18:12–13 could be found arriving in Ephesus from the east for further transportation west, including slaves for the city's slave markets, attested from inscriptions in

Figure 3.19. The tomb of shipmaster Flavius Zeuxis with a detail of the tomb's inscription.

37. The quotation comes from l. 58 of the inscription. See Kraybill, *Imperial Cult and Commerce*, 66; the translation is my altered version.

Figure 3.20. The great theater, seen from the interior.

the Square Market and from regulations concerning slave trafficking on the customs inscription.[38]

At the east end of "Harbor Street" stands the great theater of Ephesus (see fig. 3.20). Originally constructed during the Hellenistic period, it was expanded to its present dimensions over the course of a century beginning in about AD 40.[39] An inscription suggests that this was the regular place of meeting for the city council (the *boulē*), a group of perhaps two hundred men, into the early second century.[40] The theater, however, could accommodate a vast crowd of between twenty-one thousand and twenty-five thousand spectators.[41] It was here that the author of Acts set the riot that probably convinced Paul that it was time for him to move on from Ephesus (Acts 19:21–41). In that instructive episode, we see the intersection of economic interests, civic pride, the prominence of particular deities, and the ease with which local populations could be rallied by these factors against a foreign cult.

38. Shaner, "Ephesus," 372, 374; Harrison, "Epigraphic Portrait," 37–38.
39. Wilson, *Biblical Turkey*, 218.
40. Horsley, *New Documents*, 4:8.
41. For the lower estimate, see Wilson, *Biblical Turkey*, 218; for the higher, Fairchild, *Christian Origins*, 36.

Figure 3.21. The largely unexcavated interior of the Ephesus stadium, looking south toward the entrances.

The street that ran north from the Embolos past the great theater continued farther north to a gymnasium complex that began just diagonally across from the theater. A gymnasium was a staple, central institution in any Greek city, a center for learning and practicing the athletic skills—like boxing, wrestling, the pancratium, running, and the javelin throw—distantly related to the martial training of the Classical Greek city-states. It was also a place for the education and formation of youth into the citizenry of the future. During the Roman period, gymnasiums were typically joined to bath complexes to complete the experience of attending fully to the fitness and care of the body.

This same road led eventually to a vast, U-shaped stadium (see fig. 3.21). During the Hellenistic period, this had been a simple earthen stadium like the one at Olympia in Greece. During Nero's reign, it was reconfigured in stone with typical stadium seating over arched passageways.[42] It had the capacity to seat twenty thousand to twenty-five thousand spectators viewing the action on its field of 100 by 765 feet.[43] The stadium and theater were home to the *Ephesia*, an annual series of games drawing competitors from throughout the province and involving both athletic and artistic competitions, including music and dance.[44] These and other regularly held games were another venue in which imperial ideology entered the public consciousness. Not only were such games often held explicitly in honor of one or another emperor, but they could also include, among their poetical competitions, events for selecting the best hymns and speeches praising the deified emperors. A roster of winners from games held in honor of Augustus in Neapolis (Naples), Italy, in AD 94 included the names of those who were judged to have produced the best poetical work and the best laudatory speech for "the god Augustus," "the goddess Livia," "the god Claudius," "the god Vespasian," and "the god Titus" (see

42. Fairchild, *Christian Origins*, 23.

43. Worth, *Seven Cities of the Apocalypse and Greco-Asian Culture*, 22; Fairchild, *Christian Origins*, 37.

44. Murphy-O'Connor, *St. Paul's Ephesus*, 199.

Figure 3.22. One of several wall-sized stone slabs celebrating the winners of imperial games held in Naples in AD 94. This particular slab is dedicated to the winners of the contests in praise of the deified emperors and family members. Six of these winners came from either Smyrna or Pergamum. Orators in Roman Asia were well practiced in creating such hymns and speeches.

fig. 3.22). Notably, Domitian himself won "best poetical work" praising his deceased and deified brother.

Another principal egress from the city's fortifications could be found beyond the stadium—the Coressian Gate, from which the great Artemision, the city's pride, would have been clearly visible in the distance.

Artemis Ephesia

As was true in every major city in the Roman world, the residents of Ephesus were devoted to many deities. For example, the worship of the Phrygian mother goddess and symbol of fertility, Cybele, is attested in a shrine that stands on the far north side of Mount Pion (see fig. 3.23). Her cult myth involved, according to one version at least, the madness and self-castration of her lover, Attis, after he had broken faith with her—an act that was thenceforth to be replicated by her eunuch priests (Ovid, *Fasti* 4.241–44). Religious rites called "mysteries," which initiated individuals into a personal, protective relationship with a deity, were celebrated in honor of Demeter and her daughter Persephone, whose story was closely related to the agricultural cycle of each year.[45] Extensive evidence of private devotion to Aphrodite, Dionysus, and Isis was discovered in houses throughout the city. A public altar was dedicated to the Egyptian deities Serapis, Isis, and Anubis as early as the third century BC.[46] A monumental temple would be erected to Serapis, probably

45. Rogers, "Ephesian Tale," 72.
46. Walters, "Egyptian Religions," 284.

Figure 3.23. Left: One of many votive steles dedicated to Cybele at Ephesus. She is flanked by Zeus and, perhaps, by Attis, her lover. She holds a patera, a shallow bowl used in ritual offerings of wine, and is accompanied by one or more lions, the animals that drove her chariot. Right: A bust of Serapis, the Hellenized adaptation of the Egyptian god Osiris. Worship of Serapis, Isis, and Harpocrates spread widely throughout the Greek world in the Hellenistic and Roman periods.
Author photo, courtesy of the Ephesus Archaeological Museum, Türkiye (left), and the Louvre, France (right).

in conjunction with his consort Isis and their son, Harpocrates (Horus), just west of the commercial forum in the second century AD, suggesting a growing following throughout the first century (see fig. 3.23).

Ephesus was known throughout the eastern Mediterranean, however, as a city specially devoted to Artemis. Artemis was worshiped in many of the cities of Asia Minor (for example at Magnesia, Didyma, Sardis, and Perga), but Ephesus was home to her greatest temple. Very little remains today of the Artemision. Throughout the Byzantine and later periods, the perfectly cut stones of the derelict temple were quarried for new buildings (see fig. 3.24). In the first century, however, the great Temple of Artemis was one of the seven wonders of the ancient world—indeed, the crowning marvel among them according to the traveler Antipater of Sidon (*Greek Anthology* 9.58). It was a major destination for pilgrims and tourists from across the Mediterranean. With a footprint of 220 by 425 feet, the Artemision covered four times as much ground as the Parthenon in Athens. Double rows of columns 6.5 feet in diameter and 65 feet high stood around the temple's perimeter, supporting its

Figure 3.24. Left: The scant remains of the once-great Artemision. Right: A model of the temple based on the description in Pliny the Elder, *Nat.* 36.21.95–97.
Author photo, courtesy of the Ephesus Archaeological Museum, Türkiye.

roof (see fig. 3.25). These were arranged in rows of 8 on the shorter side and 20 on the longer side, with a total of 127 columns (Pliny the Elder, *Nat.* 36.21.95–97; Vitruvius, *De arch.* 3.2.7).[47] A grand altar stood about 100 feet in front of the temple itself.[48] Worship and sacrifices were conducted decorously in front of, and not within, the house of the goddess. A shrine to Augustus may also have been incorporated into this famous Artemision in the early Imperial period.[49]

In addition to being the most prominent religious site in the area, the temple also served major commercial functions. It was the ancient equivalent of a bank, using the proceeds from the lands owned by "the goddess" as capital to be lent out at interest and serving as a sacred depository for major sums of money, for both private and public funds (Caesar, *Civil Wars* 3.33, 105; Dio Chrysostom, *Or.* 31.54–55). Aelius Aristides (*Or.* 23.24) called it "the bank of all Asia."[50] Its activities were supported by

Figure 3.25. A single column drum sculpted with life-sized figures in low relief: Death (left) and Hermes (right) escorting either Alcestis or Eurydice to the underworld. Similar mythic scenes would have adorned many of the lower column drums in the Artemision.
Author photo, courtesy of the British Museum, England.

47. Murphy-O'Connor, *St. Paul's Ephesus*, 116–18.
48. Murphy-O'Connor, *St. Paul's Ephesus*, 22.
49. Price, *Rituals and Power*, 254.
50. Quoted in Murphy-O'Connor, *St. Paul's Ephesus*, 65.

Figure 3.26. Left: Artemis as represented throughout Asia and its neighboring provinces. This cult image was found buried beneath the Prytaneion, likely a miniature version of the cult statue housed in the great Artemision. Right: Artemis (or Diana) in her typically Greek form.

Right: Author photo, courtesy of the Louvre, France. Left: Author photo, courtesy of the Ephesus Archaeological Museum, Türkiye.

an immense staff of priests, functionaries, and temple slaves.

The Artemision sat less than a mile's walk from the Coressian Gate (the northern gate of Roman Ephesus) and about a mile and a quarter from the Magnesian Gate (the city's eastern gate). An annual calendar of sacred processions featuring Artemis connected the city with her temple. One itinerary brought the sacred images of Artemis and other cult images and paraphernalia from the temple to the Magnesian Gate, through the civic agora, down the Embolos, past the Square Market and theater, and out the Coressian Gate, to return ultimately to the Artemision. Over 250 participants might be involved in the typical sacred procession, carrying the images on platforms, singing, and carrying out various offerings at sacred locations throughout the city.[51] The month of Artemisia (March–April) was a period of increased cultic activity and festivals honoring Artemis, with processions, sacrifices, public feasts, various entertainments (poetry, drama), and athletic competitions filling the events calendar.[52]

We may be more familiar with Artemis, or Diana, as she is portrayed in the Greek or Roman art of Europe—as a divine huntress, often with bow at the ready and deer at her feet. Although Greek-style images of Artemis were found in private homes in Ephesus, this was not her public face in Asia Minor.[53] Cult statues show her as a mother goddess, still flanked by two deer, her chest covered with symbols of fertility (see fig. 3.26). It is debated

51. Xenophon of Ephesus, *Ephesian Tale* 1.2–3; Knibbe, "*Via Sacra Ephesiaca*," 153–54; Murphy-O'Connor, *St. Paul's Ephesus*, 177–79.

52. Worth, *Seven Cities of the Apocalypse and Greco-Asian Culture*, 45–47.

53. Aurenhammer, "Sculptures of Gods," 254, 276.

Figure 3.27. A silver cistophorus (a silver coin equal to four denarii) of Claudius featuring "Dian[a] Ephe[sia]" and her great temple on the reverse.
Used by permission of Classical Numismatic Group, LLC (Triton XIV, lot 649).

whether the dozens of protuberances on the cult figure's front should be understood as breasts (so Minucius Felix, *Octavius* 23.5), eggs, or even the testicles of bulls.[54] It is clear, however, that the more ancient worship of a regional fertility goddess was melded at an early stage with the worship of Artemis. She wears a peculiar headdress on which several buildings are carved in relief—perhaps representing the city of Ephesus itself, with Artemis as its personal patron and protector.[55] Representations of the cult statue or the facade of the Artemision (with the cult statue plainly visible within) appear frequently on provincial coin mintages. These coins bear the legend "Diana Ephesia" or "Artemis Ephesia," attesting to the city's pride in their identification with their patron goddess as they laid special claim to her as, in some sense, their own (see fig. 3.27).

Inscriptions found throughout Ephesus bear witness to the importance of both Artemis and the Roman emperor for the life of the city. One such inscription begins with a dedication to both "Ephesian Artemis" and Augustus and goes on to honor a member of the Ephesian elite named Vibius Salutaris as "philartemis kai philosebastos" (a friend of Artemis and friend of Augustus). Vibius had shown his devotion by underwriting the cost of a new, regular religious procession celebrating Artemis, the imperial gods, and the various tribes of the Ephesian people. What gives Vibius honor in this city is his piety toward and investment in the civic cults of Artemis and the emperor.[56]

In the Acts of the Apostles, a local concessioner named Demetrius, whose trade in miniature silver shrines of Artemis Ephesia depended on the reputation and worship of the goddess, is remembered to have successfully rallied thousands of Ephesus's citizens to gather in the theater to protest Paul's evangelistic activity (and success) around AD 54. A generation later, Artemis remained a prominent feature of the religious and civic landscape of Ephesus—a primary example of the kind of "idol of . . . stone" that the majority of the inhabitants of the city and, indeed, the province refused to renounce (Rev. 9:20).

54. Murphy-O'Connor, *St. Paul's Ephesus*, 7.
55. Murphy-O'Connor, *St. Paul's Ephesus*, 21.
56. Rogers, "Ephesian Tale," 87.

Ephesus and Developments in the Imperial Cult

By the time John wrote Revelation, the point of greatest conflict between the Christian movement and the city was moving away from Artemis and more fully toward the worship of the emperors, as the latter became a new focus for civic pride and identity, particularly in the context of competition among the leading cities of the province of Asia.

For most of the first century, Pergamum and Smyrna were the epicenters of the provincial imperial cult in Asia. Augustus and the Roman Senate granted the Pergamenes the honor of building the province's principal temple to the emperor Augustus and the goddess Roma in 29 BC, making it the center for the worship of Augustus in the province. Smyrna would rise to Pergamum's stature in AD 26, when it was selected from among eleven cities in Asia (including Ephesus and Pergamum) competing to host the provincial cult of Augustus's successor Tiberius, along with Tiberius's mother Livia and the Roman Senate. While a provincial imperial cult temple belonged, in some sense, to the whole province, cities within the province competed vigorously for the honor of hosting the provincial cult in their particular city.[57] Such grants conferred significant honor upon a city above its peers and also became a visible symbol of the emperor's favor toward the city, even as the city proposing to host the temple expressed its exuberant gratitude and loyalty toward the imperial family.

Ephesus had long had its local (municipal-level) temples of Julius and Augustus but was finally granted the honor of housing the leading temple of the provincial cult of a particular emperor in the late first century AD in response to the city's bid to undertake a massive temple, likely proposed to honor the emperor Domitian (ruled AD 81 to 96).[58] The new temple would be inaugurated in AD 89/90.[59] It is, in fact, unclear whether the temple was to be dedicated to more than one member of the Flavian line. It was referred to as "Asia's Shared Temple of the Augusti in Ephesus" (rather than simply the "Temple of Domitian") in inscriptions, particularly inscriptions made by representatives of other cities who thus claimed a share in the temple even while conceding its placement "in Ephesus."[60] One such inscription was discovered

57. Friesen, *Twice Neokoros*, 18.

58. It is possible that Ephesus had been awarded a provincial temple late in the reign of Nero but then lost this after Nero's death and the Senate's condemnation of his memory. This is, at least, one interpretation of the city's use of the title *neōkoros* on coins minted in AD 65 and 66, in contrast with the usual explanation that this reflects the city's relationship with Artemis. Burrell, *Neokoroi*, 60–62.

59. Friesen, *Twice Neokoros*, 41–49. See deSilva, *Week in the Life*, for a historical novella of the days leading up to this event.

60. Friesen, *Imperial Cults*, 45–46.

on the base of a votive statue erected by the people of Aphrodisias (see fig. 3.28) and reads as follows:

> To Emperor [[Domitian]] Caesar Sebastos [[Germanicus]] when Marcus Fulvius Gillo was serving as proconsul: The citizenry of the Aphrodisians, devotees of Caesar, being free and self-governing from the beginning by the favor of the Sebastoi, erected [this statue] by its own favor on account of its reverence for the Sebastoi and its goodwill toward the neokorate city of the Ephesians, for Asia's shared Temple of the Sebastoi in Ephesus.[61]

Figure 3.28. The dedicatory inscription erected by the city of Aphrodisias in "Asia's Shared Temple of the Augusti in Ephesus."

The inscriptions make clear that it was dedicated at first *at least* to Domitian and later associated only with his deceased and divinized father, Vespasian. Domitian himself had fallen so significantly out of favor with the Senate as to have suffered the condemnation of his memory—the opposite of the apotheosis that his father and brother (Titus) had enjoyed upon their passing.[62] Indeed, in this particular inscription, the words supplied above in double brackets were chiseled out of the original inscription and replaced rather awkwardly with the words "god" and "Vespasian" after Domitian's death and the Senate's action.[63]

The city fathers selected a prominent plateau on the west side of the civic forum (see fig. 3.29). Engineers artificially extended this plateau to an area of 280 by 210 feet by means of a vaulted and arched brickwork substructure to accommodate the grandiose plans for this temple and its surrounding courts and porticoes.[64] Worshipers approached from the Embolos, entering a broad plaza adorned on its east side by a new fountain erected in AD 92 or

61. *IEph* 233, based on the text and translation in Friesen, *Twice Neokoros*, 32–33; see also discussion in Friesen, *Imperial Cults*, 44–48. A similar dedicatory inscription erected by the citizens of Philadelphia has also been discovered.

62. Price, *Rituals and Power*, 178, 255.

63. Titus's name never explicitly appears in inscriptions connected with this temple, though he might still have been among the "Augusti/Sebastoi" revered here (Price, *Rituals and Power*, 255). This is, in part, dependent on the identification of the cult statue whose remains were discovered on the site (see below).

64. Shaner, "Ephesus," 379.

Figure 3.29. A view of the artificially extended plateau created for the Temple of Domitian.

Figure 3.30. The remains of the three-story facade and grand staircase giving access to the precinct of the Temple of Domitian above. The scant remains of the temple's crepidoma (stepped platform) are visible atop the plateau.

93 by the Pollio family.[65] They faced a grand, three-story facade with Doric columns supporting the bottom level, Ionic columns supporting the middle level, and Corinthian columns supporting the third—a tribute to the Flavian Amphitheater in Rome, a major construction project begun under Vespasian and completed by Titus (see fig. 3.30). Across the second and third levels, every column bore the life-sized, carved relief of a human figure. According to one interpretation, each of these represented a god, some known from Greek and Roman religion, some more local like Attis and Cybele, some imported from the far reaches of the empire like Isis of Egypt, as if the pantheons of every nation had assembled here to bless those who approached to worship at the temple of the living god Domitian and to demonstrate their own support for

65. *IEph* 415; Worth, *Seven Cities of the Apocalypse and Greco-Asian Culture*, 19.

Figure 3.31. The excavated remains of the crepidoma and brick substructure of the Temple of Domitian.

imperial rule.[66] An alternative interpretation, however, suggests that these figures represent subjugated people groups across the empire, similar to a number of the high-relief friezes that once adorned the Sebasteion at Aphrodisias, which would be in keeping with the military images on the altar. In this case, the theme would be conquest, not piety.[67]

Worshipers ascended by means of a grand staircase to the temple courtyard. Excavations on the top of the plateau have uncovered parts of the original temple itself, including the raised, 80-by-110-foot platform on which the temple sat, approached on all sides by six steps, and the temple's foundations (see fig. 3.31). The temple had single rows of eight columns front and back and thirteen columns on the longer sides.[68] It was surrounded by a broad courtyard with columned porticoes on three sides. An altar stood before the temple, ornately engraved with sacrificial scenes (such as a garlanded bull, bound to the altar and ready to be sacrificed) and scenes commemorating

66. Friesen, *Imperial Cults*, 50–51; *Twice Neokoros*, 72–75; Biguzzi, "Ephesus," 283.

67. Burrell, *Neokoroi*, 64. Burrell believes that the altar and entrance facade were only added in the second century (63).

68. Shaner, "Ephesus," 380.

Figure 3.32. Left: The remains of a colossal cult statue from the Temple of Domitian. Right: The altar, decorated with a frieze of armor and shields.
Author photo, courtesy of the Ephesus Archaeological Museum, Türkiye.

Domitian's military victories. At least one colossal statue of an emperor, estimated to have stood more than 20 feet high, was housed within the temple. The identity of the emperor represented by this statue is disputed, with some scholars favoring Domitian and others favoring his elder brother, Titus (see fig. 3.32).[69] In either case, the statue presented the Flavian dynast as the larger-than-life and greater-than-human figure that an emperor was believed and experienced to be. The head and left forearm, measuring 4 and 6 feet, respectively, are all that remain. The hand once grasped a spear, suggesting that the pose of the statue resembled that of Augustus's statue in the Temple of Roma and Augustus in Pergamum.

The temple involved a good number of the provincial elite in its "staff." There was a chief priest of the cult of Domitian, of course, as well as a person who served as a *neōkoros*, a temple warden overseeing and largely subsidizing the maintenance of the temple. Inscriptions attest to fourteen people selected to serve as *thesmodoi*, or singers at the sacrifices, and at least nine *theologoi*, composers and reciters of hymns and other works in praise of the members of the imperial family.[70] Tiberius Claudius Aristion, one of the wealthiest patrons in Ephesus during the last decades of the first century, served as chief priest in AD 89 and *neōkoros* in AD 90.[71]

69. Price excludes the possibility that the statue represents Titus on the basis of the existing inscriptions that only name (first) Domitian and (then) Vespasian as the particular emperor worshiped at this site (*Rituals and Power*, 187, 197). He claims that the statue "could pass for any of the Flavians" (255). Friesen regards it as certain that the statue represents Titus, and thus that Titus was among the recipients of cult worship at this site (*Imperial Cults*, 46, 50; *Twice Neokoros*, 60–62). The unfinished rear of the statue, especially the hollowed-out head, required placement against a wall, suggesting that this was, in fact, a cult statue from the sanctuary (the *cella*) itself. Biguzzi, "Ephesus," 284–85; Friesen, *Twice Neokoros*, 62.

70. Burrell, *Neokoroi*, 66.

71. Burrell, *Neokoroi*, 66; deSilva, *Week in the Life*.

Figure 3.33. The remains of the "Baths of the Sebastoi." The palaestra, or exercise yard, would have sat in the foreground.

Another massive, related project took place beside the harbor on the north side of Harbor Street. This involved the construction (possibly the expansion) of a sprawling bath and gymnasium complex in preparation for the inauguration of Olympic-style games in honor of Domitian (see fig. 3.33). These facilities included a gymnasium complex of 260 by 220 yards, an open-air palaestra (a rectangular courtyard where all the principal exercises and combat sports were practiced) of 260 by 390 yards, and a complete Roman bath facility, the "Baths of the Sebastoi [the Augusti, or Emperors]."[72] Altogether, it covered an area of over 70,000 square yards, making it one of the largest such complexes of its time. The facilities remained unfinished the first time that the games were held here in honor of Domitian in AD 89, but they were completed by AD 92/93 in time for the next cycle.[73] The facilities themselves bore a dedicatory inscription to Domitian by none other than Tiberius Claudius Aristion.[74] Similar festivals including extensive athletic competitions (the *koina Asias*) were held in honor of Rome and Augustus, rotating between Ephesus, Smyrna, and Pergamum, each on its own five-year cycle.[75] Lesser versions of the games were held in Miletus, Cyzicus, Tralles, Sardis, Philadelphia, and Laodicea. Ephesus along with Aphrodisias and Laodicea also hosted *epinikia* festivals—games commemorating a particular Roman

72. Biguzzi, "Ephesus," 287. See Friesen, *Twice Neokoros*, 123–51, for a detailed description of the structure and its function. Irenaeus (in *Haer.* 3.3.4) narrates the story, likely legendary, of John the apostle running out of one of the bath complexes in Ephesus when a rival Christian teacher named Cerinthus entered, lest God make the ceiling collapse upon the heretic and those unfortunates caught with him.

73. Biguzzi, "Ephesus," 287; Friesen, *Imperial Cults*, 74.

74. P. Scherrer, *Ephesus*, 176.

75. Arnold, "Festivals of Ephesus," 20.

Figure 3.34. An inscription honoring the emperor Domitian (name chiseled out) and "the neokorate citizenry of the Ephesians."

victory.[76] The sports calendar was yet another prominent reminder of the place of the Roman emperor in the world of the citizens of the cities of Asia.

Ephesus thus finally gained the honor of being named *neōkoros* or "temple-warden" of a provincial imperial cult in the Roman province of Asia.[77] The city took evident pride in having achieved this honor, for a great number of public inscriptions would henceforth speak of "the council and people of the temple-warden (*neōkoros*) city of the Ephesians" (see fig. 3.34). The introduction of Ephesus's new status as a neokorate city into the city's self-identification in inscriptions was a bold innovation. The imperial cult was now at the very heart of civic identity and pride.

This was no less true for Pergamum, whose leaders (after Ephesus had also won and began to promote itself using the title that Pergamum had previously enjoyed for over a century) began to include this title in their own self-identification in inscriptions. They found a way to reassert their precedence at the same time: They would not be "the temple-warden city

76. Arnold, "Festivals of Ephesus," 21.

77. The city had previously been informally identified as *neōkoros* of the goddess Artemis (see Acts 19:35). It is possible, as Friesen (*Twice Neokoros*, 53–54, 56–57) suggests, that Ephesus immediately sought to claim to be "twice *neōkoros*" on the basis of its hosting of the principal Temple of Artemis in the Greek world and, now, the Temple of the Sebastoi. Two coins that are datable to AD 89/90 appear to make this claim on the city's behalf, though Ephesus appears to have been quickly warned not to claim more than a single neokorate because doing so would be to jump to the front of the line, as it were, ahead of Pergamum and Smyrna, both of which had been imperial *neōkoros* cities long before Ephesus. Burrell (*Neokoroi*, 65), however, claims on the basis of two studies that these coins have been recut/reworked by a modern forger to make them more valuable and, thus, have no historical value regarding Ephesus's self-identification in that year.

Figure 3.35. Two statues (or partial statues) of priests of the imperial cult. Their crowns originally sported miniature busts of members of the imperial household.
Left: Author photo, courtesy of the Aphrodisias Museum, Türkiye. Right: Author photo, courtesy of Ephesus Archaeological Museum, Türkiye.

of the Pergamenes" but rather "the *first-to-be-named*-temple-warden city of the Pergamenes." Under Trajan (ruled AD 98–117), Pergamum would be granted the privilege of hosting the provincial cult of that emperor, building a monumental temple to him on the very brow of their acropolis, for which they were awarded a second neokorate and began to speak of their city as "twice-named-temple-warden." Smyrna, not to be outdone, was granted by Trajan's successor Hadrian (ruled AD 117–138) to host a provincial cult in his own honor and thus also became a "twice-named-temple-warden" city.

The Ephesians would not allow both Smyrna and Pergamum to "pull ahead" of them, however, in regard to what had become a coveted honor. They successfully lobbied for the privilege of *also* hosting a provincial cult of Hadrian. This would be the first time that an emperor allowed two different cities to host provincial temples to himself.[78] The result was a monument erected to Hadrian, identified with "Olympian Zeus" (hence often referred to as the Olympieion), near the harbor.[79] The temple itself had a footprint of 36 by 65 yards but sat in the midst of an expansive precinct with dimensions of 246 by 380 yards (see figs. 3.36, 3.37).[80] The precinct was, in turn, surrounded by porticoes supported by columns in the Corinthian order. The complex dwarfed all other compounds in the city other than the adjacent Harbor Baths and Gymnasium.

78. Burrell, *Neokoroi*, 66.

79. Guides almost uniformly present the little shrine on the Embolos as the "Temple of Hadrian," but that diminutive building, dedicated to Artemis, Hadrian, and the Ephesian people, served a different function (Burrell, *Neokoroi*, 80). The Olympieion is also not to be confused with the temple to Zeus that Pausanias (*Descr.* 7.2.8–9) located outside of the city walls between the Magnesian Gate and the Temple of Artemis. Burrell, *Neokoroi*, 68.

80. Burrell, *Neokoroi*, 68.

Figure 3.36. The foundations of the Temple of Hadrian (the Olympieion).

Figure 3.37. A model of the Temple of Hadrian complex. Author photo, courtesy of the Ephesos Museum, Vienna.

Figure 3.38. An honorific inscription for a benefactor erected by "the council and citizenry of the Ephesians, the first and great mother city of Asia and twice *neōkoros* of the emperors." This inscription was preserved from weathering and thus preserves the typical coloring that made the lettering of inscriptions stand out.

The award of a second neokorate, adding to the reputation and luster of the city, was something Ephesus was quick to broadcast in its self-identification in inscriptions, styling itself now "twice temple-warden of the emperors" (see fig. 3.38). The Pergamenes, predictably, maintained their edge over their rivals by referring to themselves as "the *first*-to-be-named-*twice*-temple-warden."

Modern readers of Revelation may have difficulty understanding the unpopularity—indeed the resentment and danger—that Christians faced if they took an open stance against the worship of the emperor in cities like Ephesus and Pergamum. It may be even more difficult to understand the local enthusiasm for the cults of men-turned-gods. But when we begin to understand how civic identity, civic pride, civic standing in the region, and civic well-being were all tied to the imperial cult, we may begin to appreciate more fully what a threat the Christian gospel was, with its call to "fear God and give him glory" (Rev. 14:7)—him, and no other. Nevertheless, John called the Christians in Ephesus (who would have heard John's references to a beast and its organized cult as a trenchant critique of the

Figure 3.39. A selection of bronze lamps on lampstands from Roman Asia. The ubiquity of such furniture makes it highly unlikely that the addressees of Revelation would think of seven menorahs rather than seven single lampstands like these when hearing John's description of the glorified Christ standing "in the midst of seven lampstands" (Rev. 1:12–13, 20).

Left: Author photo, courtesy of the Aphrodisias Museum, Türkiye. Center: Author photo, courtesy of the Ephesus Archaeological Museum, Türkiye. Right: Author photo, courtesy of the Akhisar Museum, Türkiye.

Roman emperor and the worship offered to him throughout the province) to consistent and uncompromising witness to their neighbors that there was indeed only one God and that the pretensions of Rome and its emperors were utterly demonic.[81]

The congregations in Ephesus appear to have risen to the challenges before them. When the soldiers transporting the bishop Ignatius of Antioch to Rome for execution under Trajan paused in Smyrna, Ephesus was among the cities that sent a delegation to the Christian hero to encourage him and receive letters of instruction from him. It required significant boldness to openly associate *as Christians* with a person condemned for his promotion of the Christian movement. They appear to have continued to exercise discernment in regard to new winds of teaching (*Eph.* 9.1), but Ignatius also bears witness to the outpouring of love the congregations showed him in the persons of their representatives (1.1–2; 2.1). The eventual triumph of Christianity in Ephesus is dramatically illustrated in the remains of the Church of Mary the Theotokos

81. On Revelation 13 and the Roman imperial cult, see Friesen, *Imperial Cults*, 135–217; deSilva, *Seeing Things*, 93–116, 193–228, 257–84; *Unholy Allegiances*, 21–76.

Figure 3.40. Top: The chancel area of the Church of Mary the Theotokos. Bottom: The nave.

("the Mother of God"; see fig. 3.40). The church was built around AD 500 using the shell of the southern portico of the massive Temple of Hadrian, which had by then been dismantled to its very foundations.

4

SMYRNA

The city of Smyrna sat 44 miles north of Ephesus along a major road that extended to Pergamum and beyond.[1] Although Smyrna had a long history even before the Classical age of Greece, the history of the Smyrna that was home to the Christians addressed by John began only after Alexander the Great's rise to power. The old city had been built around a defensible peak 2 miles from the shoreline, thriving until it was taken and largely destroyed first by the Lydian kingdom in the late seventh century BC and then by the Persian Empire in the mid-sixth century BC.[2]

The remnants of Smyrna became little more than a cluster of villages until Alexander and his successors reestablished the city, this time at a small distance removed from the original site (Pausanias, *Descr.* 7.5.1–3; Strabo, *Geogr.* 14.1.37). The new city would not sit on the fortified hill but beside the shore, so that it could enjoy the benefits of the natural harbor at the coast. While it would come to be eclipsed in maritime trade by Ephesus, the harbor in Smyrna remained a great asset and kept Smyrna firmly on the commercial map. As İzmir remains an important hub for shipping, all traces of the original harbor have since been overbuilt and buried beneath the modern harbor installations.

Because the modern city of İzmir sits atop the Roman-period city of Smyrna, very little of the ancient city has been excavated. Literary, numismatic, and epigraphic evidence, however, still permit substantial recovery of the features of the Roman city. Smyrna's population during the first and

1. Calculated using "The Stanford Geospatial Model of the Roman World."
2. Hemer, *Letters*, 60–61; Wilson, *Biblical Turkey*, 312.

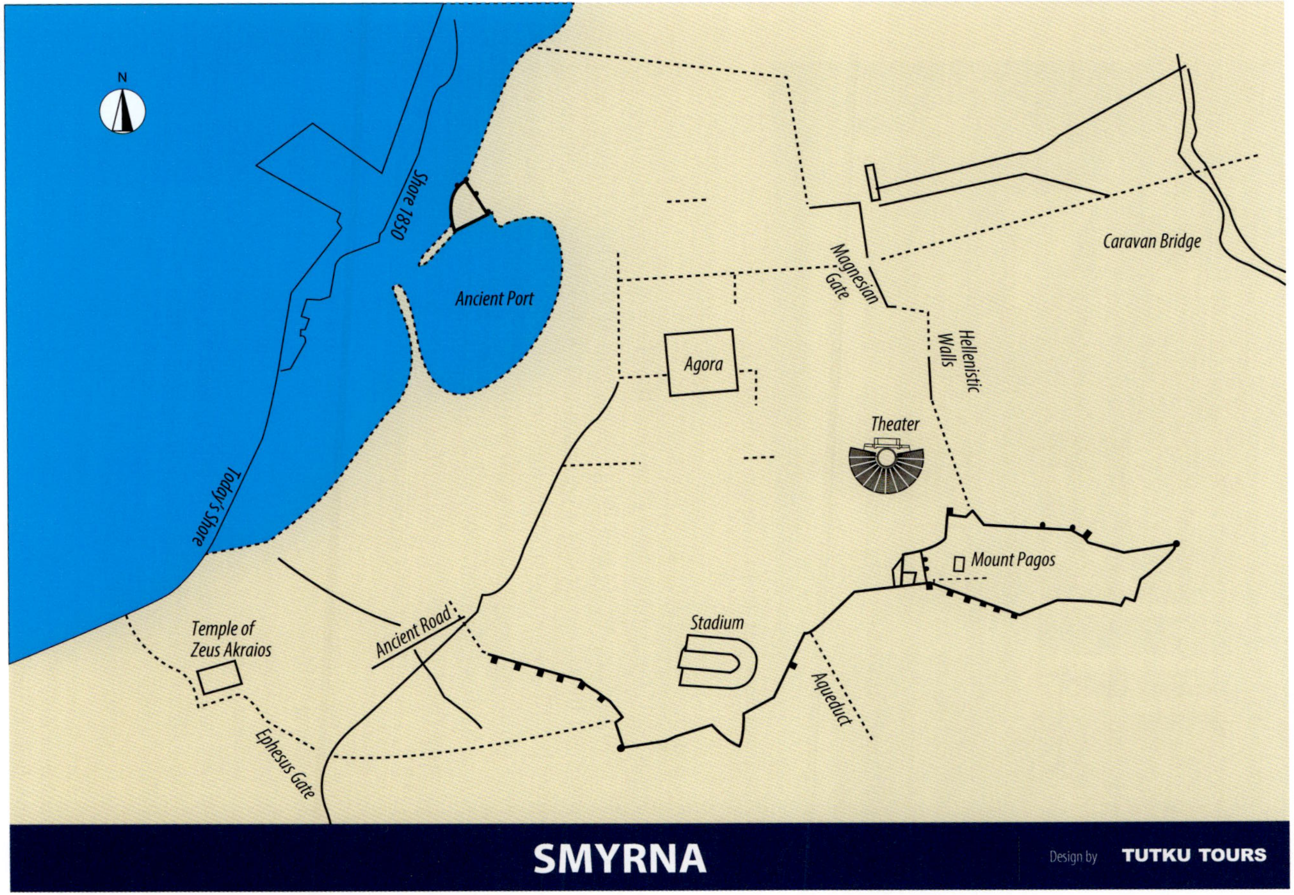

Figure 4.1. Map of sites related to ancient Smyrna in modern İzmir.

Author photo, courtesy of Todd Bolen.

Figure 4.2. The archaic Temple of Athena, destroyed by the Persians in 545 BC.

second centuries AD may have risen above one hundred thousand inhabitants,[3] making it, alongside Ephesus and Pergamum, one of the three largest cities in the province.[4] It was no doubt a splendid city. Aelius Aristides, speaking of the city's landscape in the mid-second century AD, writes: "All the way down to the shore it is resplendent with gymnasia, agoras, theaters, sacred precincts, and harbors, beautiful works of nature vying with those wrought by man . . . and there is nothing which does not serve both for ornament and use" (*Or.* 17:8, 11). Strabo also speaks expansively of its grandeur:

> Their city is now the most beautiful of all; a part of it is on a mountain and walled, but the greater part of it is in the plain near the harbour and near the Metroüm and near the gymnasium. The division into streets is exceptionally good, in straight lines as far as possible; and the streets are paved with stone; and there are large quadrangular porticoes, with both lower and upper stories. There is also a library; and the Homereium, a quadrangular portico containing a shrine and wooden statue of Homer; for the Smyrnaeans also lay especial claim to the poet; and indeed a bronze coin of theirs is called Homereium. (*Geogr.* 14.1.37)[5]

3. Wilson, *Biblical Turkey*, 310.
4. C. Koester, *Revelation*, 271–72.
5. Strabo, *Geography of Strabo*, 6:246–47.

Figure 4.4. A votive stele of Cybele, flanked by her iconic pair of lions and accompanied by two other deities.
Author photo, courtesy of the Arkeoloji ve Etnografya Müzesi, İzmir, Türkiye.

Figure 4.3. A cult statue of Zeus discovered in Smyrna, dating to the mid-second century AD.
Author photo, courtesy of the Louvre, France.

These and other literary references suggest that there were two prominent temples in the city marking the uppermost and lowermost ends of a road known as "The Golden Way"—a temple to Zeus and a temple to Cybele, the Phrygian mother goddess and a kind of patron goddess of Smyrna, to judge from coins minted in the city (see figs. 4.3 and 4.4).[6] Smyrna also had a cult of Dionysus, as attested by a local inscription recording that a certain Dionysicles, son of Metrodoros, began to serve as priest of Dionysus during the presidency of a certain Alexander.[7]

Like its sister and competitor cities, Smyrna was also deeply invested in the cults of Rome and its emperors. Tacitus (*Ann.* 4.56) recounts how the city had already built a temple to honor Roma in 195 BC—long before it was popular to do so in the region (see fig. 4.5).[8] In 195 BC, the Seleucid kingdom under Antiochus III to the east was at its strongest, and Antiochus was

6. Ascough, "Greco-Roman Religions," 47–48.
7. C. Koester, *Revelation*, 272; see also Aelius Aristides, *Or.* 20.20, 23.
8. Hemer, *Letters*, 70–71.

keen on establishing his hold over all of Asia Minor. The city of Carthage in North Africa was still a great power in the west and a significant threat to Rome's dominance in the Mediterranean. The outcome of their struggle was still uncertain at that time. Smyrna's acknowledgment of the rising power of Rome in the west rather than the established Greco-Syrian kingdom to the east was a sign of extraordinary faith in Rome and its destiny.

This loyalty would be long remembered. In the first century BC, the Roman senator Cicero spoke of Smyrna as "a city . . . of our most trusty and longstanding allies" (*Philippics* 11.2.5 [p. 461]) and the historian Livy would remember the city as demonstrating exceptional loyalty to Rome (*History of Rome* 38.39.11). The

Figure 4.5. A cult image of the goddess Roma from the Capitoline Museum in Rome.

Figure 4.6. A Roman-period road uncovered in İzmir.

Figure 4.7. A locally minted coin celebrating Smyrna's new temple to Tiberius, Livia, and the Senate. One side features the temple itself with the cult image of Tiberius visible. Tiberius wears a toga draped over his head in the fashion of a priest, recalling his role in the Roman world as *Pontifex Maximus* (Friesen, *Imperial Cults,* 38). The busts of Livia and the Senate (personified as a young man) are featured on the reverse side.
Used by permission of Classical Numismatic Group, LLC (auction 69, lot 991).

Temple of Roma continued to be active in the first century AD. An inscription from the time of Nero lists several offices connected with this shrine, all held in that particular year by a single, highly motivated individual. These include the offices of chief priest, sebastophant (revealer of the cult image of the emperor in the context of celebrating "imperial mysteries"), and agonothete (director and chief subsidizer of athletic games honoring Roma).[9]

By the early decades of the third century AD, Smyrna had been awarded the honor of being named *neōkoros* three times. The city was eager to publicize the fact, as a popular coin minting featuring the three imperial temples on its reverse demonstrates. Smyrna had won its first neokorate in AD 26, when it successfully petitioned the Senate for the honor of erecting a temple and establishing a cult for Tiberius, his mother Livia, and the Senate of Rome, beating out ten rival cities for the privilege (Tacitus, *Ann.* 4.55–56; see fig. 4.7).[10] It was, in large measure, Smyrna's long history of admiration and support for Rome that made it a front-runner and, finally, the winner in this competition. The province's evident enthusiasm for sponsoring a provincial temple to Tiberius may have been particularly stoked by their successful prosecution before the imperial court of a corrupt proconsul and an overreaching procurator.[11] Smyrna would not use the title of *neōkoros* in its self-identification in inscriptions or on coins until after Ephesus had begun the practice in AD 89.

The city received a second neokorate in connection with a new temple to Hadrian.[12] This project was probably initiated between AD 124 and 129 in response to Hadrian's gift to Smyrna of ten million denarii, which funded a new grain market and a magnificent gymnasium.[13] Smyrna's exuberance for this

9. Knight, "Was Roma the Scarlet Harlot?," 115, citing *ISmyrna* 591.

10. Price, *Rituals and Power*, 64–65, 258.

11. Burrell, *Neokoroi*, 38, and Friesen, *Imperial Cults*, 36–37, referring to events in Tacitus, *Ann.* 3.66–69; 4.15. Burrell thinks this more likely than the common view that the enthusiasm was a response to the emperor's generosity in earthquake relief a decade earlier.

12. Price, *Rituals and Power*, 67, 258; Burrell, *Neokoroi*, 42–44.

13. Burrell, *Neokoroi*, 43.

Figure 4.8. A dedicatory inscription to the emperor Hadrian calling him "Olympian," "Savior," and "Founder" of the city.

Figure 4.9. A statue of a priest of the imperial cult from the second century AD.

Author photo, courtesy of the Arkeoloji ve Etnografya Müzesi, İzmir, Türkiye.

emperor is evident from the titles used to describe him in an inscription that was found in the civic forum: "The emperor Trajan Hadrian Caesar Augustus, *Olympios*, Savior, and Founder" (see fig. 4.8). The title *Olympios* (Olympian) equated Hadrian with the god Zeus, often called "Olympian Zeus." The title "Founder" attributed to Hadrian's generosity the gift of a new beginning, a new era, for Smyrna; the title "Savior," of course, refers to Hadrian as the city's deliverer, using language that had already become prominent in Christian circles to speak of Jesus's accomplishments and significance.

Smyrna would win a third neokorate with its successful bid to build a temple to Caracalla, the son of and successor to Septimius Severus, in the early third century.[14] Several inscriptions found in the civic forum attest to the prominence of the imperial cult and its priests in this city (see fig. 4.9). One inscription, in which Smyrna boasts of its greatness in the midst of other cities of Asia on account of its having received the honor of a neokorate three times, honors a certain Julius Menekleus Diophantes, an Asiarch (a leading figure in the provincial council), for gladiatorial games that he provided for

14. Price, *Rituals and Power*, 258.

Figure 4.10. A civic inscription honoring Julius Menekleus Diophantes.

Figure 4.11. An inscription in the forum honoring Claudius Aristophanes Aurelianus, "*neōkoros* of the emperors."

five days at his own expense (see fig. 4.10). Another inscription graced the base of a statue of Claudius Aristophanes Aurelianus, a chief priest of the imperial cult prior to the city's third neokorate (see fig. 4.11).

Roman Smyrna was well supplied with water, brought by aqueducts to vast cisterns located on the hill above the city and distributed thence to public and private sites throughout the city (see figs. 4.12, 4.13). A large theater was carved into the side of the hill overlooking the city and its harbor, and the remains of the stage building and the lower section of the cavea remain visible in the midst of a sprawling modern residential area (see fig. 4.14). Some

Figure 4.12. Two Roman-period aqueducts, located 2 miles south of the agora, that brought fresh water to Smyrna.

Figure 4.13. The interior of a large early Roman-period cistern atop Mount Pagus, the area of Smyrna's acropolis.

Figure 4.14. The theater's partially excavated stage building and lower cavea (the seating area).

Figure 4.15. A bronze statue of a runner.

Author photo, courtesy of the Arkeoloji ve Etnografya Müzesi, İzmir, Türkiye.

of the more ornate seats reserved for dignitaries have also been recovered. It is thought that the theater was once able to accommodate sixteen thousand spectators.[15] The ancient stadium has also been located on an artificially leveled area of the hill descending from Mount Pagus, only the contours of which are visible around the buildings that have been erected over it (see fig. 4.15).

The most extensive and accessible remains uncovered to date are those of the state agora, or civic forum. The city had been devastated by an earthquake in AD 178, with the result that the older forum had to be rebuilt with significant aid from the emperor Marcus Aurelius and his family.[16] Aelius Aristides

15. Wilson, *Biblical Turkey*, 312.
16. Wilson, *Biblical Turkey*, 313.

Figure 4.16. A portion of the carved reliefs that once adorned the periphery of the Altar of Zeus in the middle of the forum.
Author photo, courtesy of the Arkeoloji ve Etnografya Müzesi, İzmir, Türkiye.

Figure 4.17. An altar from the bouleuterion, or council chamber, attesting to the inseparability of religion and politics in the Greco-Roman city.
Author photo, courtesy of the İzmir Museum of History and Art, Türkiye.

(*Or.* 20), a resident of Smyrna around that time, called them the "new founders" of the city.[17] An arch still bears the portrait of Faustina the Younger, wife of Marcus Aurelius, in honor of the imperial household's support.[18] The agora was once graced with statues of members of the imperial family; one statue base, still standing on the site, bears the inscription "Fadilla, daughter of Augustus Caesar Marcus Aurelius Antoninus."

The civic forum was rebuilt around an open court of about 394 by 262 feet. An altar to Zeus once stood in the center of the forum, a reminder of the watchful care of the gods and the obligations of the city to its divine protectors. Part of the facade of this monument now stands in the Arkeoloji ve Etnografya Müzesi (Museum of Archaeology and Ethnography) in İzmir, Türkiye. In deep relief and in figures significantly larger than life-size, it shows Poseidon seated, with Demeter and Artemis standing beside him (see fig. 4.16).

The east and west sides of the courtyard were lined with two-story, colonnaded porticoes, each 59 feet wide. On the north side stood a two-story colonnaded building patterned after a basilica (essentially three long covered aisles, with the central aisle—the nave—being wider and taller than the two outside aisles), running the length of the forum and sporting a depth of about 90 feet. The basilica was erected over a foundation of an arched, vaulted basement (see fig. 4.18).

17. Burrell, *Neokoroi*, 48.
18. Wilson, *Biblical Turkey*, 313.

Figure 4.18. The remains of the basilica in Smyrna's second-century forum.

This basement served as a shopping arcade, which could be entered from the main road behind the forum so as to preserve the decorum of the basilica and civic areas above. Further excavations have followed the shopping arcade, uncovering a large cryptoporticus (a portico that is mostly or entirely underground, hence "hidden") with much of its original plaster still intact—and, in this plaster, a wealth of graffiti, sometimes in the form of charcoal markings, sometimes in the form of messages or drawings scratched into the plaster. Several of these graffiti bear witness to the phenomenon called isopsephism—the equating of a text with its numerical equivalent and a number of variations of this game. Isopsephisms are possible in languages such as Greek, Latin, and Hebrew, where the letters of the alphabet are also used as numerals. Several graffiti in the passageways beneath the agora are professions of love for a woman identified only by a number—the sum of the letters in her name:

> "I love her whose number is 616."
> "I love her whose number is 731."
> "I love her whose number is 1308."[19]

19. Inscriptions T.22.1, T.24.2, and T.27.3 in Bagnall et al., *Graffiti*, 226, 236, and 267, respectively.

Similar graffiti have been found scratched into the walls of taverns and similar establishments in Pompeii. A hypothetical graffito might read, "I love her whose number is 157." This would prompt bored readers to figure out a variety of ways in which letters functioning as numbers could add up to 157. In Latin, one might posit L (50), L, L, V (5), I (1), I and land on the name "Livilla" as a possibility. In the examples from Smyrna above, "1308" might lead one to the Greek name "Tychē" (tau = 300; upsilon = 400; chi = 600; eta = 8).[20] A clearly Christian graffito even announces itself with the word *isopsepha* ("equal sums") and then lists two words: *kyrios* (lord) and *pistis* (faith), words whose letters both add up to 800.[21] While the graffiti in Smyrna appear to date from after the restoration of the forum by Marcus Aurelius (thus after AD 178), the practice in Pompeii shows it to have been well established by the mid-first century. In his biography of Nero, Suetonius (*Nero* 39.2) also tells of a slur that circulated after the suspicious death of Nero's mother, Agrippina, involving this numerical game: "A new calculation: Nero killed his own mother."[22] In Greek, the letters of Nero's name and the letters in the phrase "he killed his own mother" both have the same sum: 1005. The Jewish authors of several of the *Sibylline Oracles* identify successive emperors by the number of their first initial (*Sib. Or.* 5.12–51) and Jesus by the number 888, the sum of the letters of his name in Greek, *Iēsous* (iota = 10; eta = 8; sigma = 200; omicron = 70; upsilon = 400; sigma = 200; see *Sib. Or.* 1.141–45).

As early as the second century, this was identified as the proper background for solving this cryptic statement in Revelation 13:18: "Here is wisdom. Let the person with understanding count up the number of the beast, for it is the number of a man, and his number is 666." The solution that seems the most compelling to most scholars is "Nero Caesar." Written in Hebrew letters, Nero's name reads *nrwn qsr* and totals 666 (n = 50; r = 200; w = 6; n = 50; q = 100; s = 60; r = 200). This solution is particularly attractive because it also accounts for an early textual variant that presents the sum of the beast's name as "616," a sum that results from adding up the numerical values of the Hebrew transliteration of the *Latin* form of Nero's name (*Nero*) rather than its *Greek* form (*Nerōn*).[23] The missing final Hebrew letter *nun* accounts for the difference of 50. In this reading, John uses the figure of Nero to characterize the principate as a whole. In Nero—not only in his excesses and indulgence but all the more in his brutal repression of John's Christian brothers and sisters in Rome—one can see the ugliness of the principate exposed. John

20. Bagnall et al., *Graffiti*, 267.
21. Bagnall et al., *Graffiti*, 423.
22. My translation.
23. This variant is attested as early as the late second century (see Irenaeus, *Haer.* 5.30.1–4).

might well have thought of this as an irrefutable certainty, for the Greek word for "beast," *thērion*, transliterated into Hebrew as *thrywn*, also adds up to 666 (tau = 400; resh = 200; yod = 10; waw = 6; nun = 50).[24]

The piecemeal efforts at archaeology in İzmir have yet to uncover evidence of the Jewish community that figures so prominently in the glorified Christ's oracle to the Christians in Smyrna (Rev. 2:8–11). Inscriptional evidence is also largely lacking until the second century AD. Nevertheless, it is highly probable that Smyrna enjoyed the same organized Jewish presence that many of its sister cities did throughout the early Roman period. John identifies some facet of the local Jewish community's activity in Smyrna that he calls "slander" (*blasphēmia*) as a source of significant danger to the Christians there.[25] The close connection here between their "slander" and potential legal penalties suggests "denunciation of Christians before Roman or civic authorities."[26] Acts provides early examples of this sort of activity (Acts 17:5–9; 18:12–17), which is quite understandable not simply as an aggressive posture against maverick Jews like Paul, who were promoting a particular messiah and a new way of life, but as a defensive posture seeking to affirm before these (Roman) authorities that the Jews living in their city wanted nothing to do with a revolutionary condemned and crucified by a Roman prefect in their motherland. The local Jewish community was likely acting chiefly to protect "the [fragile] good standing and good relations which the Jewish community had established for itself within the city," whatever theological objections that they might have had to the Christian group's message and its practical implications.[27]

The origins of the Christian community or communities in Smyrna are unknown. Acts 19:26 attributes church planting throughout Roman Asia beyond the city of Ephesus to Paul's missionary work, perhaps through residents of other cities coming to Ephesus and hearing and connecting with Paul and his team or through Paul and his associates making short trips to nearby cities. We know that one of Paul's associates—Epaphras—took the gospel to Colossae, Laodicea, and Hierapolis, perhaps while Paul was working in the ministry hub of Ephesus (Col. 1:7–8; 4:13). It is quite possible that other members of Paul's team took the gospel to Smyrna during the same period,

24. Bauckham, *Climax of Prophecy*, 389.

25. The "blasphemy" in view is not speech against God (as English-speakers might most naturally understand the term) but slander against the Christians themselves, likely taking the form of formal denunciations. Witherington, *Revelation*, 100–101; Beale, *Book of Revelation*, 240.

26. Aune, *Revelation 1–5*, 162; so also C. Koester, *Revelation*, 274.

27. Dunn, *Acts of the Apostles*, 183. Dunn writes this in regard to the opposition Paul and his team encountered in Pisidian Antioch (Acts 13), but his observation is more widely applicable.

which is all the more likely as Smyrna was a more important city and far closer to Ephesus than any of the cities where Epaphras was known to have taken the gospel (see, e.g., Acts 19:10, 26). However, Polycarp, the bishop of the Christians in Smyrna in the early to mid-second century, claims that Smyrna had not yet been evangelized when Paul wrote his letter to the Christians in Philippi (Polycarp, *Phil.* 11.3), which suggests that no Christian community had been established until the mid-60s or later.[28]

At some point during the Flavian period, then, the local Jewish community decided that it was necessary to make it clear to the local authorities that this group that appeared to be so closely related—worshiping the same God, reading the same sacred texts, claiming the same spiritual heritage—was not, in fact, representative of the Jewish community, its views, or its loyalties. An act as simple as providing the local authorities with lists of registered members of the synagogue would still leave Christians—who were abstaining from the cults of the gods and emperor like Jews were, but who were *not* Jews—susceptible to closer investigation. The unwanted attention and pressure this would put on the Christian community led John to write some of his harshest words as the glorified Christ denies to the church's denouncers the right to claim to be "Jews" and calls them "a synagogue of Satan." Scholars and theologians have become very sensitive to how language in the New Testament has been used and has contributed to anti-Judaism throughout the history of the church, culminating in the Holocaust.[29] It is important to hear the epithet "synagogue of Satan" against the background of Jewish groups using such language to label other Jewish rival groups. For example, the Qumran community spoke of fellow Jews who were outside of their group as "the congregation of Beliar" (1QH 2.22; 1QM 4.9), and Jesus's detractors accused him of acting in league with Beelzebul (Matt. 9:34; Luke 11:15). Such language is typical for sectarian in-fighting.

Why would John think of members of his own ethnic group, who shared many of the same commitments as John himself, as a "synagogue of Satan"? It is tempting to look beyond the mere fact that the Jewish community's response to Christians in Smyrna (and Philadelphia) put the latter in greater

28. Fairchild, *Christian Origins*, 147.

29. Scholars who are particularly sensitive to this often promote alternative, less plausible scenarios behind the oracles to Smyrna and Philadelphia—for example, the suggestion that "synagogues of Satan" refers to Gentile promoters and practitioners of Judaism (Gaston, "Jewish Communities," 21; see the presentation and critique of such views in Mayo, *Those Who Call*, 51–76). Such scholars are too quick to dismiss ancient testimonies to Jewish antagonism toward Christians as mere Christian propaganda. It is difficult to avoid the opinion that they are engaged in revisionist propaganda of their own, even though their reasons for doing so are intelligible enough in the theological climate of the post-Holocaust era.

jeopardy and to consider the implications of a major shift in practice that was imposed on Jews in AD 70. Jews had for centuries been accustomed to collecting the annual contribution of two denarii from all adult male Jews and to sending this money to Jerusalem for the support of the temple and its sacrifices—and they zealously defended their right to do so. This was an important point of connection for them, a means by which to affirm their own stake in the routine offerings made there to the God of Israel.

Figure 4.19. A cistophorus minted by Domitian showing the facade of the restored Temple of Jupiter Capitolinus on the reverse with the cult images of Juno, Jupiter, and Minerva visible in the interior.

Author photo, courtesy of the Schloss Museum, Tübingen, Germany.

In the wake of the First Jewish Revolt, which ended in the destruction of Jerusalem and its temple in AD 70, the emperor Vespasian—who, with his son, Titus, had personally led the Roman and auxiliary forces in the suppression of the revolt—introduced a stunning innovation to this practice. Jews would continue to take up their accustomed collection—now to include Jews of both genders and expanded age brackets—and pay this to the imperial treasury to help fund the reconstruction and operations of the Temple of Jupiter Capitolinus in Rome that had been destroyed in the course of the civil wars of AD 68–69 (Josephus, *J.W.* 7.218; Dio Cassius, *Hist. rom.* 46.7.2; see fig. 4.19).[30] While Vespasian might have considered this to be a lenient penalty in terms of the war reparations levied upon a rebellious *ethnos*, the Jews were now faced with the dilemma of having to buy continued toleration at the cost of contributing to a pagan cult, taking what belonged to God and rendering it to Caesar and *his* chief god. John might well have looked with scorn and condemnation on his fellow Jews' acquiescence to such a policy, which he would have regarded as compromising their own witness and loyalty to the one true God.[31] John held to the view shared by other Jews that demons were the ultimate recipients of the worship that Gentiles offered to their so-called gods (Rev. 9:20; cf. Ps. 106:37; Bar. 4:7; 1 Cor. 10:20–21). It was an easy inference to regard the chief of demons (Satan) as standing behind the idols of the Gentiles' chief god (Jupiter or Zeus). John, of course, promoted a policy of zero compromise among his own congregations in regard to the worship, loyalty, and witness due "him who made heaven and earth and sea and springs of water" (Rev. 14:7).

30. See, further, Smallwood, *Jews Under Roman Rule*, 371–76.
31. Kraybill, *Imperial Cult and Commerce*, 184.

As we have seen, Smyrna showed significant devotion to the Roman emperors in the form of the imperial cult. This would also make the question of loyalty—of "faithfulness unto death" (Rev. 2:10)—a principal issue for the Christians living within its jurisdiction, as they would come more and more to be forced to choose between loyalty to Caesar and loyalty to Christ. The issue of loyalty to the emperor and the traditional gods was a major factor in the growing tension between Christians and the civic authorities throughout Asia Minor and its surrounding provinces—witness the famous correspondence between Pliny the Younger, governor of Bithynia and Pontus, and the emperor Trajan from about AD 110 (Pliny, *Ep.* 10.96–97; see pp. 92–93 below). It is likely that these questions of religious loyalty would have been at the fore of the trials that the glorified Christ predicted for the near future of the Christians in late first-century Smyrna.

In the middle of the second century, Smyrna would become the scene of a great drama of faith as Polycarp, the elderly bishop of the Christian congregation there, was brought to trial in the arena before the provincial governor. The governor might not have known the details of Christian faith and practice, but he knew that it drew people away from giving the gods—including the emperors—their due and that this Christ (and his kingdom) was a rival to Rome and its emperors. This could not be tolerated in the city of Rome's "most trusty and longstanding allies." The governor therefore gave Polycarp an ultimatum: "Swear by Caesar's fortune; change your mind; say, 'Away with the atheists,'" or face death in the stadium (*Martyrdom of Polycarp* 9.2).[32] The local police chief urged the old man, "What harm is it to say 'Caesar is Lord' and to offer a sacrifice?" (8.2). But Polycarp could not bring himself to show disloyalty to so great a benefactor as Jesus: "For eighty-six years I have served him, and he has wronged me in no way. How, then, can I revile my king, who rescued me?" (9.3). As a result, the elderly bishop was burned at the stake and, when the fires failed to end his life, stabbed to death.

John called the Christians in Smyrna, as in the other six cities he addressed, to take up a position of no compromise with the domination system of Rome and its self-glorifying and self-deifying claims. The glorified Christ urges his followers not to yield to the demands to prove themselves loyal subjects of Rome and her emperor, even under the coercive pressure of being thrown into prison, but rather to prove themselves loyal subjects of God and his Messiah: "Be faithful to the point of death, and I will give you the crown of life" (Rev. 2:10). The "crown," better visualized here as a "wreath," was a familiar image in Smyrna and throughout the Greco-Roman world. It was given to

32. Translations from the Martyrdom of Polycarp are my own.

Figure 4.20. A gold-leaf wreath such as is frequently found in funerary settings adorning the deceased.

Author photo, courtesy of the Archaeological Museum of Thessaloniki, Greece.

Author photo, courtesy of the Istanbul Archaeological Museums, Türkiye.

Figure 4.21. Wreaths decorating a grave stele for two deceased daughters, denoting their preservation of their virtue. The stele is decorated with other items thought to be appropriate to young women—mirrors, combs, spindles for making yarn, and cosmetic baskets.

the winning athlete; it adorned the military conqueror. It also showed up in funerary settings, as the bodies of the deceased were frequently adorned with gold-leaf wreaths, and their grave steles often sported wreaths in carved relief (see figs. 4.20, 4.21).[33] Such wreaths were testimonies to a life well lived, the value and virtue of which were sealed by death, not ended by it. Whichever of these backgrounds John has in mind, his message is clear: Dying for loyalty to Jesus does not mark one as a deviant or a loser but rather as a winner, a conqueror, a person who lived and died virtuously, and who would continue to live and enjoy honor in the greater empire of God.

33. Over one hundred funerary inscriptions from Smyrna, dating between the third and first centuries BC, incorporate the image of a wreath. Horsley, *New Documents*, 3:52.

5

PERGAMUM

Pergamum, once the capital of the Attalid kingdom of Pergamum, sat 66 miles north of Smyrna along the major road that continued south to Ephesus and north to Adramyteion (a.k.a. Adramyttium) and other cities along the coast.[1] Its population is estimated to have been between one hundred twenty thousand and two hundred thousand during the early Roman period,[2] somewhat smaller than Ephesus and on par with Smyrna. Like Ephesus, Pergamum has been the focus of extensive excavation work, resulting in the recovery of a great many structures and an excellent sense of the layout of the Roman city.

Many of the monuments and inscriptions on hand to be seen even in first-century Roman Pergamum would have kept the residents mindful of the dynasty of the Attalid kings who had ruled Pergamum prior to 133 BC. In the struggles between Alexander's offspring and generals following Alexander's death, Lysimachus, a former commander and close confidant of Alexander, gained control of western Asia, including Pergamum. He entrusted a great amount of his war chest to his friend and steward, Philetaerus, in the stronghold of Pergamum. Philetaerus served Lysimachus faithfully for two more decades, but, in the ongoing strife between the successors, he revolted against Lysimachus and allied himself with the Seleucid kings as their client. After his death, his nephew and heir, Eumenes I (263–241 BC), successfully broke away from the Seleucid overlords and established a kingdom of Pergamum, taking the title "king." He was followed, in turn, by Attalus I (241–197 BC), a nephew

1. Calculated using "The Stanford Geospatial Model of the Roman World."
2. Worth, *Seven Cities of the Apocalypse and Greco-Asian Culture*, 111.

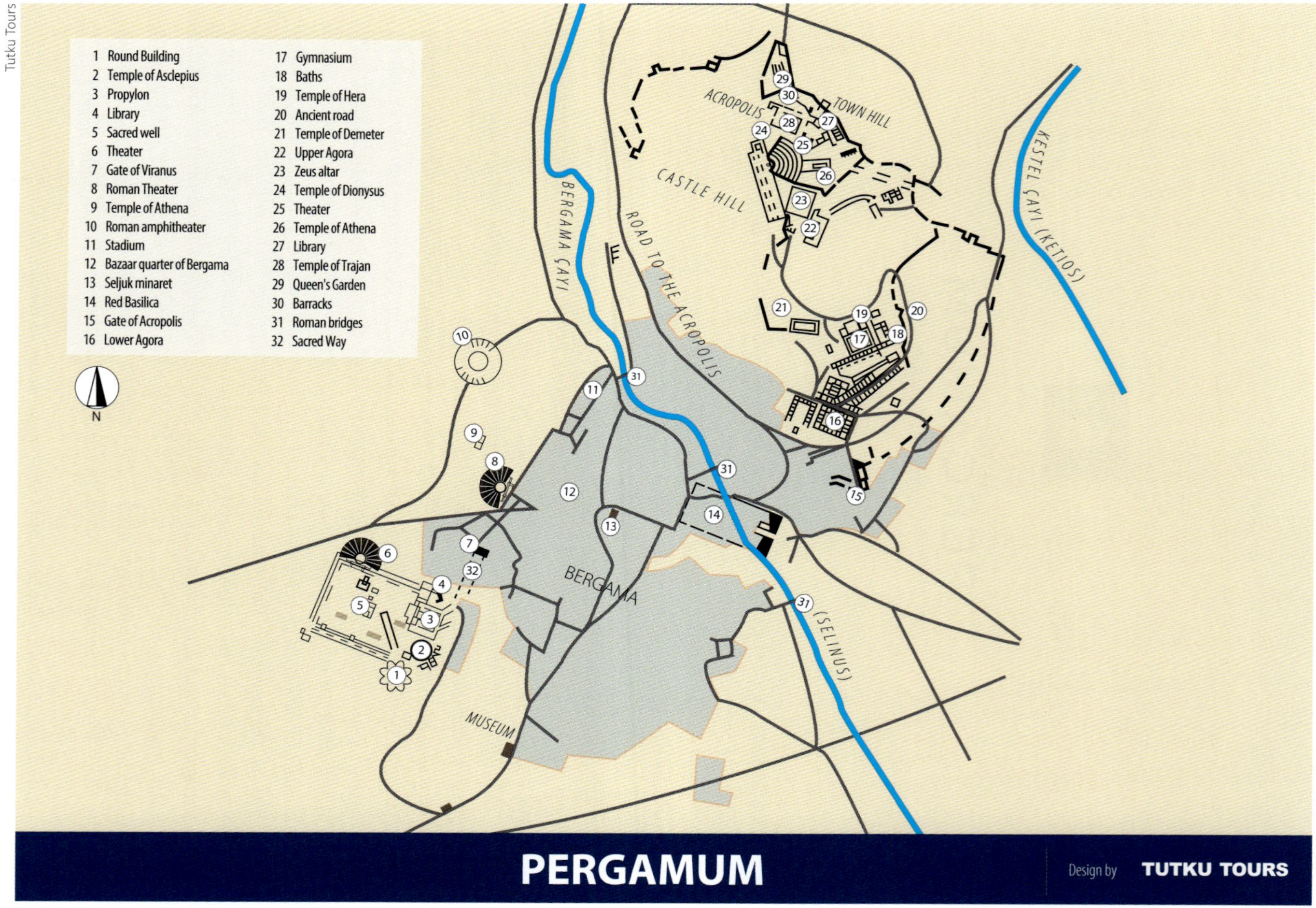

Figure 5.1. Map of the excavated features of ancient Pergamum.

Figure 5.2. Hellenistic-period fortifications near the gate of the Pergamum acropolis.

of Philetaerus by another brother, who protected Pergamene independence from both the ambitious Seleucids and the Galatians in central Anatolia, and then by Eumenes II (197–159 BC), son of Attalus I, who was instrumental in leveraging Roman power against the Seleucid Antiochus III, destroying Seleucid ambitions of ever retaking Asia. Following next were Attalus II (159–138 BC), the brother of Eumenes II and younger son of Attalus I, and, finally, Attalus III (138–133 BC), the son of Eumenes II. The heirless Attalus III willed his kingdom to the Roman Republic upon his untimely death.[3]

Pergamum was one of the chief cities of the Roman province of Asia, with Ephesus and Smyrna as its primary rivals. Its acropolis dominated the city and the landscape, towering more than 1,000 feet above the surrounding plains.[4] During the Attalid period, the city was largely confined to the hill of the acropolis (see figs. 5.2, 5.3), though the residential areas moved increasingly

Figure 5.3. Friedrich Thiersch's 1882 conceptualization of the acropolis at its peak. The Altar of Zeus is in the foreground and the Temple of Trajan in the background. The temple and sacred precincts of Athena stand between them.

3. Strabo, *Geogr.* 13.4.1–2; Hemer, *Letters*, 79–81.
4. Hemer, *Letters*, 78.

and expansively into the valley below during the later Hellenistic period and throughout the Roman period. A siphon system brought water up from the rivers below to the acropolis above. It was Pergamum that introduced this technology to Roman engineers, who used it advantageously throughout the empire.[5]

Pergamum and the Imperial Cult

One of the city's greatest claims to fame in the province was the honor of having been named *neōkoros* of the first provincial imperial cult in Asia. Permission to build a temple to honor Augustus was granted to Pergamum in 29 BC (Dio Cassius, *Hist. rom.* 51.20.6–9), and the project was completed and the temple inaugurated by 19 BC.[6] As both Suetonius (*Aug.* 52) and coin issues confirm, the temple was dedicated not only to Augustus himself but also, at Augustus's request, to the goddess Roma. This was a politic move on Augustus's part as the Senate and people of Rome would see themselves honored by the provinces alongside Augustus and, thus, be less susceptible to feeling envy and alienation at the worship offered the living emperor. The Pergamenes would no doubt also have found this emendation perfectly natural and appropriate, as they had already erected a temple to the goddess Roma in 98 BC.[7] Augustus simultaneously granted a similar honor to Nicomedia in the neighboring province of Bithynia to the north and northeast of Asia. It is important to bear in mind that such temples were not an imposition from above; rather, the initiative came from the elite residents of the cities of Roman Asia.[8]

No archaeological remains of the temple have been positively identified, and its location within the city is a matter of conjecture, though the agora at the foot of the acropolis has been suggested as an appropriate location.[9] A resident of Pergamum named Telephus had written an extensive treatise on this famous temple in the second century AD, but this document was

5. Wilson, *Biblical Turkey*, 281. On the water supply system of Pergamum, see, further, Crouch, *Water Management*, 43–46, 104–8, 329–33.

6. Burrell, *Neokoroi*, 19. Tiberius later referred to this imperially authorized temple as the precedent he himself followed for accepting a proposed temple to himself, his mother Livia, and the Roman Senate in Smyrna fifty years later: "The divine Augustus did not forbid the institution of a temple to himself and to the city of Rome in Pergamum, and I view all his deeds and words as carrying the force of law." Tacitus, *Ann.* 4.37, my translation.

7. Worth, *Seven Cities of the Apocalypse and Roman Culture*, 113.

8. Burrell, *Neokoroi*, 18.

9. Price, *Rituals and Power*, 137.

Figure 5.4. A silver cistophoric tetradrachm of Claudius with the facade of the Temple of Rome and Augustus at Pergamum on the reverse, clearly showing the cult images.
Numismatica Ars Classica NAC AG, Auction 64, lot 2482

also unfortunately lost to posterity.[10] Coins issued with the authority of the provincial council of Asia under Augustus, Claudius, Nero, Vespasian, Domitian, Nerva, and Trajan, however, feature the facade of this temple and reveal something of its contents.[11] A coin issued during Augustus's reign shows a temple on a five-step crepidoma with six columns supporting its front architrave. In later issues, the middle four columns are removed to reveal the two cult images within the temple.[12] Augustus appears standing in military armor; the goddess Roma stands next to him, draped in a feminine toga, her left hand holding a cornucopia as a symbol of prosperity, her right hand extending a victor's wreath as if to place it upon Augustus's head (see fig. 5.4). As the seat of the provincial cult of Augustus, an association popularized on the currency of the province, this temple and its activity is frequently identified as the ground for John's description of the city as the location of "Satan's throne" (Rev. 2:13).[13]

The temple provided many individuals with the opportunity to participate and thereby to gain honor for themselves locally. An individual member of the elite would also be awarded the title and office of *neōkoros* (see figs. 5.5, 5.6). Another office was that of chief priest; inscriptions bear further witness to a "panegyriarch" (a person who would lead the chorus in hymns of praise) and a choir of three dozen or more men, the *hymnodoi* (hymn singers) of the divine Augustus and Rome.[14] These *hymnodoi* represent an often-overlooked feature of the imperial cult—not just ritual but worship in the form of recitations of praise for various imperial figures and their accomplishments, an important facet indeed of the legitimation of their authority promoted by these cults. When John composes Revelation, he fills it with hymns sung to God and to God's Anointed, Jesus. These hymns, echoed by the hymns sung by the worshiping assemblies that gathered to hear Revelation read, become an ongoing counter-proclamation concerning who deserves worship, whose authority is legitimate, and, therefore, who deserves humanity's ultimate allegiance and obedience. Olympic-style games were also initiated in honor of

10. Price, *Rituals and Power*, 133.
11. Knight, "Was Roma the Scarlet Harlot?," 112.
12. See also Friesen, *Imperial Cults*, 29–30.
13. Hemer, *Letters*, 87; Wilson, *Biblical Turkey*, 285.
14. Burrell, *Neokoroi*, 21–22.

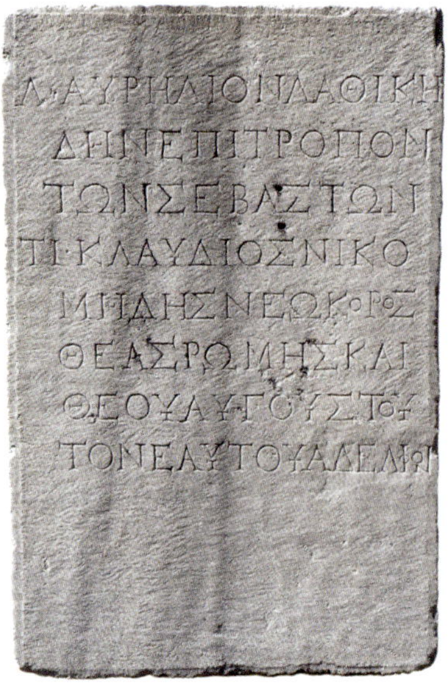

Figure 5.5. "Ti. Claudius Nicomedes, *neōkoros* of the goddess Roma and god Augustus, [honors] his brother, L. Aurelius Lathikedes, guardian [*epitropos*] of the emperors."

Figure 5.6. "The youth [*neoi*] honored Gaius Julius Sacerdotatus, *neōkoros* of the goddess Roma and god Augustus Caesar, priest of Tiberius Claudius Nero, and gymnasiarch for the twelfth *Sebaste Romaia* for the five gymnasia" for his financial support for the games and the athletes' expenses related to the same (Friesen, *Imperial Cults*, 31).

Augustus and Rome, as attested in inscriptions from 20 BC and later. These were at first called the *Rhomaia Sebasta* after both honorands but later came to be referred to by the more general name of *Koina Augusteia* (the Augustan games sponsored by the provincial council, the *Koinon Asias*) alongside similar games in Smyrna and, eventually, Ephesus.[15] These games offered local elites the opportunity to serve as agonothetes, gaining recognition and honor at the games at the cost of heavily subsidizing their activities.

Smyrna would be named *neōkoros* for the temple to Tiberius, Livia, and the Senate in AD 26, and Ephesus would finally win the title for the temple to the Flavian emperors inaugurated in AD 89. After Ephesus began to flaunt its recent acquisition of the title in civic inscriptions both within its municipality and abroad, the Pergamenes, sensitive to their place in the pecking order among the cities of Asia, began to assert their more ancient honor in their own civic inscriptions. One such inscription in the ancient gymnasium in Pergamum honoring the director of the facility (the "gymnasiarch"; see fig. 5.29) identifies

15. Burrell, *Neokoroi*, 21.

Figure 5.7. A view of the southern and eastern colonnades surrounding the Temple of Trajan and its courtyard. The temple is visible in the center.

the city and its leaders as "the council and the people of the Pergamenes, the first to be awarded the title of 'temple-warden'" (*neōkoros*). Pergamum thus claimed continuing preeminence over its rival for having been thus distinguished first in the province.

The Pergamenes were not content, however, merely to have been "first" to win this honor. Shortly after Ephesus had won the title for its temple to Domitian, Pergamum was granted the right to host the provincial cult of the emperor Trajan and, with it, a second award of a neokorate. The city invested in a massive temple dedicated to Trajan and to Zeus Philios, "preserver of friendships and alliances."[16] This temple and its precincts were placed conspicuously at the center of the side of the acropolis overlooking the city below (see fig. 5.7). An artificial extension of the temple's platform using the barrel-vaulted arch technique found also in the substructure of the Temple of Domitian in Ephesus allowed part of the new temple complex to jut out upon an artificial brow of the acropolis. Set on a podium 10 feet high, with a footprint of 60 by 80 feet and rising to a height of 60 feet, the temple to Trajan (the Traianeum) towered above the worshipers and passersby, a testimony to the city's enthusiasm for the emperor and estimation of his greatness. Its architrave was supported by six Corinthian columns on each of its shorter sides

16. Price, *Rituals and Power*, 137, 252; Burrell, *Neokoroi*, 23.

Figure 5.8. The Temple of Trajan, viewed from the front corner.

Figure 5.9. A dedicatory inscription to Trajan, "lord of earth and sea," on the premises of the Traianeum. The city identifies itself as "twice *neōkoros*" in this inscription.

and nine on its longer sides (see fig. 5.8).[17] The temple sat in the midst of a courtyard of 220 by 160 feet that was itself surrounded by tall colonnaded porticoes on its north, east, and south sides, with no colonnade obscuring the view of the temple from below. Pieces of statues of Zeus, Trajan, and Hadrian have been found on site, their scale suggesting cult images about 15 feet tall.[18] This was, notably, the first time a *second* imperial neokorate had been awarded to a city.[19] Civic inscriptions bear witness to the city's pride in its renewed preeminence among the cities of Asia: Its civic body began to refer to itself in inscriptions as "the council and people of the Pergamenes, twice awarded the neokorate" (see fig. 5.9).

Ephesus continued the competition after Trajan's death, winning the privilege of building

17. Worth, *Seven Cities of the Apocalypse and Greco-Asian Culture*, 115.
18. Burrell, *Neokoroi*, 27.
19. Burrell, *Neokoroi*, 42.

Figure 5.10. An honorific inscription erected by "the council and citizenry of the mother city [*metropolis*] of Asia and first-to-be-twice-*neōkoros* city of the Pergamenes," standing in the courtyard of the Asclepion. The key phrase appears on the third and fourth lines.

a temple consecrated to Trajan's successor, Hadrian, and, with it, its own second award of a neokorate. Thus Ephesus began to refer to itself also as "twice *neōkoros*" in its civic inscriptions. The city fathers of Pergamum, however, did not relinquish their claim to preeminence in the province: Inscriptions found in the Asclepion speak of "the people and council of the *first*-to-be-twice-named-*neōkoros* city of the Pergamenes" (see fig. 5.10).

This story of civic competition demonstrates the strength of the connections between civic identity and pride and support for the imperial cult. This competition appears only to have begun in earnest during the reign of Domitian, specifically following the erection of Ephesus's temple in AD 89. Nevertheless, it attests to the growing investment of the local elites in the imperial cult and the relationship of the imperial cult to a city's regional prominence at the very time that Christian witness *against* the legitimacy of the imperial cult and resistance to participation were becoming sharper. Even if John would not have identified a particular imperial cult site as the "throne of Satan," the conflict between the Pergamenes and the Christians in their midst can certainly be attributed, in part at least, to their differing views of this particular cult.

Figure 5.11. A statue base bearing this dedicatory inscription: "Aulus Julius Quadratus, *neōkoros* and priest of Dionysus, with his mother, Julia Urbana, [honors] emperor Caesar Trajan Hadrian Augustus, savior and benefactor, son of the god Trajan Parthicus, son of the god Nerva."

PLINY THE YOUNGER AND THE TRIALS OF CHRISTIANS

Pliny the Younger served as the proconsular governor of the provinces of Bithynia and Pontus, conjoined provinces north and northeast of Roman Asia, in AD 112–113. He left to posterity a collection of his letters, among which are 121 letters he exchanged with the emperor Trajan during his year as governor. One of those letters sheds a great deal of light on the kind of situation that John seems to have envisioned Christians facing in the near future, especially in Revelation 13:11–17. Pliny has been presented with accusations denouncing people in his province as "Christians" and, in part because of the number of those accused and imperiled, he writes to the emperor for confirmation or correction of the procedures he has been following.

Pliny admits that he had not possessed firm knowledge of what "being a Christian" entailed—a gap in his knowledge that he sought to fill by torturing two female slaves who, he learned, were "deaconesses" in the movement. He evidently knew enough, however, to regard self-identification as a Christian as a punishable offense in and of itself, particularly because Christians were known to refuse to sacrifice to the empire's gods and to the emperor himself. He describes in a chillingly matter-of-fact manner the sort of encounter for which John prepared his congregations:

> This is the line I have taken with all persons brought before me on the charge of being Christians. I have asked them in person if they are Christians, and if they admit it, I repeat the question a second and third time, with a warning of punishment awaiting them. If they persist, I order them to be led away for execution; for, whatever the nature of their admission, I am convinced that their stubbornness and unshakable obstinacy ought not to go unpunished. . . . I considered that I should dismiss any who denied that they were or ever had been Christians when they had repeated after me a formula of invocation to the gods and had made offerings of wine and incense to your statue (which I had ordered to be brought into court for this purpose along with the images of the gods), and furthermore had reviled the name of Christ: none of which things, I understand, any genuine Christian can be induced to do.[a]

Pliny inquires whether those who had been Christians but claim to have left the group, proving this by offering worship to the images of Trajan and the gods, ought to be pardoned, suggesting that keeping the possibility of pardon open in this way would help to reclaim significant numbers of people who may have strayed and to revive popular attention to traditional religious rites.

Trajan confirmed Pliny in this policy. Those who showed proper piety to the gods when thus confronted would be pardoned.

Pliny thus provides us with our oldest surviving account of legal proceedings against individuals on the charge of professing Christianity. An easy way of escape was left open: Offer a little incense and wine and utter perhaps two little words—*Anathema Christos*. John, however, urges his congregations to prepare themselves to hold fast to the testimony of Jesus to the end. It is a great testimony to John that, in the clash between the confession of Christ and loyalty to the emperor that he foresaw, Christ-followers would indeed choose faithfulness unto death and, thereby, keep the testimony about Jesus alive in the Roman world for centuries.

a. Pliny the Younger, *Ep.* 10.96. Quotation is from Radice, *Letters of the Younger Pliny*, 293–94.

The Altar of Zeus and Temple of Athena

The cult of the emperor and Roma, however, was merely one facet of religion in the city of Pergamum—and a relatively recent arrival. Several gods of the traditional Greco-Roman pantheon were worshiped in splendid shrines and temples studding the acropolis and spread throughout the city below. Many of the religious sites atop the acropolis would have been prominently visible even from far away (see fig. 5.12).

Before the Temple of Trajan was constructed, the brow of the acropolis was dominated by the Great Altar of Zeus and the Temple of Athena. Throughout

Figure 5.12. The acropolis of Pergamum, viewed from the west. The Temple of Trajan is visible top left, the theater top center, and the area where the Altar of Zeus once stood top right.

the first century, the Altar of Zeus, located on the southern crest of the acropolis, was the most distinctive and most prominently visible structure overlooking Pergamum (see figs. 5.3, 5.13, 5.14). Construction was begun in the early to mid-second century BC under Eumenes II, likely in connection with (and financed by fresh spoils from) his victory over the Galatians invading his kingdom from the east in 183 BC. The massive throne-like altar complex resembled an open-air temple, complete with columned porticoes flanking its staircase

Figure 5.13. The crepidoma (stepped platform) on which the Altar of Zeus once stood.

Figure 5.14. The reconstructed front of the Altar of Zeus.

Figure 5.15. Remains of images of Cybele and Attis from the terrace of the Altar of Zeus.
Author photo, courtesy of the Pergamonmuseum, Germany.

and surrounding its inner courtyards. The whole had a footprint of about 120 by 110 feet and rose to a height of 40 feet.[20] The altar sat within the inner courtyard. A grand stairway of twenty-eight steps led to the altar platform 30 feet above the ground.[21] The reconstructed monument now sits in the Pergamonmuseum in Berlin (see figs. 5.13, 5.14). The altar was adorned with nearly 400 linear feet of frieze, its scenes carved about 7 feet high. The frieze around the structure's perimeter depicted the mythological battle between the Olympian gods and the giants, with Zeus and Athena prominently featured on the front side. An interior frieze depicted scenes from the myth of Heracles's son, Telephus, the legendary founder of Pergamum.[22] The roof of the porticoes surrounding the Great Altar of Zeus was decorated with statues of gods (like Athena and Poseidon), tritons, griffins, horses, and the like (see figs. 5.15, 5.16).[23] An L-shaped agora or forum was set just below the precincts of the Altar of Zeus. The identification of some of the buildings as warehouses makes it likely that this particular forum served as a commercial center in the old city.[24]

On a plateau just above the Altar of Zeus sat the Temple of Athena, originally constructed in the fourth century BC (see fig. 5.18).[25] The 40-by-70-foot temple appears to have had a double sanctuary, with the deities facing

Figure 5.16. A statue of Zeus from the terrace of the Altar of Zeus, dated to the second century BC.
Author photo, courtesy of the Pergamonmuseum, Germany.

20. Wilson, *Biblical Turkey*, 285.
21. Worth, *Seven Cities of the Apocalypse and Greco-Asian Culture*, 132.
22. Vos, *Archaeology*, 330–31. For a detailed account of the monument, see Kästner, "Architecture of the Great Altar."
23. Picón and Hemingway, *Pergamon*, 196–200.
24. Kekeç, *Pergamon*, 36.
25. Kekeç, *Pergamon*, 37.

Figure 5.17. The precincts of the Temple of Athena.

opposite directions. As Zeus and Athena were both the protectors of Pergamum, it would make sense for Zeus to have been the second deity worshiped at this site. The temple was built close to the edge of the acropolis, with its large courtyard extending away from the precipice (see fig. 5.17). The sacred precincts were expanded with colonnaded porticoes and an elegant gate (called a propylon) bearing the inscription "King Eumenes [II] to Athena Victory-Bearer." The false balcony of this gateway was decorated with reliefs of shields, armor, and weaponry, most likely representing the weapons of the defeated Gauls in Galatia, as this was the major military threat resolved during Eumenes II's time (see fig. 5.19).[26] The facades of both the temple and the propylon

Figure 5.18. A cult statue of Athena Parthenos and the facade of her temple, re-erected in the Pergamonmuseum in Berlin.

26. Habicht, "Seleucids," 328, 330.

Figure 5.19. Left: The facade of the propylon at the entrance to the sacred precincts of Athena (courtesy of Magnus Manske). Right: Frieze detail.

have been re-erected in the Pergamonmuseum, along with a cult statue of Athena.

An inscription bears witness to purity regulations for entering the Athena temple, a reminder that concerns for purity and pollution were common to Jews, Greeks, and Romans. This particular inscription prescribes abstaining from intercourse with one's spouse for the previous day, with anyone else for the previous two days, and performing ceremonial washings as well as abstaining from contact with a corpse or a woman in childbirth for two days.[27]

Eumenes II also established a library adjacent to the sacred precincts of Athena. If the library did indeed boast a collection of two hundred thousand scrolls at one point, a good portion of these would have had to have been stored someplace other than the five rooms of the library complex.[28] That certain ancient kings took special pride in possessing great libraries—indeed, sought to amass the *greatest* library—is exemplified in the rivalry of Ptolemy II, king of Egypt and patron of the great library of Alexandria, and Eumenes II. Upon learning of Eumenes's ambition, Ptolemy significantly curtailed the export of papyrus. This led, in turn, to the Pergamenes' invention of parchment (called *pergamentum* in Pliny, *Nat.* 13.21.70), a writing medium made from the scraped skins of goats, and the development of the codex.[29] Pergamum thereafter became a major exporter of parchment.

27. Worth, *Seven Cities of the Apocalypse and Greco-Asian Culture*, 113.

28. Kekeç, *Pergamon*, 40; Fairchild, *Christian Origins*, 165.

29. Plutarch (*Antony* 58.5) recounts that Mark Antony presented Cleopatra with the two hundred thousand scrolls of Pergamum's library, Asia Minor being within Mark Antony's jurisdiction, but it is far from clear if this involved the physical transfer of the library to Egypt. On the library at Pergamum, see Casson, *Libraries in the Ancient World*, 48–53.

The palaces of the Attalid kings lay to the north and east of the library and Athena temple. These generally followed the peristyle pattern—rooms for various purposes arranged around a central, open-air courtyard, the courtyard itself being surrounded by columned porticoes. After the kingdom passed into Roman hands, these palaces came to serve as barracks for soldiers, with some areas converted into storerooms and arsenals. A *heroon* (a shrine to a hero), likely dedicated to the cult of the Attalid kings, stood at the south edge of the line of palaces and Athena temple.[30] This consisted essentially of a courtyard leading to the shrine, with a number of smaller rooms and a fellowship hall. It appears to have been built in the midst of (and to some extent *over*) a residential area.

Additional Public Buildings and Religious Sites

A great theater—the steepest in the province of Asia—was built into the hill southwest of the Athena temple (see fig. 5.20). It was begun in the third century BC and eventually renovated and expanded during the Roman period

Figure 5.20. The theater viewed from the Traianeum.

30. Cimok, *Pergamum*, 9; Kekeç, *Pergamon*, 28–29.

Figure 5.21. The Temple of Dionysus.

to accommodate as many as ten thousand spectators in eighty rows of stone benches.[31] A pathway leading north-northwest from the stage area of the theater led to the Temple of Dionysus, appropriately linked to the theater's activities (see fig. 5.21). The performance of Greek tragedies and the worship of Dionysus were often connected, as in the Greater Dionysiac Festival in Athens, in honor of which Sophocles, Aeschylus, and Euripides wrote their famous plays, including *Oedipus the King*, *Agamemnon*, and *The Bacchae* (respectively). The temple, itself about 40 by 65 feet, sat atop a podium fitted with a tall staircase of twenty-five steps. It had its origins in the Hellenistic period but, in its present form, reflects renovations from the third century AD.[32]

Following the main road down from the upper toward the lower acropolis, one passes a Hellenistic-period bathhouse and exercise area and, farther down, a complex consisting of a small Roman bath, an odeon, and an opulent cult room honoring a Pergamene named Diodoros Pasparos from the first century BC, as well as some oil, grain, and wine shops.[33] One does not have to travel far, however, before coming to another complex of major cultic sites.

31. Fairchild, *Christian Origins*, 162, 165; Wilson, *Biblical Turkey*, 285.
32. Fairchild, *Christian Origins*, 159.
33. Kekeç, *Pergamon*, 54.

Figure 5.22. The sacred precinct of the Temple of Demeter midway down the southern slope of the acropolis.

Figure 5.23. A portion of the relief that once adorned the altar before the Temple of Demeter. A priestess holds a torch and a patera (a shallow bowl for offering incense, grain, or wine) while a bull awaits sacrifice. Author photo, courtesy of the Bergama Museum, Türkiye.

On a large shelf halfway down the southern slope of the acropolis sit the expansive precincts of the Temple of Demeter, the goddess of abundant harvest (see fig. 5.22). The complex occupies a space of about 125 by 250 feet. The altar proper (about 25 by 8 feet) sits in the middle of the precinct with the remains of the sanctuary of the goddess behind it. The altar was adorned with sacrificial scenes, such as a relief of a priestess of Demeter, standing beside the altar, preparing to sacrifice a bull to the goddess (see fig. 5.23). One major difference between ancient temples and modern religious practice is that the worshipers tended to gather respectfully *outside* the house of the god, with the rituals and sacrifices conducted on an altar in front of the god's house. The Temple of Demeter was originally built by the predecessors of the Attalid kings—Philetaerus and his brother Eumenes (father of Eumenes I)—in honor of their mother. It was expanded and renovated

Figure 5.24. The crepidoma and pieces of the architrave of the small Temple of Hera overlooking the gymnasium.

Figure 5.25. A portion of the dedicatory inscription from the Hera temple, which reads "King Attalus to Hera B[ounaia?]."
Author photo, courtesy of the Bergama Museum, Türkiye.

by their successors. One significant improvement was the creation of stadium seating along the northern side of the courtyard sufficient to accommodate about eight hundred worshipers.[34]

East of the Temple of Demeter sat the Temple of Hera, the wife of Zeus. An inscription found in situ shows this temple to have been built by Attalus II (159–138 BC). Building it atop a platform approached by twelve steps helped to make the smallish temple more impressive (see figs. 5.24, 5.25). A modest cult hall dedicated to Dionysos, the main building measuring about 75 by 30 feet, was located nearby in the midst of what was a (rather exclusive) residential area.[35] A large, open rectangular space was surrounded by stone couches (now covered by weeds) set about 4 feet above the level of the central courtyard. Once furnished with cushions, these couches provided devotees with a comfortable, communal dining experience. A stone shelf for food and drink ran around the inside perimeter, not quite a foot below the level of the couches. A small altar suitable for incense and libations, now fallen, once stood in the center of the room, its presence and its rites reminding the diners of their divine host (see fig. 5.26).

The Temple of Hera overlooked the grand gymnasium and bath complex of Pergamum. The first iteration was constructed under Eumenes II, but it

34. Cimok, *Pergamum*, 54.
35. See discussion in Wulf-Rheidt, "Hellenistic and Roman Houses."

Figure 5.26. A room for cultic meals in honor of Dionysus.

continued to be expanded and modified throughout the Roman period.[36] Because of the nature of the landscape, the complex featured a three-tiered plan. The whole had overall dimensions of 490 by 650 feet over its three terraces.

The upper level housed the principal facilities—a sprawling palaestra and two bath complexes. The palaestra was surrounded by colonnaded porticoes on at least three of its sides, which were in turn surrounded by halls that could be put to various uses (including educational purposes; see fig. 5.27). The complex was furnished with a one-thousand-seat odeon in its northwest corner and a small temple to Asclepius. The bath complexes followed the typical course of the Roman bath, including cold pools, warm pools, saunas, and rooms for massages and cleansing one's skin with olive oil and a good scraping with strigils (see figs. 5.28, 5.30). A second, lower tier offered a running track for the younger teenage boys; the third and lowest tier was allocated for children, including an exercise area and classroom spaces. A shrine to Hermes and Heracles, the patron gods of the gymnasium and athletics in general (no doubt because of their representation of speed and strength, respectively), was part of the middle gymnasium complex.[37]

36. Wilson, *Biblical Turkey*, 286.
37. Worth, *Seven Cities of the Apocalypse and Greco-Asian Culture*, 111.

Figure 5.27. The upper level of the gymnasium from the northwest corner. The small theater is visible on the lower left. The bath complex is in the left background.

Figure 5.28. The remains of the upper gymnasium bath complex.

Figure 5.29. An inscription erected by "the council and the citizenry of the first-to-be-*neōkoros* Pergamenes" honoring a gymnasiarch (an overseer and financier of the activities in the gymnasium) who was also the son of a "high priest of Asia."

Figure 5.30. Three bronze strigils, used to scrape off oil and dirt.

Author photo, courtesy of the Bergama Museum, Türkiye.

Another agora or forum of about 120 by 200 feet, which was surrounded by the customary columned porticoes, was constructed below and south of the gymnasium as part of Eumenes II's expansion of the city. Eumenes also created a new perimeter of defensive fortifications. Its principal access point—the Gate of Eumenes—was located just west of this forum. The entryway was guarded from above by soldiers stationed on three towers.

Figure 5.31. The brick substructure of "Red Hall," once a temple to the Egyptian gods, later repurposed as a Christian church.

One other monument merits mention—namely, the Serapeion (informally known as "Red Hall"), located about 500 yards south of the acropolis (see fig. 5.31). Built in the second century AD under Hadrian, this massive temple was likely dedicated to the Egyptian deities Serapis (Osiris), Isis, and Harpocrates (Horus), though other Egyptian gods may have been represented here as well. The shrine had a footprint of approximately 200 by 70 feet and rose to a height of at least 60 feet. It was flanked by two circular buildings, each with a diameter of 50 feet, and approached through a broad forecourt surrounded by columned porticoes.[38] Only the brick substructure remains—the veneer of marble slabs has long since been reappropriated for other buildings and uses. Although built after Revelation was written, the construction of such a magnificent edifice to the Egyptian gods suggests a devotee base that had been growing in Pergamum throughout the first century. The chief point of interest for readers of Revelation is that one of the statues within this temple was found to have an apparatus of piping that allowed a priest, speaking from a chamber beneath the cult statue, to make it appear that the cult image could speak to its worshipers (see fig. 5.32). John's vision of a local beast causing a cult image of the first beast to speak (Rev. 13:15) was not beyond the special effects technology of his time.[39]

38. Kekeç, *Pergamon*, 75; Worth, *Seven Cities of the Apocalypse and Greco-Asian Culture*, 114.

39. For a wealth of literary allusions to this and other cultic special effects, see S. Scherrer, "Signs and Wonders."

Figure 5.32. The principal cult image once sat atop this platform. From a special room beneath, accessible by a stairway, a priest could make the image seem to speak.

Figure 5.33. A Roman-period bridge over the Selinus River, south of the acropolis, still in use as a pedestrian bridge today.

Beginning in the Hellenistic period and increasingly in the Roman period, the major residential areas of the city spread from the lower slopes of the hill into and across the valley beneath the acropolis, all under the watchful eyes of the gods above, even as the modern city of Bergama does today (sporting a population of one hundred thousand, perhaps not far off from the population in the first century). To the southwest of the acropolis lie the remains of three principal public buildings from the Roman period— a stadium, a theater, and, unusually in Anatolia, an amphitheater (a structure akin to the Colosseum in Rome for gladiatorial and similar fights), all making the public entertainments of the Roman period more accessible to the resident population.

The Asclepion

Further to the southwest of the acropolis lies an Asclepion, a kind of religious healing resort dedicated to Asclepius, the son of Apollo and the god of medicine and healing, whose interventions would be sought in these sanctuaries

Figure 5.34. The well-preserved head from a Roman-period statue of Asclepius, likely a copy of the cult statue once housed in the Pergamum Asclepion. The scale suggests that the complete statue would have stood 12 feet high.
Author photo, courtesy of the Museo Archeologico Regionale Paolo Orsi, Italy.

Figure 5.35. Asclepius.
Author photo, courtesy of the Antalya Archaeological Museum, Türkiye.

(see figs. 5.34, 5.35). There were many such facilities in the ancient world, another celebrated one being located in Corinth.

In its earliest phase, it was a more-or-less private sanctuary built in the fourth century BC by Archias, son of Aristaechmus, in gratitude for healing received at the Asclepion in Epidaurus, Greece. The Attalid kings Eumenes I (ruled 263–241 BC) and Eumenes II (ruled 197–159 BC) dramatically expanded it. The Hellenistic-period sanctuary housed three temples dedicated to Asclepius, Hygieia, and Apollo, each with the customary altar standing before the temple.[40] A distinctive feature of the temple to Asclepius involved a spring that "flows from the very steps on which the temple stands," arising, as it were, "from the temple and the feet of the Savior [Asclepius],"[41] a feature that was carefully preserved throughout the renovations and expansions that would occur into the Roman Imperial period. This water flowed into pools that were used in healing rituals and was also channeled through the buildings

40. Melfi, "Archaeology," 91.
41. Aelius Aristides, *Or.* 39.2.

Figure 5.36. A Hellenistic-period portico in the Asclepion.

set aside for devotees to sleep in, in the hope of receiving instructions for a cure or even miraculous healing itself from the god in their dreams.[42] Other springs fed stepped pools that may have been used for purification rites. A modest fee was required of those entering the sanctuary and wishing to have access to the sacred waters—and a further, more substantial fee was required of those who actually received healing as a result of their visit.[43] For Pergamene Christians, the vision of a river flowing from a throne and the invitation to receive the water of life "as a gift" in Revelation 22:1–2, 17 might call to mind, by way of contrast, the local counterfeit. Inscriptions and votive offerings suggest that the healing sanctuary remained in use throughout the first centuries BC and AD. One notable votive offering is a lock of hair, presented in a gold box, from Emperor Domitian's favored boy, Flavius Earinus, severed in a common rite of passage into adulthood.[44] A Doric stoa of no fewer than forty-five columns and a complex of twenty rooms is likely a remnant of a gymnasium complex in place by the Hellenistic period and still in use into the Roman period (see fig. 5.36).[45]

The remains visible on the archaeological site today, however, largely reflect the Hadrianic-period renovation and expansion of the complex.[46] A road lined

42. Melfi, "Archaeology," 92–93.
43. Melfi, "Archaeology," 93.
44. Melfi, "Archaeology," 101.
45. Melfi, "Archaeology," 98.
46. Levick, "Greece and Asia Minor," 626.

Figure 5.37. The tunnel leading from the principal courtyard of the Asclepion to the *abaton* (dormitory).

Figure 5.38. An excavated stretch of the "Sacred Way" looking back from the Asclepion toward the Acropolis.

with columned porticoes—the "Sacred Way"—stretched 850 yards between the foot of the acropolis and the Asclepion (see fig. 5.38).[47] The road was further adorned with statue groups of gods, philosophers, and benefactors; fountains; and a once-simple tomb (reputed to house either Telephus, the legendary founder of Pergamum, or his mother, Auge) that had been transformed into a hero shrine.[48] The Sacred Way terminated in a small forecourt of 60 by 60 feet, equipped with a central round altar, which opened into the sanctuary's main courtyard of about 400 by 300 feet, surrounded by wide, columned porticoes on the north, west, and south sides. Off the northwest corner of the courtyard stood a theater capable of seating over three thousand spectators (see fig. 5.39). The southwest corner was furnished with spacious latrines. A library and reading room stood in the northeast corner. The pavement of the main courtyard was interrupted by the small pools mentioned above, likely used for purification or healing treatments. The temples of Asclepius, Hygieia, and Apollo stood side by side in the eastern portion of the precinct along with a new temple to Zeus Asclepius Soter built in imitation of the Pantheon in Rome (see fig. 5.40).[49] In the center of the courtyard was the entrance to a long tunnel running diagonally southeast into the circular *abaton*, the dormitory where patients slept in hopes of the god communicating or effecting a cure in a dream (see fig. 5.37).

47. Worth, *Seven Cities of the Apocalypse and Greco-Asian Culture*, 117.
48. Melfi, "Archaeology," 103–4.
49. Melfi, "Archaeology," 108–9.

Figure 5.39. A view of the theater and northern colonnade of the Asclepion.

Figure 5.40. The remains of the Temple of Zeus and Asclepius in the Asclepion.

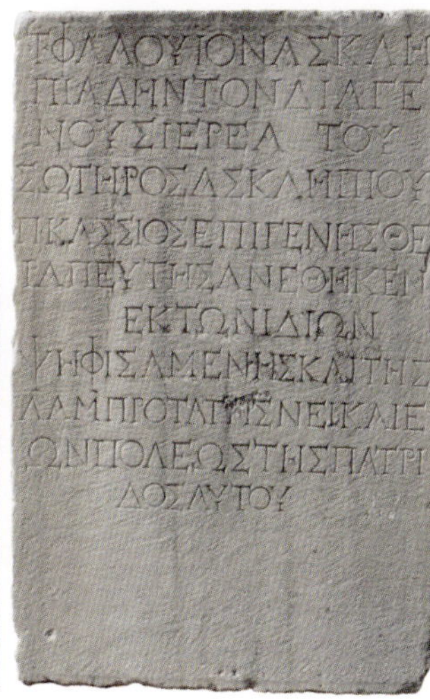

Figure 5.41. An inscription honoring a priest of "Asclepius the Savior."

Aelius Aristides, who suffered from chronic ill health, spent significant periods of time in one Asclepion or another. He recalls, during a stay here in Pergamum, how "a crowd of people clad in white, gathered in honor of the god" in the theater and how he himself "made a speech and sang the praises of the god" (*Or.* 48.30).[50] The vision of the innumerable multitude robed in white and singing praises to God and the Lamb (Rev. 7:9–17) would recall—and greatly surpass—many such gatherings in praise of the "demons and idols" (9:20) worshiped throughout the seven cities.

50. Translation from Edelstein and Edelstein, *Asclepius*, 278, quoted in Melfi, "Archaeology," 110.

THE JEWISH COMMUNITY OF PERGAMUM

A Jewish community, at least one of small to moderate size, appears to have existed in Pergamum and might have provided the seedbed for the fledgling church there, as so frequently was the case in the Mediterranean diaspora. The evidence for this Jewish community's existence is almost entirely literary. Josephus (*Ant.* 14.247–55) preserves a decree of the city council of Pergamum in favor of the Jewish people, essentially acknowledging and pledging support for the stipulations laid down by Rome concerning the Jewish state in Judea under John Hyrcanus I (high priest and head of state from 134–104 BC). The decree is quite vague and mentions nothing about a Jewish presence in Pergamum itself, but it seems highly likely that the Judean embassy would only have stopped in Pergamum on its way home to Judea from its audience with the Roman Senate because there was a Jewish community in the city that they wished to visit.[a]

In 59 BC, the governor of Asia, L. Valerius Flaccus, was accused of misappropriation of funds, including a large sum of money that had been collected by Jewish communities throughout the province for the purpose of supporting the Jerusalem temple (that is, the "temple tax" paid by adult male Jews throughout Israel and the diaspora). In the details of the charges, we learn that a small amount of the money in question had been appropriated from Jews in Pergamum, suggesting at least a small Jewish community resident in the city and its environs (Cicero, *Pro Flacco* 28.66–69). Cicero argued that Flaccus was not guilty of misappropriation but rather was enforcing an earlier edict prohibiting the transport of gold out of the province. This, in turn, tells us something of the Jews of Asia Minor's devotion to the temple and to their fulfillment of their obligation that expressed their connection to the temple, since they were willing to defy a recent edict in order to continue their practice, and also something of the importance of getting the right to do so officially recognized by Roman authorities.[b]

Finally, we might mention one important second-century AD artifact that attests to a Jewish presence in Pergamum—a small altar or table bearing an inscription that seems most naturally to speak of the God of the Jews: "God, (the) Lord, the 'one who is' forever. Zopyros (dedicated) the altar/table and the lampstand with the lamp to the Lord."[c] The designation of God not with any known name of the Greek pantheon but by the titles familiar from the Jewish Scriptures ("Lord," frequently; "the one who is," Exod. 3:14) renders it highly likely that Zopyros was a devotee of the God of Israel (though his own ethnicity cannot be determined).

a. Trebilco, *Jewish Communities*, 7–8.
b. Trebilco, *Jewish Communities*, 14–16.
c. Trebilco, *Jewish Communities*, 163.

"Satan's Throne" in Pergamum

The association of Asclepius with the serpent that is found coiled about his staff and thus is a common decorative feature throughout the Asclepion has led a few scholars to associate this complex in Pergamum with the "throne of Satan."[51] In favor of such an identification might be the fact that Asclepius came to serve as the visual representation of the city itself on coins and in carved reliefs on inscriptions—for example, on coins or adorning inscriptions celebrating the *homonoiai*, the "agreements" worked out between Ephesus (represented by the distinctive Artemis Ephesia) and Pergamum (represented by Asclepius).[52] Many scholars believe, however, that John was speaking about Pergamum's most distinctive landmark, the Altar of Zeus, when he said that Pergamum was home to "Satan's throne" (Rev. 2:13).[53] Jewish writers frequently identify the pagan gods with demons, claiming that those who worshiped idols were really worshiping demons (Ps. 106:37; Bar. 4:6–7; 1 Cor. 10:19–21; Rev. 9:20–21). Identifying the Greeks' chief god (Zeus) with Satan (the chief of the demons) would have been a natural extension of this tendency. If John is thinking of a particular monument in Pergamum as "Satan's throne"—indeed, a distinctive monument that would set "Satan's throne" in Pergamum apart from the other six cities John addresses—the Great Altar of Zeus seems to me the likeliest candidate.[54] The officially promoted view was that Rome and its emperors ruled by the will of Jupiter/Zeus and were destined by the chief of the gods to bring order, peace, and rule of law to the known world (see, e.g., Virgil, *Aen.* 1.236–37; 4.232). According to John's deconstruction of this public knowledge, however, it is "the dragon, the old serpent" (i.e., Satan; Rev. 12:9), who stands behind the many-headed beast that exercises authority over the peoples, nations, and languages of the world, and that receives worship from its awestruck subjects (13:1–4, 7–8). The Temple of Roma and Augustus in Pergamum is a manifestation of the cult of the beast and its image; temples and altars of Zeus would represent the closest parallels to shrines to the dragon that gives the beast its power.

Whether John had in mind the Great Altar of Zeus, the centers of the imperial cult, or the acropolis as a whole as a cluster of sacred sites that would be abhorrent to John, Pergamum would indeed have seemed to him

51. For example, Fairchild, *Christian Origins*, 155–56.

52. On the importance of *homonoia*, or "concord, agreement," between the three great rival cities of Asia—Ephesus, Smyrna, and Pergamum—as they negotiated their pecking order with their shifting fortunes, see Dio Chrysostom, *Or.* 34.48; Kampmann, "*Homonoia* Politics," 376–77.

53. For a summary of views on the subject, see Aune, *Revelation 1–5*, 182–84.

54. DeSilva, *Seeing Things*, 43; Kästner, "Architecture of the Great Altar," 143.

a stronghold of Satan, perhaps the location of his very seat of power as he deceived humanity to take what was due God and give it instead to sticks and stones and pretentious human rulers. The investment of the city in these cults, however, also explains why their inhabitants would not be disposed to tolerate a movement of people in their midst who claimed all their temples, their sacrifices, and their piety to be a sham—or worse.[55] It is surely no coincidence that the theological program of the rival Christian teachers whom John labels "Nicolaitans" and identifies with Balaam, the historic prophet of compromise (see Num. 25:1–3; 31:15–16), found a following among the Christians of this city (Rev. 2:14–15).[56] The pressure was indeed great to find a way to pay lip service to the gods of their neighbors while holding on to their (private?) belief in one God and his Messiah. John rightly saw in the steadfast disciple Antipas, who was killed (whether as a result of judicial proceedings or simply vigilante action) because of his profession of one God to the exclusion of all others (2:13), the shape of things to come for Christians who refused to bow, as John saw it, before Satan's throne.[57]

55. Nothing at all is known of the origins of the Christian community there. It is possible that members of Paul's team or of the congregations he planted in Ephesus, 110 miles to the south, carried the gospel to other major cities in their province, as Epaphras had evangelized Colossae, Laodicea, and Hierapolis (Col. 1:7–8; 4:12–13), but this is merely conjecture.

56. Further on the Nicolaitans, see deSilva, *Seeing Things*, 59–63, 138–40; for a contrary view, see Worth, *Seven Cities of the Apocalypse and Greco-Asian Culture*, 125–30.

57. On Antipas and persecution in the background of Revelation, see deSilva, *Seeing Things*, 50–55; Worth, *Seven Cities of the Apocalypse and Roman Culture*, 112–30; *Seven Cities of the Apocalypse and Greco-Asian Culture*, 124–25.

6

THYATIRA

The city of Thyatira was founded as a military colony under Seleucus I in the early third century BC on the site of an older Lydian town.[1] After the Treaty of Apamea (190 BC) pushed the western border of the Seleucid Empire back to the Taurus Mountains, Thyatira was placed under the authority of Eumenes II of the kingdom of Pergamum. The Attalid kings constructed a road (maintained throughout the Roman period) that connected Pergamum (46 miles northwest of Thyatira), Thyatira, Sardis (38 miles southeast of Thyatira), and Laodicea, and that continued south as far as the Mediterranean coast. Thyatira's population in the first century has been estimated at around twenty-five thousand—an admittedly very rough estimate but one that at least suggests that the city was significantly smaller than the *mētropoleis* of Ephesus, Smyrna, and Pergamum.[2] The city may have had a number of Jewish residents, perhaps descendants of some of the two thousand Jewish families relocated to the Seleucid cities and colonies throughout Lydia and Phrygia by Antiochus III around 210 BC with a view to securing his interests in the territory.[3]

The physical remnants of Thyatira are inevitably disappointing to any visitor. The presence of the modern city of Akhisar atop the remains of the ancient city has made any substantial effort at excavation impossible. Inscriptions, however, reveal that Thyatira once had several gymnasiums, a theater,

1. Wilson, *Biblical Turkey*, 319.
2. Mitchell, *Celts*, 244.
3. Josephus, *Ant.* 12.148–53.

Figure 6.1. Map of the excavated remains of Thyatira in the modern city of Akhisar.

Figure 6.2. An inscription honoring Stratonikeia, a priestess of Artemis, from ancient Hierokaisara, a town 10 miles south of Thyatira.

Figure 6.3. A Roman-period altar featuring the typical motif of fruit-laden garlands and skulls or heads of sacrificial animals.
Author photo, courtesy of the Akhisar Museum, Türkiye

and multiple cult sites for both the traditional gods and the imperial cult, particularly focused on Augustus. The frequency with which Apollo and Artemis are featured on the city's coinage suggests that these were the city's principal gods. Apollo would have been a natural choice for a city that had long venerated one or another version of a "sun god" over its long life.[4] A Roman-period inscription honoring a priestess named Stratonikeia for her "pious conduct and generosity" in the course of a festival also attests to an active cult of Artemis (see fig. 6.2). A locally minted coin featuring Vespasian on the obverse and a tetrastyle (four-columned) temple with a standing figure in its interior on the reverse suggests the presence of a local imperial cult temple (see fig. 6.4).

Figure 6.4. A local bronze coin of Thyatira from the time of Vespasian featuring an otherwise unattested temple on the reverse.
Used with permission of wildwinds.com, ex Numismatik Naumann Auction 41, Lot 540, March 2016

Inscriptions also tell us that at least two local residents of Thyatira had become provincial high priests in the late first century BC. One of these priests, at least, would have overseen worship in the new Temple of Rome and

4. Wilson, "Social and Geographical World of Thyatira," 660; *Biblical Turkey*, 319.

Augustus in Pergamum, the provincial seat of emperor worship. Construction on this temple had begun in 29 BC and was completed before 19 BC.[5] An inscription located in the vicinity of the Temple of Zeus Philios and Trajan in Pergamum records the congratulations offered by the citizens of Thyatira to their neighbor for being awarded the title of *neōkoros* a second time (see fig. 6.5). Thyatira appears to have been an active supporter of the imperial cult at both the local and the provincial levels.

Figure 6.5. An inscription beside the remains of Pergamum's Temple of Trajan recording the citizenry of Thyatira's congratulations of Pergamum on being awarded its second neokorate.

The space of a city block has been partially excavated. There one can see the remnants of a colonnaded portico from the second century AD, as well as pieces of an ornate arched gate or entryway into this public space or forum (see fig. 6.6).[6] One of the more interesting inscriptions unearthed in this area

Figure 6.6. The reconstructed portion of a second-century AD arcade.

5. C. Koester, *Revelation*, 296.

6. The remains of a sixth-century basilica have also been uncovered in this area. It is unclear whether it was built to serve some administrative or judicial function or if it was built, or repurposed, for use as a church.

Figure 6.7. The inscription honoring the emperor Titus.

is an inscription honoring Titus, the son of Vespasian, who was the emperor from AD 79 to 81 (see fig. 6.7). This is the only surviving slab of an inscription that originally consisted of three or more such pieces. Not enough of the text survives to indicate what motivated this particular dedication. Vespasian and Domitian both gave attention to improving the roads around Thyatira and throughout Roman Asia, which were essential for travel and trade.[7] Titus likely also contributed to the city's infrastructure in some such way, thus being honored in this inscription. The inscription is one of the very few pieces of ancient Thyatira uncovered so far that dates firmly to the first century, near the time when John addressed one or more Christian congregations here.

Inscriptions also bear witness to the existence of a number of guilds in the city. A cluster of these were erected by members of a guild of fabric dyers, some of whom attained prominent roles in the city's cults and civic life (see fig. 6.8).[8] The early Christian convert Lydia,

Figure 6.8. Two honorific inscriptions erected by two prominent guilds (the fullers and the wool workers). The inscription on the top can be dated narrowly to AD 218–222 on the basis of the (presumed) presence of the name Antoneinon, a more formal name of the emperor Elagabalus. This name was chiseled out after Elagabalus's assassination and the condemnation of his memory by the Roman Senate (Wilson, *Biblical Turkey*, 321).

7. Magie, *Roman Rule*, 1:570. See also, for example, the inscription on a column (a milestone?) near Smyrna acknowledging Domitian's role in road construction. Kearsley, "Roman Road in Asia Minor," 23–26.

8. Graves, "What Is the Madder?," 4.

while a resident of Philippi at the time of her conversion in response to Paul's preaching there (Acts 16:14–15, 40), hailed from Thyatira and might well have learned her craft of dying fabric purple in her native city. A major source of a crimson-purple dye in Asia Minor came from the root of the madder plant (see Strabo, *Geogr.* 13.4.14), though it is possible that the dyers engaged in trade for the rarer, more expensive dye extracted from the glands of the Murex family of shellfish so as to include the uppermost echelons of their region in their clientele.[9]

There were also guilds of leather workers, tanners, weavers, wool merchants, potters, and coppersmiths.[10] These were associations of people who (generally) shared a common trade, formed for the purpose of creating occasions for socializing, networking, and professional cooperation. They also provided for a decent burial for any of their members who could not afford one. Trade associations named one or more deities as their patron gods and honored these gods at their social functions. They also became increasingly attentive to honoring the emperors as an assurance of their loyalty (and the political harmlessness of their gatherings), often adopting a particular member of the imperial family as another patron god or goddess and performing "sacrifices and other rituals including mysteries in honor of the emperor or *Sebastoi*."[11] Their fellowship meals—like many such meals in the Greco-Roman world—would often feature meat from an animal that the guild had offered in some such sacrificial ritual.[12]

All of the cities addressed by John, of course, had numerous professional associations (or "trade guilds"), such that this cannot be seen as particularly distinctive of Thyatira.[13] For example, inscriptions (again) confirm the presence of associations of "architects and fishermen, bankers and bakers, basket makers and bath workers, carpenters and cobblers, hemp-weavers and linen-weavers, silversmiths and slave dealers, wineskin-makers and wool dealers" in Roman Ephesus.[14] Smyrna similarly had its associations of goldsmiths, silversmiths, vintners, fishermen, flax workers, porters, and bankers.[15] Nevertheless, the activities and importance of these trade associations provide one important context for the emergence of Christian teachers who might seek to make room for continued participation in their activities. John accuses the

9. Graves, "What Is the Madder?," 8–16.

10. Magie, *Roman Rule*, 1:48–49, 2:812n78.

11. Harland, "Honouring the Emperor," 113.

12. Harland, "Honouring the Emperor," 113.

13. Broughton, "Roman Asia," 841–44; C. Koester, *Revelation*, 295; contra Hemer, *Letters*, 107–8.

14. Worth, *Seven Cities of the Apocalypse and Greco-Asian Culture*, 29.

15. Strabo, *Geogr.* 14.1.15; Harland, *Associations*, 39–40, 85; C. Koester, *Revelation*, 272.

Figure 6.9. An inscription honoring members of a local elite family whose members held the titles "Asiarch" and "*neōkoros* of the emperors." The names "M[arcus] Aur[elius] Priscillianus Saturninus" and "Marcus Aur[elius] Athenaeus" suggest a family of descendants of an imperial freedman of the later second century AD.

Thyatira Christian whom he calls "Jezebel" of "teaching and leading my slaves astray so that they commit fornication and eat things sacrificed to idols" (Rev. 2:20). John's language recalls the incident in Numbers that recounts the Moabites' strategies for getting the Hebrews to assimilate to them—one sure way to neutralize the threat of a formidable group of foreigners passing into one's territory: "While Israel was staying in Shittim, the men began to indulge in sexual immorality with Moabite women, who invited them to the sacrifices to their gods. The people ate the sacrificial meal and bowed down before these gods" (Num. 25:1–2 NIV). This suggests that "Jezebel" was indeed promoting a theology that would permit participation in the Christians' neighbors' religious and social activities, ever inextricably linked. A position that viewed such participation as somehow compatible with Christian identity would allow the believers to maximize the benefits of remaining embedded in trade associations as well as other civic networks. That "Jezebel" was gaining a hearing in Thyatira while the "Nicolaitans" were also enjoying influence in Pergamum suggests that a number of Christians in Asia were willing to take a far more moderate view of such matters than John would condone for the sake of continued economic and social enfranchisement.[16]

16. Harland, "Honouring the Emperor," 101. "Fornication" here might well be regarded as metaphorical, in keeping with John's use of sexual imagery throughout Revelation. Unfaithfulness to the one God and his Anointed One in matters of worship would lend itself to this metaphor, particularly in a visionary world in which two prominent inhabitants are a great prostitute and a pure bride.

Photo credit: Mark Wilson.

Figure 6.10. A wall of the Ulu Mosque, built in part from Roman-period remains.

Some remains of ancient Thyatira can be found incorporated into the buildings throughout the modern city of Akhisar. For example, the Ulu Mosque (see fig. 6.10) appears to have incorporated portions of an ancient church (testifying to the ongoing life of the Christian community in Thyatira prior to the Muslim period), which, in turn, had incorporated ashlars from a pagan temple.[17]

17. Wilson, *Biblical Turkey*, 321.

7

SARDIS

The city of Sardis (*Sardeis*) sits 60 miles east of Smyrna and 38 miles southeast of Thyatira. Sardis had a legendary past as the seat of the kingdom of Lydia. It was situated beside the Pactolus River, whose sands, rich in gold dust, gave the city a constant source of wealth. Coins made of electrum, a gold and silver alloy, were minted here as early as the seventh century BC (Herodotus, *Hist.* 1.94).[1] One of its kings, Croesus, became proverbially associated with wealth—and with folly, for provoking the Persians to war and losing his kingdom (1.47–91). The Persians extended their "Royal Road" into their newly conquered territory, linking Sardis, which they made the capital of their empire's westernmost province, with the capital city of Susa some 1,500 miles to the east.[2] This placed Sardis on a major trade and communications route that persisted into the Roman period, positioning the city for ongoing prosperity (see fig. 7.2).

Sardis surrendered to Alexander the Great on his advance through Asia Minor in 334 BC (Arrian, *Anabasis of Alexander* 1.17.306). In the struggles between Alexander's successors, Sardis finally came under Seleucid control in 281 BC and served as their western capital.[3] Taking advantage of a period of weakness, the Attalid kingdom of Pergamum seized control of Sardis in 226 BC, but Achaeus, a cousin of Antiochus III, took it back four years later. Achaeus attempted to establish it as the capital of his own breakaway

1. Hemer, *Letters*, 131.
2. Wilson, *Biblical Turkey*, 297.
3. Trebilco, *Jewish Communities*, 37; Wilson, *Biblical Turkey*, 297.

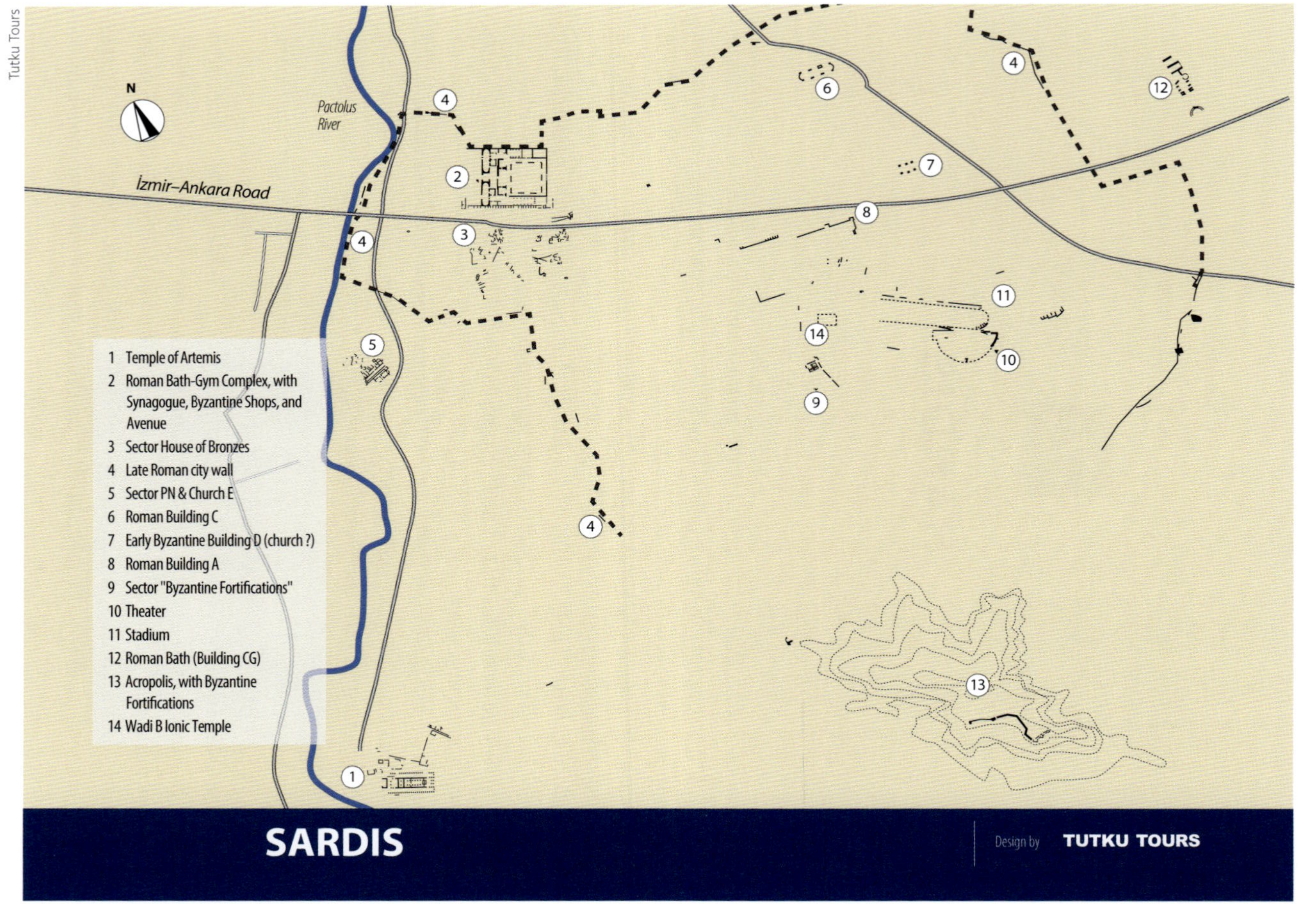

Figure 7.1. A map of the excavations at Sardis.

Figure 7.2. A partially excavated segment of the major road, renovated during the Roman period, that once connected Sardis with points as far east as Susa, one of the capital cities of the former Persian Empire.

kingdom, however, leading Antiochus III to besiege and recapture the city in 214 BC.[4] A series of letters written by Antiochus III to the city after these events was discovered inscribed on large blocks of stone that had been reused in the construction of the late Roman synagogue.[5] The city would remain in Seleucid control until Antiochus III's defeat at the battle of Magnesia in 190 BC, after which the Romans made Sardis a secure part of the kingdom of Pergamum, the whole of which was bequeathed to the Roman people upon the death of the childless King Attalus III in 133 BC.

Sardis was a major urban center with upward of sixty thousand residents during the Roman period.[6] It was one of nine cities in Asia that were regular

4. See Polybius, *Hist.* 4.48.7; 7.18.9; 8.15–21, cited in Ratté, "Reflections," 126.

5. Ratté, "Reflections," 126.

6. Hanfmann, Yegül, and Crawford, "Roman and Late Antique Period," 146. Trebilco (*Jewish Communities*, 37) estimates a population of around one hundred thousand in the second century AD. Estimates are necessarily very rough, of course, given the paucity of excavated areas on which to base any estimate. Galen (*De cognoscendis curandi* 9) gives a population of one hundred twenty thousand for the city in the later second century, likely including the populations of the villages in its hinterlands.

sites for the Roman governor to hear judicial cases that had been referred to him.[7] The Roman-period city is estimated to have covered 3 square miles.[8] Unfortunately, very little of first-century Sardis, such as might illumine the context and situation of the Christian church addressed by John, has been uncovered. The most impressive archaeological remains postdate the New Testament period by a century or more. This is due, practically, to the focus of the archaeological teams working at Sardis, which have devoted their greatest efforts to recovering the monumental buildings of the late Roman period in a limited area. It is due, historically, to an earthquake that shook the entire province in AD 17 but devastated Sardis more severely than its neighbors. As Tacitus relates the event, "In the same year, twelve important cities of Asia collapsed in an earthquake that struck at night. . . . As the disaster fell heaviest upon the Sardians, it brought them the greatest measure of charity. Caesar promised ten million sesterces and remitted for five years their [tax] payments to the Public and the Imperial Treasuries. It was voted to send a Senatorial Commissioner to inspect the present situation and initiate recovery measures."[9] It should be remembered that such aid, though generous and welcome as far as the population of Sardis was concerned, represented the redistribution of the proceeds of taxes and tribute drawn from subject populations to cities that had been known to cooperate with and support imperial rule.

Sardis, like neighboring Philadelphia, took on the epithet Caesarea as a display of gratitude, though this would drop from use in inscriptions within a generation. An inscription from a statue base found in Sardis provides another window into the city's expressions of gratitude toward "the god Tiberius Caesar Augustus," who is therein named "founder of the city and benefactor of the world."[10] All the cities affected by this earthquake and benefited by the emperor also dedicated a larger-than-life statue of Tiberius, with carved reliefs representing the patron gods or other personifications of each of the cities around the base, in Rome.[11] A smaller version of this monument, with the representations of the cities appearing in carved relief on the statue base, was placed in the port city of Puteoli (modern Pozzuoli, near Naples, Italy; see fig. 7.3).

Sardis had recovered sufficiently to compete a decade later with her sister cities for the honor of building the provincial temple to honor Tiberius,

7. Trebilco, *Jewish Communities*, 37.

8. Hanfmann, Yegül, and Crawford, "Roman and Late Antique Period," 139.

9. Tacitus, *Ann.* 2.47, trans. Hanfmann, Yegül, and Crawford, "Roman and Late Antique Period," 141.

10. Judge, "Thanksgiving to the Benefactor," 22.

11. Magie, *Roman Rule*, 1:500.

Figure 7.3. The base of the statue erected in honor of Tiberius by the cities in Roman Asia affected by the earthquake of AD 17. The visible side features representations of the patron gods of Sardis (left) and Magnesia (right).
Olga Lyubimova / CC BY-SA 4.0 / The Gallery of Ancient Art

losing out in the final round to Smyrna as a better resourced and higher-profile competitor (Tacitus, *Ann.* 4.55). Nevertheless, Sardis was still a city very much "under construction" throughout the whole of the first century, undergoing "near total urban renewal directed by Roman authorities."[12] It is believed that major roads, water delivery systems, and sewage systems were completed only thirty years later, under Claudius.[13] The monumental buildings of the city would take far longer to recover or to replace (as in the case of the gymnasium complex).

The acropolis, with the most ancient remains predating the Persian invasion, has yielded very little archaeological fruit, having been subject to centuries of erosion and collapse, and is therefore almost never visited except by devoted hikers.[14] The acropolis had been successfully taken in the city's ancient past on two occasions. In 546 BC, the Persians breached the acropolis's defenses, allegedly on account of the lack of vigilance on the part of the watchmen stationed on the ramparts above. The forces led by Antiochus III would do so again in 213 BC. It has become something of a trope in commentaries and other treatments of the oracle to Sardis (Rev. 3:1–6) to connect the glorified Lord's exhortation to "be watchful" (3:2) and the threat of bursting in on them unexpectedly like a thief (3:3) with local knowledge of these distant events.[15] Granting that the story particularly of the demise of Croesus and his empire had become proverbial in the Classical period (though more in connection with the dangerous ambiguity of oracles than with the

12. Hanfmann, Robert, and Mierse, "Hellenistic Period," 109.

13. Hanfmann, Yegül, and Crawford, "Roman and Late Antique Period," 142–43.

14. Ratté ("Reflections," 131–32) suggests that the acropolis had always been rather limited in size, accommodating chiefly its garrison and serving as a place of refuge.

15. See, e.g., Hemer, *Letters*, 133, 144; "Sardis Letter."

folly of overconfidence in one's defenses), the more obvious background for this exhortation is the body of Jesus's sayings urging this same posture of watchfulness (Matt. 24:42; 25:13; Mark 13:35, 37) and using the same image of the thief to underscore the importance of living each day with the day of the Lord foremost in one's mind (Matt. 24:43–44).

The Temple of Artemis and the Cults of Other Gods

The oldest structure of significance is the Temple of Artemis, built about two-thirds of a mile west of the acropolis. The worship of Artemis was popular throughout the cities of Roman Asia, nowhere more so than in Ephesus. The Temple of Artemis in Sardis, however, was also a marvel—the eighth largest temple in the Greek world, with eight grand Ionic columns supporting its roof on the east and west sides, and twenty columns on each of the longer sides (see fig. 7.4). The temple's footprint is about 300 by 160 feet, covering twice the area of the Parthenon in Athens. Its roof once rose to a height of over 80 feet.[16] A large stone altar sits in front of the temple (to the west), as was typical throughout the ancient world. The temple was the house of the deity; worshipers gathered respectfully outside for the rites and sacrifices.

Figure 7.4. The Temple of Artemis, seen from the rear. Note the brick substructure of a Byzantine-period church on the far left of the photo.

16. Pfeiffer and Vos, *Wycliffe Historical Geography*, 400.

Figure 7.5. The interior of the Temple of Artemis showing the remains of the wall that divided the double cella. The entirety of the rear cella is visible in the photo, including the doorway through which the cult image would have been visible from behind the temple.

Construction on this temple (which replaced an earlier Artemis temple on the site built in the sixth century BC) began in 334 BC—shortly after Alexander wrested control of Asia Minor from the Persians—but suffered major interruptions and setbacks.[17] Not least among these was the earthquake of AD 17. The Temple of Artemis was quickly rendered functional again, but none of its columns appear to have been re-erected until the early second century.[18]

At some point, Artemis appears to have come to share her temple with Zeus. It is unknown whether this occurred during the late Hellenistic or the early Roman periods.[19] The most obvious conjecture would be that the earthquake made this a more practical solution than restoring two separate temples. What is certain is that, at some point in its history, the temple's cella—the interior portion of the temple that housed the cult image of the deity—was divided into two separate cellas, one still facing the front of the temple (west) and the other facing the rear (east) (see fig. 7.5).

Soon Artemis and Zeus would also share their sacred space with the imperial gods. It is possible that both Tiberius and his mother, Livia, were honored at this site.[20] It is certain, however, that the precincts were rededicated in the mid-second century to include Antoninus Pius (ruled AD 138–161) and his wife, Faustina. If the temple's structure had not previously been altered to accommodate the worship of Zeus, it would have been altered at this time to create two sanctuaries. It is unclear how the sacred spaces were divided. One

17. Sherwin-White and Kuhrt, *From Samarkhand to Sardis*, 183.
18. Hanfmann, Yegül, and Crawford, "Roman and Late Antique Period," 143.
19. Hanfmann, Robert, and Mierse, "Hellenistic Period," 118.
20. Hanfmann, Robert, and Mierse, "Hellenistic Period," 120.

theory is that the front-facing sanctuary remained sacred to Artemis (and Zeus?) with the rear-facing sanctuary dedicated to Antoninus and Faustina; another suggests that the rear-facing sanctuary was dedicated to Zeus and Antoninus, with Artemis and Faustina sharing the front-facing sanctuary.[21]

The temple to Antoninus and Faustina won the city the title of *neōkoros* of the provincial imperial cult for the second time. The cult images of the imperial couple were massive: The heads alone measured a yard from chin to crown.[22] Fragmentary remains of heads and other parts of colossal statues have been tentatively identified as representing other members of the Antonine dynasty: Lucius Verus and his wife, Lucilla; and Marcus Aurelius and his wife, Faustina the Younger.[23] The possibility still exists, however, that one of these pairs represented the original dedicatees of the temple, Artemis and Zeus.

The award of this neokorate was, of course, a climactic development in a long history of devotion to Rome and her emperors. Inscriptions show the city to have had a cult of the goddess Roma by the late second or early first century BC and a local cult of Augustus by the late first century BC.[24] One inscription datable to 9 BC mentions a priest of Roma who also served as the *stephanophoros*, a kind of city mayor.[25] Another refers to the consecration of a statue of Gaius Caesar (who along with his brother Lucius had been one of Augustus's heirs-apparent until their untimely deaths) in the city's Temple of Augustus.[26] Sardis had also been, as mentioned above, one of two finalists in a competition involving no fewer than eleven cities of Roman Asia to host the provincial cult of Tiberius in AD 26.

Coins and inscriptions show that the provincial temple to Antoninus Pius made Sardis "twice *neōkoros*." There are no literary or archaeological clues, however, concerning what temple to what emperor *first* gave Sardis that title. Possible candidates include Claudius, Nero, Vespasian, Titus, and Nerva, depending on the original dedicatee or dedicatees of the "Temple of the Augusti" in Ephesus.[27] The remains of a temple have been partially uncovered on the northern slopes of the acropolis, built at some point during the early Imperial period.[28] A fragmentary inscription plausibly reconstructed

21. Price, *Rituals and Power*, 151–52. Wilson (*Biblical Turkey*, 298) prefers the second configuration.

22. Price, *Rituals and Power*, 187.

23. See Burrell, *Neokoroi*, 103–8, for their identification and their possible placements in the sacred precincts.

24. Hanfmann, Robert, and Mierse, "Hellenistic Period," 118; C. Koester, *Revelation*, 311.

25. Knight, "Was Roma the Scarlet Harlot?," 115.

26. Price, *Rituals and Power*, 259.

27. Burrell, *Neokoroi*, 100–101. Ascough ("Greco-Roman Religions," 44) favors Vespasian.

28. Burrell, *Neokoroi*, 100–101.

as "Adramython"—and thus a reference to the city of Adramyteion, also in the province of Asia—suggests that this was at one point a provincial temple for the imperial cult, bearing the names of the cities of the whole province inscribed around its architrave.[29] It was short-lived, however, due to the instability of the location. It remains unclear whether this temple was connected to the city's first or second imperial neokorate. If it was originally erected to house the cult of Antoninus and Faustina, the temple's early collapse would explain the unusual step that Sardis had taken, installing their cult in a remodeled temple already dedicated to Artemis and Zeus.[30] It would have simply been impractical, and possibly financially impossible, to do otherwise at that point.

The Temple of Artemis was situated close by the Pactolus stream, which ran a fairly straight course to the north and west of the city. A structure identified as a shrine to Cybele sat about 500 yards north-northeast of the Artemis temple, also near the Pactolus, in the center of what had been a gold recovery and smithing facility, processing gold sifted from the riverbed, during the period of the Lydian kingdom. Worship of Cybele, identified as the "Great Mother" goddess and famous for her eunuch priests, is well attested throughout Lydia and Asia Minor in general.[31] A fourth-century BC relief featuring Artemis and Cybele, attended by two worshipers, was found in secondary use as part of the support for a colonnade in the forecourt of the late Roman synagogue.[32]

In the absence of further excavation, inscriptions continue to provide important evidence for the religious life of Hellenistic and Roman Sardis. An inscription found on a block in secondary use in the late Roman synagogue bears witness to the existence of a Temple of Hera in the Hellenistic period and to its restoration in the Roman period after the earthquake.[33] A cult of Sabazios (a local god eventually assimilated to Dionysus) existed from at least the fourth century BC and persisted through the first century. An inscription from the late first or early second century AD (itself a reaffirmation of a fourth-century BC rule) forbids cult personnel of Zeus to participate in the mysteries of other gods, including Sabazios, Agdistis, and Ma.[34] This is particularly interesting because Greco-Roman cults were almost never

29. Burrell, *Neokoroi*, 101.

30. Burrell, *Neokoroi*, 102–3.

31. Hemer, *Letters*, 138–39.

32. Mitten and Scorziello, "Reappropriating Antiquity," 138.

33. Hanfmann, Robert, and Mierse, "Hellenistic Period," 111; Mitten and Scorziello, "Reappropriating Antiquity," 142–43.

34. Ascough, "Greco-Roman Religions," 41–43; Horsley, *New Documents*, 1:21–23.

exclusive of participation in one another. Even here, the proscription is limited to priests and other cult staff.[35]

Inscriptions and coinage suggest that Sardis also hosted active cults of Asclepius, Athena, Attis, Eros, Heracles, Hermes, Apollo, Men, and Demeter at various points during the Hellenistic and Roman periods, though it is not known to what extent these cults were also represented in architecture.[36] Hermes and Heracles were typically associated with gymnasiums in Greek cities, and it is likely that this was the case in Sardis as well.[37]

Civic Architecture

About 2,000 feet north-northeast of the acropolis sat two structures essential to entertainment in the Greco-Roman context: the theater and the stadium. A theater existed here in the Seleucid period, though it was thoroughly rebuilt in the Roman period.[38] Only the general contours of the seating area (the cavea), together with large portions of the massive retaining walls that supported the seating at the open ends, remain to be seen today (see fig. 7.6). The cavea has dimensions of about 140 yards on its east-west axis and 76 yards north-south.[39] Much of the seating itself has been removed and repurposed over the centuries. Immediately north of the theater sits the eastern end of the stadium, which remains largely unexcavated save for a few lengths of the broad arched passageway that once led under, and gave access to, the seating (see fig. 7.7). It is likely that Hellenistic Sardis already had a stadium, but it may or may not have been situated on the same site as the one currently known, which is clearly of Roman-period construction.[40]

The most prominent building standing on the site of ancient Sardis is a portion of the reconstructed gymnasium, standing about 1,400 yards north-northeast of the Artemis temple and 1,600 yards north-northwest of the acropolis (see fig. 7.8). A gymnasium had existed in Sardis already in the third

35. It is sometimes asserted that Sabazios was a corruption of Sabaoth and, thus, evidence of Jewish syncretism. This is, however, based entirely on the claim by Valerius Maximus (*Memorable Deeds and Sayings* 1.3.2) that the Jews were expelled from Rome in 139 BC as worshipers of Sabazios, a proscribed cult deity. It seems more likely that Valerius simply misunderstood the situation. Worth, *Seven Cities of the Apocalypse and Greco-Asian Culture*, 178–79.

36. Hanfmann, Robert, and Mierse, "Hellenistic Period," 118; Ascough, "Greco-Roman Religions," 44.

37. Hanfmann, Robert, and Mierse, "Hellenistic Period," 133; Ascough, "Greco-Roman Religions," 45.

38. Ratté, "Reflections," 130–31.

39. Hanfmann, Robert, and Mierse, "Hellenistic Period," 116.

40. Hanfmann, Robert, and Mierse, "Hellenistic Period," 116.

Figure 7.6. The remains of the theater prior to excavation. The visible stonework once supported the western side of the cavea, the contours of which remain clearly visible.

Figure 7.7. A portion of the unexcavated passageway running the length of the stadium and supporting the spectators' stands.

Figure 7.8. The reconstructed facade of the gymnasium complex. The broad, grassy space in front of the facade is a portion of the palaestra, once surrounded by colonnades fronting rooms and halls on its north, south, and west sides.

century BC, as Antiochus III mentions the structure in one of his edicts concerning the city (the texts of which are inscribed on several stone blocks that were repurposed in the construction of the late Roman synagogue). Moreover, the gymnasium, which combined emphases on education and athletics, was an indispensable institution for forming the next generation into good citizens in every Greek or Hellenized city. The location of the earlier Hellenistic gymnasium remains unknown.[41] The Roman-period gymnasium complex was built in a new quarter of the city in connection with the rebuilding of the city begun under Tiberius.[42] Construction appears to have begun in earnest in the second half of the first century AD. A good portion of it was probably functional by the early second century, but the ornate central court—the so-called Imperial Hall—was not completed until AD 211, the year to which the inscription that runs around its inside perimeter can be dated.[43]

The gymnasium had an expansive square forecourt (its palaestra) consisting of a field measuring approximately 200 feet on each of its sides, the whole once surrounded by porticoes sporting 100 columns facing the interior.[44] This was the location of the facility's athletic fields where wrestling, boxing, running, discus-throwing, and other events were practiced. Little of the original architecture of the forecourt and its surrounding halls remains. The massive "Imperial Hall" separating the palaestra from the bathhouse, however, has been painstakingly reconstructed. The hall's breathtaking ornamentation, together with its pious dedicatory inscription to the imperial family, has led archaeologists to suspect that it functioned not only as a grand vestibule but also as a site for the celebration of imperial cult rituals. The inscription dates to the early third century, dedicating the structure to the members of the Severan dynasty—the emperor Septimius Severus; the empress Julia Domna; and their sons, Caracalla and Geta (though the name of the latter appears to have been defaced).[45] The inscription also bears proud witness to the fact that Sardis had been twice awarded the title *neōkoros*.

Immediately behind the marble hall was a large hall containing a shallow swimming pool, or natatorium (see fig. 7.9). This may also have functioned as the frigidarium, or "cold plunge," of the bath complex. The rooms behind, which still lie largely unexcavated, would have offered the remainder of the typical features of a Roman bath—a tepidarium, a caldarium (a sauna and heated pools), dressing rooms, and spaces for massages. Lecture halls and

41. Hanfmann, Robert, and Mierse, "Hellenistic Period," 117.
42. Hanfmann, Yegül, and Crawford, "Roman and Late Antique Period," 142–43.
43. Hanfmann, Yegül, and Crawford, "Roman and Late Antique Period," 143, 145.
44. Wilson, *Biblical Turkey*, 302.
45. Wilson, *Biblical Turkey*, 302.

Figure 7.9. A swimming pool within the gymnasium/bath complex, located directly behind the imperial cult hall.

classroom spaces were also part of the complex, located in the rooms on the wings to either side of the Imperial Hall and behind the north and south colonnades of the palaestra.

The Synagogue

The third most prominent site in Sardis is a Jewish synagogue, dating in its present form from the fourth century AD.[46] The Jewish community in Sardis significantly predates this structure. When Antiochus III relocated two thousand Jewish families from Syria and Babylon to the western frontier regions of his empire, he would hardly have failed to plant some number of these families in his western capital city (Josephus, *Ant.* 12.147–53).[47] Josephus also records decrees by Roman officials confirming the traditional rights of the Jewish community in Sardis, including the right of assembly, adjudicating internal affairs, and collecting funds for the Jerusalem temple (14.235, 259–61; 16.171). In Sardis, this extended to the city's duty to provide a place for assembly (14.260–61), though the locations of the several predecessors of the excavated synagogue building remain unknown.

A surprising feature of this particular synagogue is its placement adjacent to the gymnasium complex itself, as well as its ornate decoration and construction. Indeed, the synagogue occupies a space that had previously been part of the southeastern wing of the larger gymnasium complex. It is believed that this wing was first remodeled to serve the city as a basilica (a law court, likely in addition to others already established) and was deeded to the Jewish community at some point late in the third or early in the fourth century.[48] This all

46. Gaston, "Jewish Communities," 19–20; Seager and Kraabel, "Synagogue and the Jewish Community," 173; Trebilco, *Jewish Communities*, 44.

47. So also Hanfmann, Robert, and Mierse, "Hellenistic Period," 135–36; Trebilco, *Jewish Communities*, 38.

48. Seager and Kraabel, "Synagogue and the Jewish Community," 171–73.

points to the fact that the Jews of Sardis were by that time, at least, very much at home, quite prosperous, and accepted by their Gentile neighbors to a very high degree. This is somewhat unusual in the ancient world, given typical anti-Jewish prejudice among Gentiles and the not infrequent eruptions of violence against local Jewish communities. The Jewish community here was well integrated into the life of the city.

Figure 7.10. The forecourt of the synagogue. Note the older marble krater (center) in secondary use in the central fountain.

The late Roman or early Byzantine synagogue consists of two principal rooms—an interior hall of 279 by 66 feet and a forecourt of 82 by 66 feet.[49] The forecourt was furnished with a central fountain that incorporates a large, reconstructed marble krater (a massive vessel for holding wine) from the late Hellenistic or early Roman period, perhaps originally part of a bathhouse or nymphaeum in Sardis (see fig. 7.10).[50] The main hall was able to accommodate roughly a thousand worshipers. Over eighty inscriptions have been discovered on the premises of the synagogue, providing insights into the place of the Jewish community in Sardis. For example, a number of inscriptions identify particular individuals as members of the city's chief governing body (its *boulē*, or council).[51] All of these inscriptions, however, postdate Revelation by more than two centuries and provide no secure information about the Jewish community in the first century.

The synagogue had a central table for the reading of the Torah scrolls and accompanying Scriptures (the haftorah). The table itself and its two vertical supports are spolia (reused architectural pieces) from the late Hellenistic or early Roman period.[52] Each support features a carving of an eagle holding a bundle of thunderbolts in its talons, suggestive of a connection with Zeus, who was often depicted with an eagle and, of course, armed with thunderbolts (see fig. 7.12).[53] This is quite strange, first of all given the fact that Jews tended to avoid three-dimensional depictions of animals or

49. Wilson, *Biblical Turkey*, 304.
50. Mitten and Scorziello, "Reappropriating Antiquity," 139–41.
51. Seager, "Architecture," 84–85.
52. Mitten and Scorziello, "Reappropriating Antiquity," 142–43.
53. Wilson, *Biblical Turkey*, 304.

Figure 7.11. The western half of the interior of the synagogue with the table for the reading of the law and the seats of the elders clearly visible.

Figure 7.12. One of the two blocks supporting the central table in the synagogue showing the eagle in carved relief.

people in fulfillment of the second commandment;[54] second, given the fact that the Romans had by this time twice devastated the Jews' homeland (in AD 70 and 135)—and the eagle was the most prominent symbol of Rome. Statues of lions decorated the central space of the main hall as well, perhaps repurposed from the defunct, ancient shrine of Cybele, a goddess often portrayed flanked by pairs of lions. Even if they were reimagined as representations of the Lion of Judah, identified with the tribe of Jews in Sardis who designated themselves the *Leontioi*, the carved depiction of animals in a synagogue shows a remarkable accommodation of the second commandment to Greco-Roman religious artistic practices.[55] The mosaic designs in the main hall's floor, however, were all of the more typical geometric designs with no images. The elders of the synagogue enjoyed a place of honor in semicircular seats at the far front of the main hall (the far west end). This area might also have served as a kind of community council chamber, being crafted in imitation of the typical bouleuterion (see fig. 7.11).

A distinctive structure within the synagogue is the *nomophylakion*, located in the rear (east end) of the main hall, in which the Torah scrolls were housed (see fig. 7.13).[56] This became a common feature of synagogues persisting to

54. Two-dimensional representations of human beings, animals, and mythic figures began to appear in synagogue art by the late Roman period, as in the celebrated frescoes of the Dura-Europos synagogue beside the Euphrates River in eastern Syria and the zodiac mosaic in the Beit Alpha synagogue, located about 5 miles west of Beit She'an in Israel.

55. For the use of the term *Leontioi*, see Trebilco, *Jewish Communities*, 44–45.

56. The term itself appears in a nearby inscription. See Trebilco, *Jewish Communities*, 51.

Figure 7.13. The niches at the east end of the synagogue's main hall, one of which was the *nomophylakion*. The triangular gables over the niches sport a common Hellenistic-period ornament (round shields) and are here in secondary use (Hanfmann, Robert, and Mierse, "Hellenistic Period," 118).

Figure 7.14. The mosaic inscriptions set into the floor of the synagogue's forecourt attesting to God's answering of a prayer offered by Aurelius Polyhippos, a "godfearer."

the present day (they are typically called arks, establishing a connection with the historic ark of the covenant).

The forecourt of the synagogue also sported an ornate mosaic floor, again rich in geometric patterns but not in images. Several inscriptions honoring donors have been laid within the mosaic. One, for example, reads, "Aurelius Polyhippos, a God-fearer, having prayed, fulfilled [his vow]" (see fig. 7.14).[57] Gentile adherents of the synagogue like Polyhippos may have paid for some portion of its decoration as thank offerings for answered prayers. A row of Byzantine-period shops, some of which enjoyed running water, has also been excavated along the street that runs adjacent to the south wall of the synagogue and gymnasium complex.

Colin Hemer believed that a pressing problem for the Christians in Sardis at the time of John's writing was the lure of joining the synagogue (and implicitly, at least, denying their allegiance to Jesus as the Messiah) so as to come under its aegis and exemption from participation in the imperial cult. He particularly links the language of having one's name expunged or not expunged from the rolls in the oracle to being registered (or not) on the synagogue's roster, citing the late first-century addition to the synagogue prayers, the "Benediction Against Heretics": "May the Nazarenes and the Minim suddenly perish, and may they be blotted out of the book of life and not enrolled with the righteous."[58] Having one's name expunged from God's

57. See Trebilco, *Jewish Communities*, 158–59.
58. Hemer, *Letters*, 148–49, 151–52.

Figure 7.15. The Christian church built in the southeast corner of the derelict temple of Artemis. A sixth-century expansion of the original fourth-century structure is in the foreground.

"Scroll of Life," however, was an ancient image rooted in the Pentateuch itself (Exod. 32:32–33), and thus John cannot necessarily be said to respond to recent innovations in the worship life of the synagogue when the glorified Lord promises the faithful, "I will not blot out your name from the scroll of life" (Rev. 3:5). More to the point, one is left to wonder why John never mentions the synagogue or the Jewish community in Sardis if this is the case, especially as he was not reluctant to do so in the oracles to Smyrna and Philadelphia.

The Christians whom the glorified Christ chastened in the fifth of the seven oracles that open the book of Revelation appear to have heeded Christ's warning. The church continued its living witness into the second century and beyond, until the Sassanid invasion destroyed Sardis and scattered all its inhabitants in AD 616. The most dramatic archaeological witness to this survival is the fine Byzantine chapel in the southeast corner of the precincts of the Temple of Artemis (see fig. 7.15). Worship of Christ significantly outlasted the worship of Artemis in this city. A smaller church structure has been uncovered in the near vicinity of the shrine to Cybele, another sign of the growth and, indeed, the victory of the Christ cult over the others that had enjoyed such widespread devotion in the city and surrounding region for so long.

8

PHILADELPHIA

Thirty miles southeast of Sardis sits the city of Philadelphia (*Philadelpheia*). Travel between the two cities had been facilitated since the early second century BC by a road built under the Attalid kings of Pergamum and maintained throughout the Roman period. This road would continue south to Laodicea and eventually to Side, a port city on the Mediterranean coast.[1] Philadelphia was the youngest of the seven cities addressed by John. It was founded by King Attalus II Philadelphus of Pergamum, who reigned from 159 to 138 BC.[2] Rough estimates of the population suggest a small city with ten thousand or so inhabitants in the Roman period.[3] The volcanic soil of the city's hinterlands was well suited to the production of grapes, which was a primary crop and source of income.[4] John leads us to believe that a Jewish community existed in Philadelphia with his heated comments about the synagogue there (Rev. 3:9).[5] Their origins are unknown, but it is possible that descendants of some of the thousands of Jewish families that Antiochus III had relocated to cities throughout the region around 210 BC had migrated to the new city in the second or first centuries BC.

Inscriptions tell us that Philadelphia had an active cult of the emperor Augustus by 27 BC, although not an actual temple to Augustus.[6] These

1. Wilson, "Social and Geographical World of Philadelphia," 675.
2. Wilson, "Social and Geographical World of Philadelphia," 676.
3. Worth, *Seven Cities of the Apocalypse and Greco-Asian Culture*, 194.
4. Strabo, *Geogr.* 13.4.11; Pliny the Elder, *Nat.* 14.9.74.
5. It is likely that Ignatius of Antioch's letter to the Christians in Philadelphia in the years around AD 110 also bears witness to the presence of a Jewish community there (Ignatius, *Philadelphians* 6.1).
6. *IPhil* 1428 (see also 1434, 1472, 1484); C. Koester, *Revelation*, 322; Wilson, *Biblical Turkey*, 295.

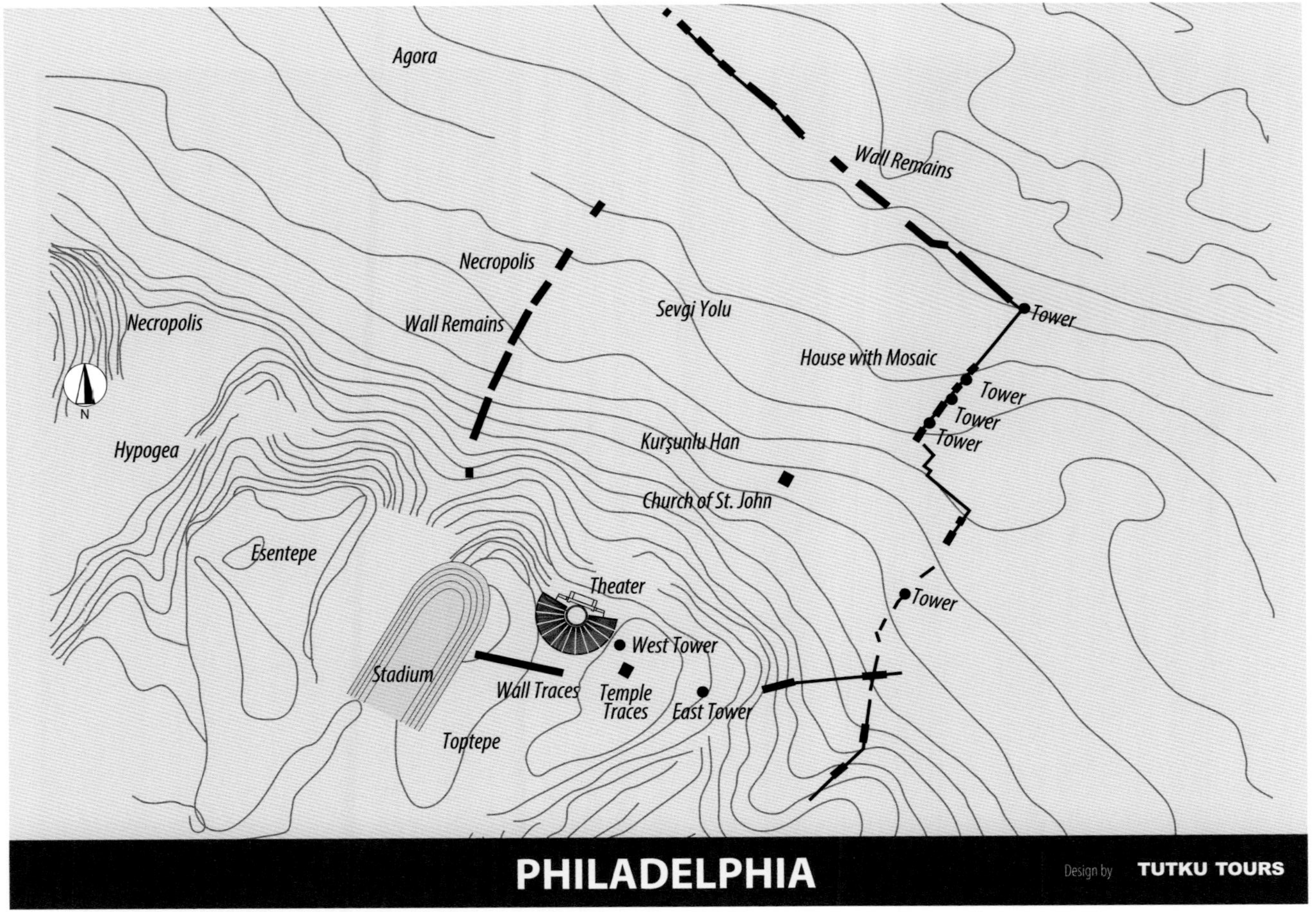

Figure 8.1. Map of the excavated features of Philadelphia in modern Alaşehir.

inscriptions also show that the city began to date events with the Battle of Actium (31 BC)—the event that marked Octavian's (Augustus's) rise to sole power—marking its "year one."[7] Philadelphia was destroyed in the earthquake of AD 17 that rocked the entire province, and it was rebuilt with the assistance of Augustus's successor, Tiberius, who provided an exemption from imperial taxes for the space of five years as well as emergency funding (Tacitus, *Ann.* 2.47).[8] Philadelphia was one of fourteen cities of Asia that expressed their gratitude to the emperor by dedicating a large statue to him in Rome, a smaller version of which was placed in the port of Puteoli (see fig. 8.2). Philadelphia also took on a second name—Neocaesarea—as another token of gratitude for its rebirth.

Figure 8.2. The base of the statue erected in honor of Tiberius featuring, on this side, the representations of the cities of Philadelphia, Tmolus, and Cyme.

Philadelphia was particularly susceptible to minor earthquakes occurring between the major ones to which the entire province was prone, with the result that the city's population did not grow appreciably during the first and second centuries and, indeed, dropped at a number of points as families relocated to villages in the hinterlands (Strabo, *Geogr.* 12.8.18). It is possible that the image of the pillar in Revelation 3:12, as a symbol of stability, would have been particularly winsome to the Christians living in this frequently shaken city, though, of course, it would be immediately meaningful and accessible to Christians in *any* city throughout the eastern Mediterranean.

The city showed its support for and loyalty to the emperors of the Flavian dynasty as well. They erected a monument in the precincts of Ephesus's "Shared Temple of the Augusti" (the temple honoring Domitian and, later, Vespasian).[9] Inscriptions also reveal that the local elites of Philadelphia constructed an imperial cult temple in their own city in the later first century (thus likely to honor Domitian) and that the city began to call itself Flavia

7. Wilson, "Social and Geographical World of Philadelphia," 677.

8. See also Suetonius, *Tib.* 48.2; Dio Cassius, *Hist. rom.* 57.17.8; Strabo, *Geogr.* 12.8.18; 13.4.8.

9. *IPhil* 1453; Friesen, *Twice Neokoros*, 157.

Figure 8.3. Keys to door locks from the early Roman period. Jesus's identification of himself in the oracle to the Christians in Philadelphia as "the one holding the key of David" (Rev. 3:7) or to John as the one having "the keys of death and of Hades" (1:18) would have evoked mental images similar to these.

Left: Author photo, courtesy of the Israel Museum, Jerusalem. Right: Author photo, courtesy of the Altes Museum, Germany.

Philadelphia to honor and, no doubt, to curry favor with the Flavian line.[10] It would not become a *neōkoros* city, however, until the reign of Caracalla (ruled AD 211–217).[11]

It has been suggested that this history of taking on new names (first Philadelphia Neocaesarea under Tiberius and Flavia Philadelphia under Domitian) *might* have lent particular poignancy to Christ's words to this congregation: "I will write on [the one who conquers] the name of my God, and the name of the city of my God, the new Jerusalem, which comes down from my God out of heaven, and my own new name" (Rev. 3:12).[12] The change from Philadelphia Neocaesarea to Flavia Philadelphia was recent enough to be reasonably expected to persist in adults' memories a decade or so later, so this is not a great stretch. In the case of Philadelphia, however, the adoption of a new name served as a sign of the city's inhabitants' gratitude and allegiance. The accent of the glorified Christ's words to these Christians falls not so much on *their* taking a new name on their own initiative as their being claimed by God and Christ as people falling under their possession and protection and being marked as people belonging to, and thus destined for, the city of the world to come.

Inscriptions and coinage also suggest that there were numerous cult sites for the traditional Greek and local gods. Coins struck in Philadelphia feature the usual pantheon on their obverses—Zeus, Dionysus, Apollo, Asclepius, Artemis, Cybele, Aphrodite, Helios, and so forth.[13] An inscription from the Roman period incidentally bears witness to the fact that devotion to the traditional gods could become an incentive to stricter morality and not merely

10. C. Koester, *Revelation*, 322.
11. Türkoğlu, "Philadelphia in Lydia," 550.
12. Ramsey, *Seven Churches*, 409–12; Hemer, *Letters*, 167, 176.
13. See at https://www.wildwinds.com/coins/greece/lydia/philadelphia/t.html, accessed January 9, 2025. See also Yamauchi, *Archaeology of New Testament Cities*, 78.

Figure 8.4. The earthen contours of the stadium.

an occasion for immorality. The rules for a private religious association stress sexual purity (the avoidance of both premarital and extramarital intercourse) as prerequisite to worship the deities—threatening the gods' curses upon those who violate these rules.[14] An inscription from the first/second centuries AD names a "high priestess of the gods of the fatherland." Several dedicatory inscriptions honoring "the Great Mother" and Hephaestus from the second and third centuries AD attest to the worship of these deities in the later Roman period.[15]

It is likely that, were extensive excavations possible, a number of structures would be discovered that might be identified as temples dedicated to the imperial cult or to several of these traditional deities. As is the case for Thyatira, however, very little of ancient Philadelphia has been excavated, since it lies beneath the modern city of Alaşehir. Thus, once again, the ongoing occupation of the space and the needs of the living make excavation highly impractical, if not impossible. Visitors to Alaşehir can find the remains of a Roman-period stadium built into a natural valley on the south side of the modern city (see fig. 8.4). The stadium, generally dated to the second or third century AD, has

14. Grant, *Hellenistic Religions*, 29.
15. Uzunoğlu and Tavukçu, "Some Inscriptions," 160–62.

Figure 8.5. A view of the cavea of the theater from behind the remains of the stage building.

been stripped of its seating, another testimony to the repurposing of good cut stone in the centuries between antiquity and the modern period.

East of the stadium sits a theater, which also dates from the second or third centuries AD (see fig. 8.5). Excavations undertaken since 2020 have exposed remains of the stage area and the vaulted passageways through which the spectators made their way into the theater itself. The materials of the orchestra floor and the lowest levels of the cavea are still present on site, having been buried as the city slipped into dereliction, but, like the stadium, this site had also almost entirely been mined for building materials now used elsewhere in the city of Alaşehir.

Between the stadium and the theater loomed the acropolis of the ancient city. Now a park (Toptepe Park), one can see a number of decorated fragments of what was once a temple that had been erected on the spot (see figs. 8.6, 8.7). (The excavated footprint of the temple has been reburied for the sake of its preservation.) It remains unclear to whom the temple was dedicated. As the city's patron deity, Zeus would be the best candidate for a temple occupying the most prominent location in the city.[16] This particular temple has

16. This is suggested not only by the number of coin issues featuring Zeus but also by the city being represented by a male, bearded, semi-nude figure on the statue base honoring Tiberius mentioned above.

Figure 8.6. A partial honorific inscription that once ran across a portion of the entablature of a monument or building on the Philadelphia acropolis. The remaining words read, "The council and the people . . . honor . . ." Mark Wilson

Figure 8.7. An ornate architectural fragment from the cornice of the second-century temple that once sat atop the Philadelphia acropolis.

been dated to the second century AD but likely represents a renovation or rebuilding of an earlier temple to the city's patron god.[17]

Figure 8.8. The brick substructure of two of the pylons that once supported the sixth-century Basilica of St. John.

The Christian community in Philadelphia addressed by John remained steadfast and survived. Several Christians from Philadelphia were executed together with Polycarp, bishop of Smyrna, in the latter's city in the mid-second century (*Martyrdom of Polycarp* 19.1). In the center of the modern city stand the remains of several of the supporting pylons of a once-towering sixth-century basilica, another witness to the perseverance and eventual triumph of Christianity throughout the region occupied by the "seven churches" (see fig. 8.8). The grounds serve as an open-air museum sporting inscriptions, statue bases, and sarcophagi from the late Roman and Byzantine periods.

17. Birol, "Roman Temple," 35 (detailed discussion on pp. 30–50); Türkoğlu, "Philadelphia in Lydia," 550.

9

LAODICEA

The last of the seven cities addressed by John is Laodicea. Antiochus II Theos, ruler of the Seleucid kingdom from 261 to 246 BC, transformed the small town of Diospolis ("Zeus's city") into a city and named it in honor of his first wife, Laodice (Pliny, *Nat.* 5.105). It was ideally situated at the intersection of two major roads. One extended from Ephesus to the east and westward through the whole of what is now Türkiye.[1] This would have been a vitally important road for Laodicea in its trade with all points west, including the many markets of Greece and Italy to which Laodicean goods would be shipped from the Ephesian harbor. The road from Ephesus spanned a river valley as it approached Laodicea from the west (the remains of the Roman-period bridge that supported it are still visible). It then entered Laodicea on the west through an ornamental gate built during Domitian's reign (see fig. 9.3).

A good portion of the road contained within the city walls, bisecting Laodicea, is well excavated, though the form in which it is preserved dates from the Byzantine period (see fig. 9.4). It left the east side of Laodicea through another gate (called the "Syrian Gate") erected in AD 84–85 and dedicated to Domitian and Zeus Soter ("Zeus the Savior") by Domitian's freedman, Tiberius Claudius Tryphon.[2] A second major road running through Laodicea led to Pergamum to the north and the seaport city of Side on the Mediterranean shore to the south.[3] The distance between Philadelphia and Laodicea

1. The distance from Ephesus to Laodicea along this road is 106 miles (calculated using "The Stanford Geospatial Model of the Roman World").

2. Şimşek, *Ancient City Laodikeia*, 4; "Urban Planning," 10.

3. Şimşek, "Urban Planning," 2.

Tutku Tours

Figure 9.1. Map of the excavations of Laodicea.

Figure 9.2. The eastern end of the street that enters the city through the "Ephesus Gate." It was a broad street with shops recessed behind colonnaded porticoes on either side. The remains of a decorative propylon dominate the foreground.

Figure 9.3. The unexcavated "Ephesus Gate" at the west end of the main street bisecting Laodicea. In its prime, it probably resembled the Frontinus Gate in Hierapolis. Both were erected in the late Flavian period.

Figure 9.4. The late Roman or Byzantine retread of the principal east-west road running through Laodicea.

along this road is approximately 56 miles.

The Hippodamian grid pattern of major streets, reflecting the layout begun from its founding under Antiochus II, is immediately evident to the person visiting the site. The city walls contained a space of about 1 square mile.[4] The presence of ancient cemeteries (*necropoleis*) surrounding the site helps determine the physical limits of the Roman city. The population of the city in the first through third centuries AD is estimated to have been around seventy to eighty thousand.[5] Literary sources bear witness to a Jewish population of several thousand by the mid-first century BC. After his term of service was ended, Flaccus, the provincial governor of Asia in 62 BC, was charged on several counts of mismanagement before the courts in Rome.[6] One of these charges was that he had seized twenty pounds of gold that had been collected in Laodicea for transport to Jerusalem (Cicero, *Pro Flacco* 28.68). If this sum of gold represents the collection of the annual contribution of two drachmas (or denarii) to the temple required of all adult male Jews, it suggests a Jewish population of about seventy-five hundred Jewish men in the district of Laodicea, besides women and children.[7] The only archaeological witnesses to their presence thus far, however, consist of a number of inscriptions and carvings of typically Jewish symbols (see fig. 9.5).

Figure 9.5. A rough carving on a pillar showing a menorah flanked by a palm branch (left) and a shofar (right). The pillar was reused in a Byzantine-period church with a bold cross engraved above the earlier symbols, surmounting the menorah.

The beginnings of communities of Christ-followers in Laodicea reach back at least to the span of Paul's lifetime, particularly the period in which he and

4. Worth, *Seven Cities of the Apocalypse and Greco-Asian Culture*, 206.
5. Şimşek, "Urban Planning," 5.
6. See Marshall, "Flaccus and the Jews of Asia," esp. 139.
7. Josephus, *Ant.* 14.241–43; Wilson, *Biblical Turkey*, 247. If the sum included a number of individual gifts and offerings over and above the didrachm, of course, then it would represent a proportionately smaller population overall.

Figure 9.6. A coin struck in Laodicea featuring Domitian and his wife, Domitia, on the obverse and a temple erected in their honor on the reverse.
The British Museum, England

his team were centered in Ephesus (AD 52–55). Laodicea sits 10 miles west-northwest of Colossae and about 6 miles south of Hierapolis. Paul credits his coworker Epaphras at least with energetic ministry among the Christian communities in all three of these cities, and it is quite possible that their founding was due to Epaphras's evangelistic activity as well: "Epaphras . . . is always wrestling in his prayers on your behalf, so that you may stand mature and fully assured in everything that God wills. For I testify for him that he has worked hard for you and for those in Laodicea and in Hierapolis" (Col. 4:12–13 NRSV). In this early period, the Christians in Laodicea gathered for worship, prayer, and instruction in the house of a woman named Nympha, whose hospitality was essential to the new community's flourishing. Paul wrote a letter to the church in Laodicea at about the same time that he wrote Colossians, instructing these two churches to exchange and read each other's letters (Col. 4:16). This letter to the Christians in Laodicea is lost unless, as some scholars argue, the Letter to the Ephesians began its life in some fashion as Paul's letter to Laodicea or functioned as a circular letter.[8]

Earthquakes were frequent throughout the Lycus valley. As a consequence of two particularly devastating ones—the first in AD 17 during Tiberius's reign and the second in AD 60 during Nero's reign—very few monumental structures from early first-century Laodicea survived (Eusebius, *Chron.* 2.154; Orosius, *Adv. pag.* 7.12). Almost everything of interest in the excavations at these sites dates from the Flavian period or later—often centuries later.

Laodicea was one of the eleven cities competing for the privilege of erecting a provincial temple for the worship of Tiberius in AD 26, though it was quickly passed over as lacking sufficient stature and resources at that point in its history due in large measure, no doubt, to its investment in rebuilding after the earthquake of AD 17 and its likely reliance, at that time, on imperial aid (Tacitus, *Ann.* 4.55). Nevertheless, like the other cities whose Christian residents were addressed by John, Laodicea would continue to invest in the imperial cult. Although the temple itself has not been identified on the site, a coin issue bears witness to the fact that the city had a local imperial temple honoring Domitian and his wife, Domitia (see fig. 9.6).[9] The depiction of the temple on the coin's reverse includes the Greek word *epinikeia* on the architrave

8. See, e.g., Hemer, *Letters*, 181; Muddiman, *Epistle to the Ephesians*, 302–5.
9. Price, *Rituals and Power*, 183; Friesen, *Imperial Cults*, 61–62.

Figure 9.7. Top: The second-century AD temple thought to be linked with Laodicea's elevation to the status of a *neōkoros* city under Commodus. Right: Detail of the ornate relief work adorning the temple's colonnades.

above the two cult images, linking the temple to the commemoration of a particular military victory under Domitian, likely his triumphs in Germany in AD 83–84 that won for him the title *Germanicus*.

Surprisingly few temples have been identified on the ground in Laodicea, perhaps on account of the extensive Christianization of the city in the late Roman and Byzantine periods. Archaeologists have excavated one sprawling temple complex near the heart of the city, however, dating from the second century AD (see fig. 9.7). The central sanctuary measures about 92 by 46 feet and is set within a courtyard surrounded by columned porticoes with exterior dimensions of 190 by 135 feet. It is unclear what deities were worshiped here when the temple was first erected. Based on artifacts discovered on the site, some scholars have suggested Apollo or Artemis, both of whom were very popular gods throughout the Roman province of Asia, or both of these deities in tandem

Figure 9.8. The western portion of the sacred forum (immediately north of the principal decumanus, or "Syria Street") that is believed to have once housed temples to Zeus and Athena.

Figure 9.9. A portion of the colonnade in the northeast quadrant of the sacred forum.

with an emperor of the Antonine period.[10] Laodicea was finally awarded the honor of being named a *neōkoros* city under Commodus, a title that was shaken after Commodus was assassinated and declared an enemy of the state in AD 192 but restored when his memory was rehabilitated under his successor, Septimius Severus, after the civil wars of 192–193.[11] The temple complex appears to have been renovated at this time, quite possibly for the occasion of its rededication to Commodus.[12] After Christianity became the official religion of the empire, the temple was decommissioned and became the city's archive.

Ongoing excavations on the north side of the site have recovered the outline of a vast forum once surrounded by colonnades and porticoes over 30 feet tall. The exterior dimensions of this forum are 420 by 800 feet. Several stretches of the colonnade have been re-erected. This space is believed to have once housed two temples from the late Hellenistic and early Roman periods. Inscriptions discovered in the area suggest that these temples were dedicated to Zeus, the city's patron deity, and to Athena (see figs. 9.8, 9.9).[13] A distinctive feature of this sacred precinct is the appearance of inscriptions acknowledging not only the names of local benefactors who supported the building of the sacred forum but also the precise amounts they spent for specific components. Thus one Publius Alfenus Varus Ducenianus is commemorated for donating ten thousand denarii to erect one stretch of ten columns.[14]

10. Şimşek, "Urban Planning," 18; *Ancient City Laodikeia*, 10.

11. Price, *Rituals and Power*, 264; Burrell, *Neokoroi*, 119–20.

12. The rededication of an existing temple for the provincial cult already had a strong precedent in Sardis.

13. Şimşek, *Ancient City Laodikeia*, 16–17; "Urban Planning," 3; Wilson, *Biblical Turkey*, 245; Cadwallader, "Lust for Recognition," 249.

14. See, further, Guizzi, "Greek and Latin Inscriptions," 170–74; Cadwallader, "Lust for Recognition," 249.

An inscription published in 2019 has led some to believe that Laodicea received the honor of being named a neokorate city during the reign of Hadrian. The inscription in question reads "The *neōkoros* city of the Laodiceans [honors] Imperator Caesar Trajan Hadrian Augustus Olympios, the benefactor and savior of the world."[15] This claim, however, has been called into question on the basis of the lack of any confirmation in the coinage produced by the city, which never uses the title *neōkoros* until the reign of Commodus and then only speaks of holding a neokorate in the singular.[16] Alan Cadwallader has suggested that the title *neōkoros* appears in this inscription in connection with the city's longtime maintenance of this grand Temple of Zeus—akin to Ephesus's informal use of the title in connection with its temple to Artemis (as in Acts 19:35), perhaps in conjunction with Laodicea's introduction of a cult statue of Hadrian Olympios into the Temple of Zeus (as happened in Pergamum in connection with their temple to Trajan and Zeus Philios).[17] The temples to Zeus and Athena, however, were dismantled and their materials incorporated into one or both of the grand Christian basilicas erected on either side of this forum in the period after Constantine. A statue of a priestess of Isis found in the vicinity suggests that a cult to the Egyptian goddess, and perhaps the larger trio of Isis, Serapis, and Horus (Harpocrates), existed in Laodicea at least by the second century AD.

Adjacent to the main east-west street and the southeast corner of the sacred forum is a square once surrounded by porticoes divided into a number of rooms. The whole space was 32 yards wide and somewhat longer in length, accessible only by steps and thus inaccessible to vehicular traffic. Dating to the late Hellenistic or early Roman period, it may have served multiple purposes over the course of a given year, from commercial activities to a staging area for festival processions (see fig. 9.10).[18]

The glorified Christ castigates the Christians in Laodicea for boasting in their wealth and self-sufficiency—an attitude that would most likely have been adopted on the basis of their participation in the larger economic prosperity enjoyed by the city as a whole. The city's (and its citizens') wealth was such that, in the wake of the devastating earthquake of AD 60, Laodicea was able to rebuild using its own local resources without relying on imperial aid

15. Guizzi, "Greek and Latin Inscriptions," quoted in Cadwallader, "Lust for Recognition," 242. The translation is my own.

16. Cadwallader, "Lust for Recognition," 243–44.

17. Cadwallader, "Lust for Recognition," 244. In this regard, Laodicea had never ceased to be "Diospolis"—that is, "Zeus's City." Pliny the Elder, *Nat.* 5.29.105.

18. Şimşek, *Ancient City Laodikeia*, 31; "Urban Planning," 12–13.

Figure 9.10. A courtyard first constructed in the Hellenistic period that may have served as a staging area for sacred processions.

(Tacitus, *Ann.* 14.27; cf. *Sib. Or.* 4.107–8). It is easy to infer that this could have become a point of pride for them.

Vitruvius (*De arch.* 8.3.14), a contemporary of Augustus, bears witness to the involvement of Laodicea and Hierapolis in the regional wool industry, breeding and raising sheep with a distinctive glossy violet-black wool. Along with Colossae, these cities were significant hubs of producing wool and textiles as well as manufacturing garments from its signature product. Given its location at the intersection of two major roads, Laodicea was well positioned to thrive from trade in the wool and clothing industries (Strabo, *Geogr.* 12.8.16). Its commercial forums were once bustling centers of industry and trade. The central agora, likely the site of one of the city's oldest markets, measures about 123 by 66 yards,[19] though archaeologists are not certain that it achieved this size by the first century (see fig. 9.11). Colonnades and covered porches once surrounded this agora, providing an important venue for merchants to offer their wares but also for people simply to meet, to exchange ideas, and to promote various philosophies and religions.

19. Şimşek, *Ancient City Laodikeia*, 12.

Figure 9.11. The central agora.

Laodicea also gained considerable wealth through its services as a banking center. In the Greek and Roman periods, temples served not only as centers for the worship of the gods but also as repositories for the wealth of a city, its institutions, its private citizens, and foreigners. This symbiosis arose not only because temples were generally well constructed and well fortified but also because of the strong social taboos against violating the sanctity of holy space. Stealing money from a neighbor's house was just theft, but removing goods from a temple was sacrilege against the gods and called down on the temple-robber the curse of human beings and gods alike.

Laodicea enjoyed all the amenities of a Greco-Roman city. In the first century, it already enjoyed a theater (the "West Theater"), built during the Hellenistic period into the northwestern slope descending from the plateau on which the city sits, and capable of seating an audience of about eight thousand (see fig. 9.12).[20] A second theater, capable of seating twelve thousand spectators, would be built into the north side of the same plateau in the second century AD (see fig. 9.13).[21] Local benefactors funded the construction of a stadium toward the end of Vespasian's reign and into the short reign of Titus.[22] This was one of the three largest in Roman Asia, able to accommodate between twenty thousand and twenty-five thousand spectators (see fig. 9.14). It appears to have been dedicated to the proconsular governor of Roman Asia at the time, Marcus Ulpius Traianus, father of the later emperor Trajan.[23]

20. Şimşek, *Ancient City Laodikeia*, 15; "Urban Planning," 17.

21. Şimşek, *Ancient City Laodikeia*, 18.

22. Şimşek, *Ancient City Laodikeia*, 22; "Urban Planning," 17.

23. Wilson, *Biblical Turkey*, 252. Craig Koester (*Revelation*, 334) reads the inscription (*ILaod* 15) differently to suggest a dedication to Titus.

Figure 9.12. The Hellenistic-period "West Theater."

Figure 9.13. The unexcavated Roman-period "north theater."

Figure 9.14. A better-preserved portion of the stands from the Flavian-period stadium. The remains of the "south bath" stretch across the top of the hill above the stands.

Figure 9.15. The Hadrianic-period bouleuterion, or city council chamber, from the civic agora in the southeast quadrant of the city.

An administrative forum appears to have been built on the south side of the city in connection with the building of the southern baths and gymnasium in the early second century under Hadrian.[24] In the center of the forum's northern side one can still see the remains of what has been identified as the bouleuterion (see fig. 9.15), the place where the city council of Laodicea would meet regularly to take care of civic business.

Visitors to Laodicea are often particularly interested to see the remains of its water system because the images of hot, cold, and lukewarm water are so forceful a part of Christ's message to and castigation of this congregation: "Would that you were hot or cold! Because you are neither hot nor cold but lukewarm, I am about to spew you out from my mouth" (Rev. 3:15–16).

Students of Revelation frequently encounter the claim that Jesus's contrast between water temperatures drew upon the geophysical setting of Laodicea vis-à-vis its neighbors, Colossae and Hierapolis. Colossae had year-round access to water from springs descending from snow-capped mountains and, thus, of a fresh, cool quality. Hierapolis was famous for its hot, mineral springs and their therapeutic properties, though these were hardly suitable

24. Şimşek, *Ancient City Laodikeia*, 20.

Figure 9.16. Travertine (marble) cascades formed by the mineral-rich hot springs immediately southeast of the city of Hierapolis.

for drinking (see fig. 9.16). Laodicea, it has often been claimed, had to pipe in their water from such hot springs which, after traveling a distance of 6 miles or so, reached a tepid state by the time it reached the city, making the mineral-rich water even more nauseating.[25]

This reading has remained attractive because of its appeal to some local features of the environment. Nevertheless, a number of factors render this interpretation unlikely. Lukewarm water from aqueducts was a common experience for residents of cities throughout the Roman Mediterranean. As Craig Koester observes, "If Laodicea's water was lukewarm, the same would have been true at Ephesus, Smyrna, Pergamum, and Sardis."[26] The water in Laodicea, though somewhat mineral-rich despite being drawn from springs south of the city (and not from the hot springs of Hierapolis or other thermal springs as commonly asserted), was deemed quite suitable for drinking by at least one experienced traveler (Strabo, *Geogr*. 13.4.14). This same traveler considered the water of Hierapolis's hot springs with their unusually rich mineral content to be entirely unsuitable for drinking—unlike the water

25. Thus Hemer, *Letters*, 186–91; Weima, *Sermons*, 239.
26. C. Koester, "Message to Laodicea," 411.

in Laodicea (13.4.14).[27] Indeed, the residents of Hierapolis had their own drinking water brought in via aqueducts from the east. An inscription dating to AD 114/115, when Cornelius Tacitus was proconsular governor of Asia, proscribes the illegal tapping of Laodicea's aqueduct, again suggesting that the water was, at the very least, perfectly adequate (even worth stealing!).[28] Calcium deposits on the interior of aqueducts and water pipes are common throughout Roman Asia, suggesting again that the water supply in Laodicea was not of a substantially lower quality than that of many other cities in Roman Asia.[29]

Scholars have therefore looked to other backgrounds against which to hear Jesus's language in the oracle to Laodicea. One prominent alternative points to banqueting practices in the ancient world. In these banquets, wine could be served heated in cauldrons or chilled with snow or ice purchased in the market to add to the diners' pleasure. Lukewarm water, on the other hand, could be served as an emetic to help to make room for the next course.[30] Indeed, in any setting those who were cold might desire a hot drink while those who were hot would crave a cold drink (Plato, *Republic* 437D), but lukewarm water was generally viewed as distasteful.[31] This has the advantage of aligning with the expectations raised in the oracle that the drink, whether cold, hot, or lukewarm, would be taken into one's mouth (whether for enjoyment or spewing) and that both the hot and the cold water were deemed positive and pleasurable.[32]

Even though a moralizing or allegorizing approach to these three temperature settings have fueled (and will no doubt continue to fuel) countless sermons, it does not appear that the glorified Lord intends this language to be part of the specific diagnosis.[33] Rather, it appears calculated to shock the

27. C. Koester, "Message to Laodicea," 410–11.

28. Wilson, "Did the Laodiceans Drink Lukewarm Water?," 80–81, 83.

29. Wilson, "Did the Laodiceans Drink Lukewarm Water?," 78.

30. Aulus Cornelius Celsus (*De Medicina* 1.3.19–23), a medical specialist active during the first half of the first century AD, also attests to the medicinal application of drinking lukewarm wine or water as an emetic.

31. C. Koester, "Message to Laodicea," 413–15.

32. The glorified Lord would therefore be referring not to the hot springs of Hierapolis but to potable water heated artificially.

33. I had myself formerly considered that "lukewarmness" was itself indicative of the problem (e.g., *Discovering Revelation*, 76; following C. Koester, *Revelation*, 344): The Laodiceans had become indistinguishable from their neighbors in terms of their witness, orientation, and practice, even as "lukewarm" water could be said to have accommodated itself entirely to its environment (hence the common phrase "room temperature"). But "room temperature" drinks are quite commonly imbibed without incident, and a closer study of the Greek word *chliaros* (rendered here "lukewarm") suggests some degree of intentional heating. Water slightly warmer than body temperature is more effective an emetic than, say, water standing at 75 degrees Fahrenheit.

Figure 9.17. The *castellum aquae*, the primary distribution node in Laodicea's water delivery system. The detail shows some of the many clay pipes leading water from this node to fountains, bathhouses, and other beneficiaries of the aqueduct bringing water to the south side of the city.

Laodicean Christ-followers into realizing the magnitude of the *danger* of their spiritual condition. Contrary to their self-assessment, they make Christ sick to his stomach and poised to purge. One of the most important areas in which the Apocalypse performs its "unveilings" is in checking the various audiences' understandings of themselves and the spiritual dangers in their situation: "You say, 'I have abundance, and I have been enriched, and I have need of nothing' and you don't perceive that you're wretched and pitiable and poor and blind and naked!" (Rev. 3:17). The Laodicean Christians' self-awareness appears to be predicated on their enjoyment of the same flourishing economic conditions enjoyed by their fellow-citizens—perhaps, as so often, taken as a sign of divine favor in and of itself—and not their maintenance of the distinctive witness and identity that would raise the glorified Christ's estimation of them.

Nevertheless, the archaeological remnants of Laodicea's water system remain a point of fascination. A significantly eroded structure is what remains of the *castellum aquae*, the point at which the aqueduct interfaced with the city's water system. An impressive feature of this system is its engineering of a siphon for the last stretch of the aqueduct that enabled the water to rise from a lower point in the valley up to the higher level of the city. A crowded network of pipes within the 20-foot-tall *castellum aquae* distributed water to different destinations in the southern city (such as the stadium baths and fountain house) as well as to other, secondary distribution nodes throughout the city (see fig. 9.17).[34]

34. Wilson, "Did the Laodiceans Drink Lukewarm Water?," 79.

Figure 9.18. The reconstructed fountain dedicated to the emperor Trajan.

Though the first-century city also had its bath complexes and public fountains, none of the bathhouses and fountains (*nymphaea*) excavated thus far can be confidently dated before the second century AD. A particularly grand—since reconstructed—fountain house is the "Trajan Nymphaeum," dated to AD 114 on the basis of its dedicatory inscription, and thus the earliest identified fountain in Laodicea (see fig. 9.18).[35] This fountain was one of many such pools where fresh water was made freely available to the city's residents and businesses.

The earliest of the excavated baths is believed to be the south bath complex above the stadium, as it bears a dedication to Hadrian.[36] This bath complex, however, may represent a renovation of an older bath complex that would have stood there in John's time.[37] This was a double bath complex arranged in two halves that mirrored each other. An apodyterium (a room for dressing and undressing) and a frigidarium (a room with one or more cold water pools) were placed at the far right and the far left. Two caldaria occupied the middlemost rooms. These functioned both as saunas and as rooms with hot water baths. The effect was achieved by creating a secondary floor raised a few feet above the main floor and directing hot air from a furnace into the resulting space. In many caldaria, ceramic pipes were

35. Şimşek, "Urban Planning," 17.
36. Wilson, *Biblical Turkey*, 254.
37. Wilson, "Neither Cold nor Hot," 15.

Figure 9.19. The interior of the central baths. The double doorway built into the large arch represents remodeling from a later stage in the structure's history.

also built into the walls to further allow the hot air to circulate and exert its heating effect more evenly. A tepidarium stood between these rooms in each half.[38] It is unclear whether these were just warm rooms or warm rooms with warm water pools.

A better-preserved bath complex on site is the central baths, immediately south of the central agora (see fig. 9.19). This was also once a complete Roman

38. A plan of the south baths can be found in Wilson, "Neither Cold nor Hot," 10. Wilson makes the novel proposal that these baths are the best context for understanding Jesus's warning since they involve areas and pools that are hot, cold, and tepid. He suggests that the tepidarium didn't really play any significant role in the experience, being more of a "heat lock" to help the caldarium retain its temperature (11) and providing "a lukewarm space for bathers moving between the hot and cold rooms" (26). But, then, there would seem to be nothing *objectionable* about this space, either, such as would explain Jesus's strong aversion to the lukewarmness of the Laodicean Christians. Wilson rejects the conviction "that hot and cold must relate to something people would take into their mouth" and that, therefore, "lukewarm applies to what would be spat out." He claims that "the text makes no explicit reference to a liquid, whether water or wine" (6). Nevertheless, Jesus does threaten to vomit the Laodiceans *from his mouth* on account of their lukewarmness, whatever this quality stands for. The Laodiceans are "unpalatable" to the glorified Lord, and this is not a consideration in the bathing experience. It is difficult to see, therefore, how the setting of the Roman bath helps us hear this warning in the manner that the Christians in Laodicea would have understood it. The setting of drinking and eating at a banquet remains far more natural to the image of vomiting.

Figure 9.20. The northern half of the interior and the baptistery of an early fourth-century basilical church at Laodicea.

bath experience, with its cold and hot pools, sauna, and warm room/pools. The structure dates from the second century AD and ceased to operate after the earthquake of AD 494, when Laodicea began its decline toward becoming an uninhabited site.

Many of the more impressive structures remaining on the archaeological site attest to the strong Christian presence in the city in the fourth century and beyond. These include small structures converted into Christian churches with clearly Christian iconography, elite homes with chapels, and large basilicas (see fig. 9.20). Laodicea was the site of a church council in AD 363 that involved some thirty bishops from Asia Minor, attesting to the ongoing life and importance of the church in this city. Thus, Laodicea also had a Christian congregation that must have responded positively to the challenges posed by John, for it did not simply blend into its surroundings but retained its distinctive identity and rose to prominence in the centuries following the Christianization of the empire.

HIERAPOLIS: PORTAL TO THE UNDERWORLD

One feature of neighboring Hierapolis seems worth mentioning in the context of the book of Revelation, which speaks on two occasions of the aperture of the abyss that is the haunt of demonic beings (Rev. 9:1–3; 20:1–3). Hierapolis had a "Plutonium" or "Ploutonion," a shrine to Hades (Latin, *Pluto*), the god of the underworld (see figs. 9.21, 9.22).[a] A deep fissure in the landscape opened up into a cavern that emitted carbon dioxide in a highly toxic concentration, proving fatal to people who ventured into it. This was identified as one of the entrances to the underworld, the realm of the dead, and became a cult site even before the city of Hierapolis was founded in the third century BC. In due course a magnificent shrine to Hades was erected over the fissure with stadium-like seating for those who came to participate in the rites.[b] Priests of Hades, specially trained to hold their breath for long periods, would carry sacrificial animals into the fissure and reemerge with the asphyxiated carcasses (Strabo, *Geogr.* 13.4.14).

a. Further on Hierapolis, see deSilva, *Archaeology and the Ministry of Paul*, 197–205, and the literature cited therein.

b. See D'Andria, "Ploutonion," for an extensive study of the archaeological remains and the history of the site's development.

Figure 9.21. The Plutonium of Hierapolis. The arched passageway beneath the statue of Hades (see detail) marks the entrance into the cavern with its deadly air.

Figure 9.22. A second-century AD statue of Hades found in the Hierapolis theater.

Author photo, courtesy of Hierapolis Archaeology Museum, Türkiye.

10

ROME

It is admittedly unusual to find a treatment of the city of Rome in books on the lived contexts of Revelation, yet according to a widely shared consensus among scholars, Rome is the (earthly) city most in view in this book. When John speaks of a "great city that rules over the kings of the earth" (Rev. 17:18) and a seven-headed beast whose "seven heads are seven hills upon which [the great prostitute] is seated" (17:9), the minds of his audiences throughout Roman Asia would have naturally latched on to the city at the center of the empire whose rule over the whole world was routinely declared, whose distinctive setting upon seven hills was routinely invoked. Poets often spoke of Rome as *urbs septicollis*, a "seven-hilled city" (see Virgil, *Georgics* 2.535; *Aen.* 6.784; Ovid, *Tristia* 1.4.69; Martial, *Epigrams* 4.64.11). Plutarch and Varro both refer to an obscure festival called Septimontium, which commemorated the city's expansion in the Republican period to encompass these seven hills (Plutarch, *Quaestiones romanae et graecae* 69; Varro, *De lingua Latina* 6.24).[1] A coin minted during the reign of Vespasian shows the goddess Roma reclining on her seven hills with a personification of the Tiber River laying at her feet (see fig. 10.2). Lest any doubt remain concerning the figure's identity, the coin also shows a wolf suckling Romulus and Remus.

Rome's prominence as the conceptual center of empire—for John, the vortex that drew the world's goods into itself and that ensured the endurance of its supremacy through violence against dissenters, enticements for its partners,

1. Connolly and Dodge, *Ancient City*, 108. The seven hills across which the city eventually spread are the Palatine, Capitoline, Quirinal, Viminal, Esquiline, Caelian, and Aventine.

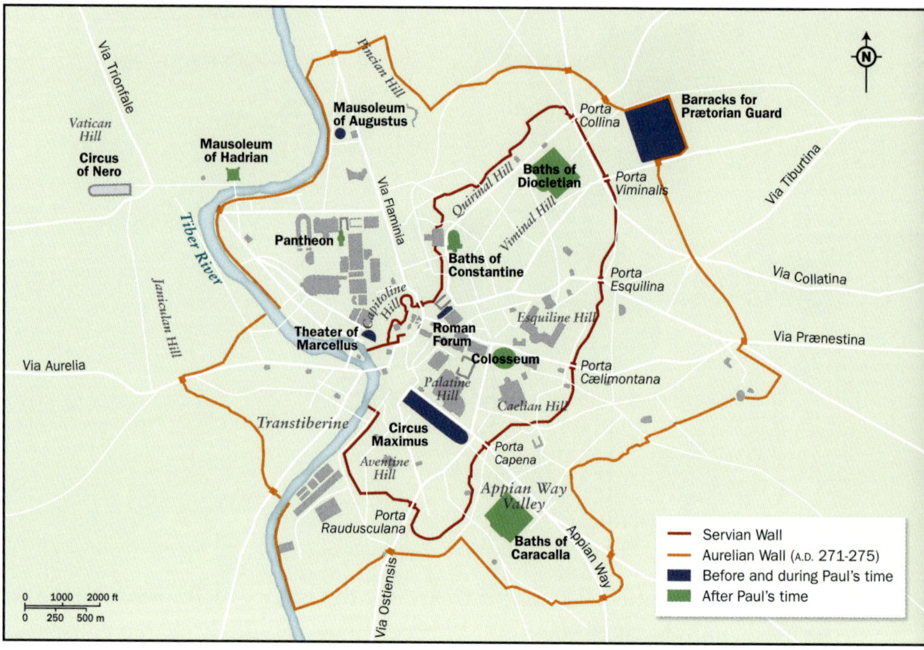

Figure 10.1. Map of Rome in the Imperial period.

Figure 10.2. A bronze sesterce of Vespasian showing the goddess Roma reposing against her seven hills.

Numismatica Ars Classica NAC AG, Auction 54, lot 361

and mythmaking about its origins, purpose, and destiny—accounts for its prominence in John's Apocalypse, even as John seeks to relativize Rome in relation to the throne of God beyond the visible skies, the *true* center of the cosmos. Rome's character, crimes, and condemnation are the subject of Revelation 16:17–19:10. Its heads of state and their activities are prominently featured in Revelation 13:1–10.

It is unlikely (though not impossible) that John had ever visited Rome firsthand. Reports of its landscape and happenings in the city, however, would circulate with the many people who had visited the city on business, visited relatives who had relocated there, or relocated from Rome themselves. The number of people Paul knew personally in Rome before ever having visited the city himself is a witness to the connections and networks people could form with Rome's inhabitants at any given time (see the list of greetings Paul sends ahead in Rom. 16:3–16). Yet, though John's knowledge of the city is most likely secondhand, archaeological discoveries supplemented by ancient literary evidence of the landmarks and developments in Rome in the decades leading up to John's prophetic ministry give us access to the secondhand impressions John may have gathered as he sought a God's-eye perspective on Roman rule.

The Economics of Empire

The city of Rome was the beating heart of the empire that encompassed the lands around the entire Mediterranean. The symbol of the eagle standing in victory and domination over the globe was an apt depiction of the power and influence of the city's power brokers. It was also the parasitic and insatiable consumer of the world's goods, for which John sharply criticizes it (Rev. 18:1–24). The grandeur of Rome was financed by siphoning off the resources and wealth of its conquered territories and vassal states around the Mediterranean through taxes and tribute.

Rome's appetite was truly staggering. One of the perks enjoyed by over two hundred thousand male heads of households in Rome was a regular supply of free grain. While the dole was likely not enough to supply the whole family, it was a noteworthy benefit—one that required a great deal of attention to logistics to ensure a steady supply from multiple provinces and the transportation necessary to keep the grain pouring in.[2] It is estimated that Rome imported eighty thousand tons of grain each year to maintain the dole.[3] The grain was duly paid for out of the annual tribute that poured into the Roman treasury from the provinces. In times of dearth, however, it was the provinces and not the capital that had to deal with the shortfall in harvests. An ironic monument to the massive amounts of supplies of staples that passed through the port at the base of the Aventine Hill beside the Tiber is the so-called Monte Testaccio, a 120-foot-high mountain made from the discarded amphorae and other clay vessels used (chiefly) to bring olive oil to Rome from Spain and North Africa (see fig. 10.3).[4]

Rome's appetites were, however, omnivorous. Its elite inhabitants craved not only staple products but also whatever luxuries every corner of the empire could afford them. In a speech delivered in praise of the city of Rome (*On Rome* 10–13), Aelius Aristides speaks thus of the benefits the Roman imperial economy brings to the mother city:

> The sea extends like a girdle in the middle of the civilized world and of your dominion. Around it lie the great continents, . . . ever offering to you in full

2. For more on the scope and logistics of sustaining the population of Rome, see Erdkamp, "Food Supply," 262–77.
3. Bang, "Forum on Trade," 296.
4. Connolly and Dodge, *Ancient City*, 127; Claridge, *Rome*, 402.

Figure 10.3. The artificial mountain, Monte Testaccio, made up of over fifty million broken amphorae.

> measure something of their own. Whatever the seasons make grow and whatever countries and rivers and lakes and arts of Greeks and barbarians produce are brought from every land and sea, so that if one wished to see all these things, that person must behold them either by visiting the entire civilized world or by coming to this city. For whatever is grown and made among each people cannot fail to be here at all times and in abundance. And here the merchant vessels come carrying these many products from all regions in every season . . . so that the city appears a kind of common marketplace of the world. One can see cargoes from India and, if you will, even from Arabia Felix in such numbers that one might surmise that in those lands the trees will have been stripped bare and that the inhabitants of these lands, if they need anything, must come here and beg for a share of their own. . . . Your farms are Egypt, Sicily and the civilized part of Africa. Arrivals and departures by sea never cease.[5]

While Rome could celebrate the availability of a world of goods in its marketplaces as a consequence of its imperial achievements, trees stripped bare of their bark and fruit could hardly have been good news for India and Arabia! Embedding the image of provincials coming to Rome as suppliants to obtain what had once been readily available in their homelands in a speech in praise of Rome is either stunningly naive or grimly sarcastic on Aristides's part. On John's lips, the speech would have been caustically so (cf. Rev. 18:11–13).

Augustus and the Architecture of Ideology

The public architecture of the city was designed above all to impress, to create a visual image that matched its leaders' propaganda about its greatness,

5. Translation from Oliver, *Ruling Power*, 896, modified.

Figure 10.4. The podium of the Temple of the deified Julius.

its eternity, and its achievement. Brick and marble everywhere gave eloquent testimony to Rome's grandeur, power, and wealth. We will focus first on the architectural projects undertaken by Octavian, upon whom the title "Augustus" was bestowed by the Senate in 27 BC, particularly those that laid the foundations for the ideology that would legitimate not only his own rule but that of his successors for centuries to come.[6]

Octavian had been adopted by Julius Caesar, who had no son of his own,[7] though Octavian's biological parents were still living. Such adoption of adult children was essentially Julius's way of naming Octavian his heir, not only to his estates but also to the loyalty of his client base. This became an essential claim to Octavian's legitimacy and an indispensable source of his power and influence. The fact that the Senate declared his adoptive father to be a god after his assassination in 44 BC significantly improved the legitimacy of Octavian's position. In 42 BC, in concert with his fellow triumvirs, Marc Antony and Aemilius Lepidus, Octavian ordered a temple to be erected to the deified Julius in the heart of the Roman Forum. Only parts of the podium remain, including the temple's most distinctive feature—a concave area in the front of the podium surrounding the site where the body of Julius had been cremated (see fig. 10.4).[8] This temple became a constant reminder of the divine power

6. A more extensive exploration of the civic, religious, and domestic structures of Rome extant in the early Imperial period can be found in deSilva, *Archaeology and the Ministry of Paul*, 254–82. For the sake of avoiding excessive redundancy with the treatment there, I focus here only on facets more relevant to Revelation.

7. Not counting Caesarion, Caesar's illegitimate son by Cleopatra VII, whom he did not formally acknowledge as his own.

8. Guidobaldi, *Roman Forum*, 36; Claridge, *Rome*, 100–101.

Figure 10.5. A silver denarius minted under Augustus. The reverse bears the image of the comet that was interpreted as the spirit of Julius ascending to the realm of the gods along with the legend "the deified Julius." Many such mintages circulated during Augustus's reign, reaffirming his connection with the god, Julius.
Used by permission of Classical Numismatic Group, LLC (190011).

Figure 10.6. An earlier denarius minted while Octavian was still part of the triumvirate with the facade of the Temple of the deified Julius on the reverse, clearly showing the cult image.
Used by permission of Classical Numismatic Group, LLC (auction 424, lot 366).

that stood behind Augustus's leadership of the empire. As the adopted son of Julius, Augustus became *Divi Filius*, "son of the deified one" (in Greek, simply *huios theou*, "son of a god"), a title included in almost every public inscription and on many coin legends (see figs. 10.5 and 10.6).

His adoption by Julius Caesar also inducted Octavian/Augustus into the legendary genealogy of the former's family. When Julius Caesar had expanded the Republican Forum, creating a subsidiary "Forum of Caesar," he provided it not only with additional public spaces for offices, meetings, and the conducting of the business of empire but also with a new temple to *Venus Genetrix*.[9] The epithet of the goddess (*Genetrix*) refers to the myth of Venus's having given birth to Aeneas, the survivor of the Trojan War and mythical hero of the Roman people whose story is told in Virgil's *Aeneid*. Julius also traced the mythical ancestry of the Julii family line back through Aeneas's son Ascanius—also called Iulus—to the goddess, making his new forum a blatant witness to his own propaganda (see fig. 10.7). As the adopted son of Julius, Augustus shared in this divine lineage.

After Julius was assassinated, Octavian and Marc Antony vowed to avenge his death and punish the conspirators, led by the famous Brutus and Cassius. Octavian's partnership with Antony outlived Brutus and Cassius only by a decade. Antony's alliance with Cleopatra VII, Egypt's last queen, proved a fatal mistake. Octavian emerged as the protector of Rome's interests and enjoyed the strong support of the Senate and people of Rome, while Antony and Cleopatra were represented as threats to the empire's unity, with Antony being labeled a traitor to his own people. Two years

9. Claridge, *Rome*, 163–68.

after Antony's defeat in the naval battle near Actium in 31 BC, a triumphal arch was built to celebrate Octavian's victory over him (see fig. 10.8).[10] This arch was erected near the center of the Roman Forum spanning the Temple

Figure 10.7. Two carved reliefs from the Sebasteion (the shrine of Augustus) in Aphrodisias, a city in Roman Asia. Left: Venus and Anchises look upon their son, Aeneas. Right: Aeneas flees the doomed city of Troy taking his father upon his shoulders and his son by his hand while Venus shelters and guides them. Even in Roman Asia, the myth of Augustus's connection with Venus was known and promoted.

Figure 10.8. The remains of the Arch of Octavian/Augustus in the Roman Forum.

10. Guidobaldi, *Roman Forum*, 37; Claridge, *Rome*, 101–2.

of Castor and Pollux (see fig. 10.9) and the Temple of the deified Julius, completed in the same year.

Figure 10.9. The podium, three remaining columns, and partial architrave of the Temple of Castor and Pollux.

This placement was fittingly symbolic. Castor and Pollux were twins and half brothers at the same time: Both were born of Leda, but Pollux had been sired by Zeus disguised as a swan while Castor was the son of Leda's mortal husband. They were famous for their brotherly affection, typified in Pollux's gift of half of his immortality to Castor so that they could share six months in Olympus at the price of sharing six months in Hades. They are seen in the constellation Gemini and were the patron gods of sailors and cavalry.[11] Castor was thus also an important precedent for a mortal becoming divine, potentially easing developments for the emperors and their worship in Rome after their deaths.

The rise of Augustus to sole power was celebrated as the beginning of a new, golden age of peace and stability. "Peace" became the watchword of the new regime, the source of the legitimacy of Augustus's power. Perhaps the most significant monument to the *Pax Augusti*—the Augustan Peace—is the Altar of the Augustan Peace (*Ara Pacis Augusti*), once erected in the northeastern portion of the Campus Martius, now reassembled and housed in a museum next to Augustus's mausoleum (see fig. 10.10). This particular monument was decreed by the Senate in 13 BC in honor of Augustus's pacification of Spain and Gaul.[12] The altar itself is housed at the top of a flight of steps inside a nearly square monument of about 40 by 36 feet.[13] A carved relief on the two shorter sides of the altar displays a religious procession in which Augustus and his extended family take conspicuous part (along with senators, lictors, and priests).[14]

11. See Strabo, *Geogr.* 1.3.2: "The Dioscuri were called 'guardians of the sea' and 'saviours of sailors'" (p. 177). The twin brothers watched over the path of the Alexandrian grain ship that took Paul from Malta to Puteoli as the ship's figurehead (Acts 28:11).

12. Claridge, *Rome*, 207.

13. Claridge, *Rome*, 209.

14. Pescarin, *Rome*, 70–71; Claridge, *Rome*, 210–13.

Figure 10.10. The "Altar of the Augustan Peace."

Augustus had a pair of Egyptian obelisks from the time of Ramses II transported to Rome as trophies after his victory over Antony and Cleopatra at Actium in 31 BC. He placed them in prominent locations as perpetual reminders of his successful end to the civil war. One was erected in the Campus Martius (or Field of Mars) northwest of the Forum and used as the needle of a solar meridian, a kind of sundial that marked out the progression of a solar year, allowing the civil calendar to keep in step with the solar calendar. A long strip of metal was laid out beside the obelisk and engraved such that, at noon every day, the shadow of the tip of the obelisk pointed to the date and indicated important seasonal transitions like the solstices and equinoxes. A new

Figure 10.11. Augustus functioning as a priest. Note the shallow bowl in his right hand, used for pouring out offerings of incense, wine, or grain over a fire burning on an altar. In a delicious twist of irony, John depicts seven angels using these bowls (*phialai*) to pour out God's wrath on those who have persisted in worshiping idols and the demonic powers behind them (Rev. 16:1).

inscription on the obelisk declared, "The Emperor Caesar Augustus, Son of the Deified, Chief Priest, with Egypt restored to the power of the Roman people, gave this as a gift to the Sun."[15]

Augustus also selected a site in the northernmost part of the Campus Martius for his mausoleum. This was a great round, marble-faced brick tomb with a diameter of almost 100 yards and rising to an estimated height of 50 yards when it was still complete.[16] It was also the site of a massive and long inscription celebrating the achievements of Augustus's career, written by Augustus himself shortly before his death—the "Acts Accomplished by the Divine Augustus" (*Res Gestae Divi Augusti*).[17] The text is known from copies of the inscription discovered in the province of Galatia, west of Roman Asia. The fullest surviving version was found at the Temple of Rome and Augustus at Ancyra, the provincial capital; fragmentary versions were found at the Augusteum in Pisidian Antioch and another sanctuary of Augustus in Apollonia.[18] Though scholars caution against assuming that the inscription was published empire-wide, its language was clearly made available in a province adjacent to Asia, and the *Koinon Asias* might well have made provision for it in the precinct of the Temple of Rome and Augustus at Pergamum at the very least, given their evident devotion.

Developments Under Nero

Tiberius, Caligula, and Claudius altered the face of Rome relatively little. Its landscape was dramatically transformed, however, during Nero's reign. In part, this was the result of the great fire of AD 64 that completely razed three of the city's fourteen districts and caused significant damage to seven others.[19] In part, it was the result of Nero's quest to create what was, in his inflated opinion, a palace worthy of an emperor. Prior to the great fire, Nero had incorporated or overbuilt a number of the imperial palaces on the Palatine Hill to create his Domus Transitoria—so named because it already stretched beyond the confines of the Hill toward the Esquiline to the northeast. Excavations beneath the Domus Flavia (Domitian's palace) revealed an ornate

15. Claridge, *Rome*, 216. The inscription is dated to 10 BC. The same inscription was carved into a sister obelisk that once graced the *spina* of the Circus Maximus and now stands in the Piazza del Populo.

16. Claridge, *Rome*, 204–5.

17. The descriptor *divi* (deified) was added after Augustus's death and formal deification by the Senate. A translation and helpful notes can be found in Danker, *Benefactor*, 256–80. See also Cooley, *Res Gestae*, for a fresh edition, translation, and rich commentary.

18. Cooley, *Res Gestae*, 7–18.

19. Segala and Sciortino, *Domus Aurea*, 5.

fountain in a porphyry-columned pavilion believed to have belonged to Nero's first palace. Portions of the so-called Domus Tiberiana ("Tiberius's" palace) are now believed also to represent Nero's modifications in conjunction with his Domus Transitoria.[20]

Nero had grander visions for his palace, however, and the fire of AD 64 gave him the opportunity to realize them, raising widespread suspicion about Nero's own involvement in that fire that had to be diverted (Suetonius, *Nero* 38; Tacitus, *Ann.* 15.38–42, 44). Having appropriated more than 150 acres in the heart of the city in the wake of the destruction, Nero set about creating his Domus Aurea (Golden House), a vast complex of palaces, gardens, lakes, and other recreational areas that spanned the Palatine and Esquiline Hills. Suetonius (*Nero* 31) describes it thus:

> The entrance hall was large enough to contain a huge statue of himself, 120 feet high; and the pillared arcade ran for a whole mile. An enormous pool, like a sea, was surrounded by buildings made to resemble cities, and by a landscaped garden consisting of ploughed fields, vineyards, pastures, and woodlands—where every variety of domestic and wild animal roamed about. Parts of the house were overlaid with gold and studded with precious stones and mother-of-pearl. All the dining rooms had ceilings of fretted ivory, the panels of which could slide back and let a rain of flowers, or perfume from hidden sprinklers, shower upon his guests. The main dining room was circular, and its roof revolved, day and night, in time with the sky. Sea water, or sulphur water, was always on tap in the baths.[21]

One cannot help but wonder if John had caught wind of this project and constructed his New Jerusalem in such a way as to mock and put to shame the beast's wildest ambitions.

Nero's personal residence remained the rebuilt palace on the Palatine itself. An example of both the achievement and the extravagance of the complex is the recently excavated domed dining room of which Suetonius had written. A remarkable system of gears, powered by skillfully harnessed water pressure, allowed the painted dome to rotate, giving guests the illusion of being under the revolving night sky.[22] To the north, in the valley between hills, he had an enormous artificial lake created, surrounded by porticoes and various buildings, filling it—and supplying the new bathhouses of his complex—with water diverted from an aqueduct. He turned the eastern wall

20. Segala and Sciortino, *Domus Aurea*, 5–6.
21. Suetonius, *Twelve Caesars*, 229.
22. Falconi, "Nero's Rotating Banquet Hall."

Figure 10.12. The octagonal dining room of Nero's pavilion.
Davide Mauro / CC BY-SA 4.0 / Wikimedia Commons

Figure 10.13. An excavated hallway of the Domus Aurea pavilion with a statue of the muse of dancing and the dramatic chorus.
Howard Hudson / CC BY-SA 3.0 / Wikipedia

Figure 10.14. Top: A frescoed ceiling in the Domus Aurea. Right: A frescoed wall from the palace of Nero's wife, Poppaea, in Oplontis, providing a better sense of the color and liveliness of Neronian-period frescoes in their heyday.

Top: Tyler Bell / CC BY 2.0 / Wikimedia Commons

of the Temple of the Divine Claudius into a tall fountain house, supplied from the same aqueduct.[23]

A vast pavilion was constructed on the Oppian Hill (a southern spur of the Esquiline Hill), chiefly for entertainment and pleasure. Its excavated remains are the best-preserved remnants of Nero's Domus Aurea and the ones most readily accessible to the public. Their state of preservation is largely due to Trajan's decision to fill in the structure and use it as part of the foundation for his expansive public baths. The site was discovered by accident in the fifteenth century and became a favorite attraction for artists, who found inspiration in the frescoes beneath, and for adventurer-tourists (see fig. 10.14). As a result

23. Segala and Sciortino, *Domus Aurea*, 10.

of increasing exposure to the elements as more of the rooms were cleared, the site has suffered a great deal of damage over the past five centuries. An octagonal room at the heart of the pavilion stands as an example of the opulent and impressive structures provided for dining there (see fig. 10.12). Broad openings in five of the eight sides gave access to other rooms and corridors; openings in the remaining three afforded lofty views of the gardens, parks, and lake below. Another dining room was made to resemble a cave with a cascading waterfall at one end, emptying into a pool. Nero had sent several of his agents into Greece and Asia to appropriate works of Greek art to decorate his new palace, pavilion, and grounds (see fig. 10.13). Pergamum was among the cities particularly plundered.[24]

Between the palace and the pavilion were vast parks, fields, terraced gardens, vineyards, and forests. According to Tacitus, these represented the greatest extravagance, given the demand for real estate in the capital: "Its wonders were not so much customary and commonplace luxuries like gold and jewels, but lawns and lakes and faked rusticity—woods here, open spaces and views there" (*Ann.* 15.42).[25] Nero had also prepared a suitably grand entryway for this complex. The vestibule was a porticoed courtyard of vast dimensions—even if we doubt Suetonius's estimate of a mile in length!—and housed the famed colossal, 120-foot-tall statue of Nero as the sun god Helios (*Nero* 31; cf. Pliny the Elder, *Nat.* 34.46).

Surviving reactions to Nero's "improvements" of the city are predictably negative. Suetonius preserves a verse that apparently circulated in criticism of Nero's remodeling efforts: "Rome is now a single house: try moving to Veii, citizens, if this house does not soon occupy Veii as well!" (*Nero* 39).[26] Martial similarly recollected with bitterness the time when "in the entire city there stood a single house" (*Spec.* 2).[27] It is possible that Nero had intended to open large portions of the Domus Aurea to the public—for example, the vestibule, the parks, and the gardens.[28] Time, however, was not on his side; he would be driven to commit suicide in AD 68, four years after the great fire, and his Domus Aurea was not yet fully completed by that time.

Tacitus informs us that Nero also gave attention to rebuilding the city itself beyond his Golden House, putting certain safeguards in place to reduce the risk of another devastating fire, including incorporating a certain proportion

24. Magie, *Roman Rule*, 1:564.
25. Tacitus, *Annals of Imperial Rome*, 364.
26. Quoted in Segala and Sciortino, *Domus Aurea*, 10. Veii is a city 10 miles northwest of Rome.
27. Quoted in Roman, "Martial and the City of Rome," 93.
28. Griffin, *Nero*, 137–41.

of stone, keeping a greater distance between buildings, doubling up the walls between attached houses, improving the water supply to the whole of the city, and requiring all householders to keep certain supplies for extinguishing fires on hand (*Ann.* 15.42–43).

The great fire had far-reaching effects, two of which would have been of particular importance to John. The first concerns the fate of large numbers of Christians in the capital. Nero diverted suspicion from himself by casting blame on the members of this unpopular group. His ability to do so alerts us to the fact that Christians were already an identifiable group in Rome distinct from the Jewish population *and* that its members lived in sufficiently high tension with their neighbors for this scapegoating to be perpetrated without resistance—and perhaps even with pleasure—by the general population of the city. Tacitus's report on these events is as follows:

> To suppress this rumour, Nero fabricated scapegoats—and punished with every refinement the notoriously depraved Christians (as they were popularly called).[29] Their originator, Christ, had been executed in Tiberius' reign by the governor of Judaea, Pontius Pilatus. But in spite of this temporary setback the deadly superstition had broken out afresh, not only in Judaea (where the mischief had started) but even in Rome. . . .
>
> First, Nero had self-acknowledged Christians arrested. Then, on their information, large numbers of others were condemned—not so much for incendiarism as for their anti-social tendencies. Their deaths were made farcical. Dressed in wild animals' skins, they were torn to pieces by dogs, or crucified, or made into torches to be ignited after dark as substitutes for daylight. Nero provided his Gardens for the spectacle, and exhibited displays in the Circus. (*Ann.* 15.44)[30]

Tacitus refers here to a racecourse or hippodrome on the west bank of the Tiber River. Indeed, its connection with the martyrdoms of Christians—and above all the martyrdom of Peter—explains why the site would later be chosen for the construction of the Basilica of St. Peter at the heart of the present-day Vatican City.

The second far-reaching effect of this fire concerns events in the Judean homeland. Because of the immense and immediate need for rebuilding the capitol (as well as fulfilling his own ambitions for remaking the face of the city) Nero sent special collection agents to a number of provinces and likely ordered all his governors and other provincial representatives to extract as

29. The Latin *Christiani* (Greek, *Christianoi*) essentially means "Christ-partisans" or "Christ-followers." It is formed on the basis of the same suffix that gives us "Herodians" (that is, "partisans of Herod's line").

30. Tacitus, *Annals of Imperial Rome*, 365–66.

much wealth as possible from the provinces. One of his representatives—Gessius Florus, the procurator overseeing the subprovince of Judea between AD 64 and 66—sent his troops into the treasuries of the Jerusalem temple to appropriate seventeen talents of silver.[31] While Josephus presents this essentially as an act of plunder, it seems likely that Florus was indeed duly fulfilling an imperial order, though, of course, violating Judean sensibilities and the holiness of the temple to do so.[32] Both Tacitus (*Ann.* 15.45) and Suetonius (*Nero* 38) assert that Nero had bled both Rome and its provinces dry in the wake of the great fire to fund his building efforts, going so far as to have his agents rob temples near and far not only of the deposits in their treasuries but even of images of the gods themselves, were they made of gold or silver.

In the aftermath of this act, some inhabitants of Jerusalem staged protests while others mocked the procurator, going about the streets with cups and bowls begging copper coins for the poor Roman. Florus responded with extreme prejudice, unleashing his troops on protestors and, when the local population would not produce those who indulged in the mockery, summarily crucifying a number of Jerusalemites—including some who held Roman citizenship and were legally to be spared any such treatment. These exchanges contributed to the escalation of grievances that led to the outbreak of the First Jewish Revolt in AD 66 and, four years later, to the devastation of Jerusalem and its temple.

These events were bound to make a lasting impression on John the Seer and, indeed, on all devotees of the God of Israel, whether Jew or Christian. When John sees a beast rising from the abyss to murder God's witnesses (Rev. 11:7), or understands this beast to have been granted "to make war against the holy ones and to conquer them" (13:7), or sees "the great city that has dominion over the kings of the earth" (17:18) as a prostitute "drunk with the blood of the holy ones and with the blood of Jesus's witnesses" (17:6), he no doubt counted Nero's victims in the tally. Indeed, Nero's actions against Christians appear to have been the first incident in which imperial agents took an interest in discovering, condemning, and brutally executing Christ-followers in the empire. This might well account for John's fixation on Nero as revealing something central about the character of Roman rule.[33] In him,

31. Nero himself had no scruples about appropriating the treasures of the temples in Rome itself (Suetonius, *Nero* 32), so there is no reason to doubt he would have given such orders to his representatives abroad.

32. See the discussion in Mason, *History*, 316–18.

33. I think here of Nero's name as a highly plausible solution to the riddle of the number 666 (Rev. 13:18) as well as the resonances of Rev. 17:10–11 with the legend of Nero returning that not only filled the popular imagination of the later first century but also inspired a number of revolutionary pretenders in AD 69, 80, and 88 (see Tacitus, *Hist.* 2.8–9; Dio Cassius, *Hist. rom.* 66.19.3;

the beast reared its ugliest head and showed something of its essential, anti-Christian character—suggesting also the shape of things to come, which, in fact, the history of the next two centuries played out.

Rome Under Vespasian, Titus, and Domitian

After Nero's death, the Roman Empire was plunged again into civil war, this time lasting only a single but devastating year (AD 68–69). The legions in Spain declared their commander, Sertorius Galba, emperor a few months prior to Nero's well-reasoned suicide in June of AD 68 (see fig. 10.15). Galba was, in turn, assassinated by the agents of Marcus Salvius Otho, who was declared emperor by the Senate with the support of the Praetorian Guard in January of AD 69 (see fig. 10.16, left). Earlier that same month, however, the legions in Germany had already declared their own commander, Aulus Vitellius, emperor (see fig. 10.16, right). When Otho's troops could not prevail over those of Vitellius, Otho also prudently committed suicide in April of AD 69. Vitellius's victory would be short-lived as well, as the legions of Vespasian stationed in Alexandria declared for *their* commander by July. Mucianus, the governor of Syria and a staunch supporter of Vespasian, led his legions eastward, picking up substantial support from other legions along the way, and engaged the legions of Vitellius in northern Italy. The latter was defeated, but it took a further two months for Vitellius to be dispatched and Vespasian established as emperor in Rome.[34]

Figure 10.15. A gold aureus minted under Galba, prematurely promoting "Rome reborn" by virtue of his accession and supplanting of Nero.
Numismatica Ars Classica NAC AG, Auction 67, lot 127

Figure 10.16. Left: A silver denarius minted under Otho. Right: A gold aureus minted under Vitellius.
Author photo, courtesy of the Altes Museum, Germany.

By December of AD 69, a new dynasty was established. For the next twenty-six years, Vespasian and, successively, his two sons Titus and Domitian would provide stable continuity of

and Suetonius, *Nero* 57.2, respectively) and echoes throughout contemporaneous literature (see, e.g., *Sib. Or.* 4.119–27, 133–39; 5.28–29, 33–35, 137–50, 363–69; Dio Chrysostom, *Or.* 21.10). For further discussion, see deSilva, *Discovering Revelation*, 135–37, 149.

34. The events of AD 69 are recounted in great detail in Tacitus, *Historiae* (*Histories*).

governance for the empire (see fig. 10.17). John plausibly has these events, and this outcome, in view when he speaks of a mortal blow to one of the beast's heads (Rev. 13:3), which is also understood as a mortal blow to the beast itself (13:12, 14), having been healed. The year 68–69 provoked both the fear and the hope, depending on one's attitude toward Roman rule, that the great empire would collapse as a result of these internal upheavals. Josephus, reflecting upon this year, declares "the Roman state" to have been "saved beyond expectation" as a result of Vespasian's accession (*J.W.* 4.657).[35] The author of 4 Ezra, writing in the same genre and near the same time as John's Revelation, creates a detailed allegory of imperial rule in the figure of a great eagle-like beast with twelve wings and three heads. The interpreting angel explains the facet of the vision relevant here, thus: "As for your hearing a voice that spoke, coming not from the eagle's heads but from the midst of its body, this is the interpretation: In the midst of the time of that kingdom great struggles shall arise, and it shall be in danger of falling; nevertheless it shall not fall then but shall regain its former power" (4 Ezra [= 2 Esdras] 12:17–18 NRSV). The recovery of the empire from the civil wars of 68–69 was widely regarded as nothing less than a marvel.[36]

Figure 10.17. A sesterce minted under Vespasian showing the emperor helping Roma to rise to her feet once more.
Numismatica Ars Classica NAC AG, Auction 25, lot 410

Figure 10.18. One of many coin mintages under Vespasian commemorating the Roman victory in Judea and Galilee. The reverse shows a male Jewish captive, his hands bound behind him, and a lamenting woman, likely a personification of the territory, seated beneath a date palm, a standard symbol for Judea. The legend, "Judea Capta," suggests the addition of a new province to the empire (and not merely the suppression of a revolt) and, in fact, Judea was first organized as an independent province, as opposed to a subprovince of Syria, in AD 70.
Used by permission of Classical Numismatic Group, LLC (Triton VIII, lot 1007).

Under Vespasian, Jesus's dire predictions of the siege and destruction of Jerusalem as related in Luke 21:20–24 came to pass.[37] Vespasian, general of

35. Translation from Josephus, *Jewish War*, 3:195.
36. So also Bauckham, *Climax of Prophecy*, 441–44.
37. A careful comparison of Mark 13:3–24 and Luke 21:7–25 shows Luke to have interpreted Jesus's murky saying concerning "the abomination of desolation" or "desolating sacrilege" (Mark 13:14–19) in light of the siege and destruction of Jerusalem (Luke 21:20–24), probably

Figure 10.19. A small relief on the highest point of the arch's interior shows Titus mounting to the heavens on the back of an eagle, likely a representation of Jupiter, to take his place among the gods.

the legions in Alexandria, had already begun putting down the First Jewish Revolt of AD 66 when his attention was diverted westward in a bid for the imperial throne. He left his eldest son, Titus, in charge of the siege of Jerusalem, which he completed by AD 70. Jerusalem and its temple were left in ruins, the temple never to be rebuilt (see fig. 10.18). An inordinate number of lives were lost.[38] Tens of thousands of able-bodied males were sold off as slaves, in part to recover the costs of the war. Thousands were taken simply to be slaughtered in gladiatorial games held both in the east and in Rome. Again the great prostitute was drunk with "the blood of all who had been slain on the earth" (Rev. 18:24). Again the inhabitants of the earth had cause to exclaim, "Who is like the beast, and who can make war against it?" (13:4).

This victory left its mark on the city of Rome in a number of ways. The famous Arch of Titus at the east entrance to the Roman Forum, erected

---

with the advantage of hindsight that Mark did not yet enjoy, writing as he did prior to the calamity in Jerusalem.

38. Tacitus (*Hist.* 5.13) reports that 600,000 people were trapped within Jerusalem's walls during the final siege. Josephus, known for inflating numbers, claims that the casualties amounted to 1.1 million dead and 97,000 taken as prisoners of war to be sold as slaves or to die in the arena (*J.W.* 6.420).

Figure 10.20. The dedicatory inscription on the Arch of Titus.

Figure 10.21. The Arch of Titus erected at the east end of the Roman Forum.

shortly after Titus's untimely death in AD 81, commemorated Titus's successful suppression of the First Jewish Revolt (see fig. 10.21).[39] Two carved reliefs on the inner walls of the arch show scenes from the triumphal procession awarded to Titus by the Senate immediately following his victory. The first relief shows Titus riding in a chariot drawn by four horses and led in procession by the goddess Roma herself (see fig. 10.23). Behind Titus stands the winged figure of Victory, holding a wreath over the conquering general's head. The second relief depicts the spoils from the temple of Jerusalem carried aloft (notably the seven-branched candelabra, the gold trumpets, and the table of the showbread), along with several Jewish slaves led as human spoils of war (see fig. 10.22). A dedicatory inscription above the arch reads, "The Senate and people of Rome to the divine Titus Vespasian Augustus, son of the deified Vespasian" (see fig. 10.20), titles that John would certainly have considered "names of blasphemy" (Rev. 13:1).[40]

39. Claridge, *Rome*, 121–23. This was actually the *second* such triumphal arch; another had been erected for Titus earlier near the Circus Maximus.

40. "The Senate and the people of Rome" (*Senatus populusque Romanorum*) is incidentally the source of the famous acronym *SPQR* seen everywhere in Rome and on things Roman.

Figure 10.22. The important relief on an inner wall of the Arch of Titus showing the furniture of the Jerusalem temple being carried in triumphal procession.

Figure 10.23. Another scene from Titus's triumphal procession showing the commander in his chariot.

Figure 10.24. The scant remains of the Forum of Peace, which was once dominated by Vespasian's Temple of Peace.

After successfully bringing an end to the civil wars of AD 68–69 and the First Jewish Revolt of 66–70, Vespasian constructed the Temple of Peace and its expansive courtyards and colonnades (see fig. 10.24). This became another major northward extension of the Roman Forum, providing additional public spaces for business, imperial administration, and gathering. Vespasian displayed a great variety of artistic treasures within the new temple, many of them assembled from the private spaces of Nero's Domus Aurea and, thus, "returned" to the people who could now access them.[41] Prominent among the treasures displayed were the sacred furnishings from the Jerusalem temple (Josephus, *J.W.* 7.158–62).[42] The emphasis on peace in Vespasian's propaganda was directed at presenting him as a new Augustus,

41. Roman, "Martial and the City," 96.

42. Claridge, *Rome*, 171–72. The remains of an artifact of particular importance for reconstructing ancient Rome was discovered in a room inside the Temple of Peace complex—the *Forma Urbis*, a marble map of Rome created in the early decades of the third century. When it was complete, it measured 60 by 43 feet and was affixed to a wall. It is outstanding in its level of detail, showing every shop, every room in a *domus* or public building, every column in every portico. Only 10 to 15 percent of the original map survives in 1,186 fragments ("Stanford Digital Forma Urbis Romae Project").

whose rise to power was similarly celebrated as bringing an end to civil war and provincial rebellion.

Vespasian also began construction on the massive Flavian Amphitheater, more popularly known as the Colosseum.[43] Vespasian made a powerful statement here. He returned to the use of the people of Rome a large piece of the land that Nero had co-opted for his Domus Aurea. Indeed, this required first the draining and filling in of Nero's immense lake, over which the new construction took shape. The poet Martial celebrated the transformation thus:

> Here, where the starry Colossus sees the constellations closer at hand
> and high scaffolding rises in the middle of the road,
> the hated halls of the savage king used to gleam,
> and in the entire city there stood a single house.
> Here, where the revered mass of the far-seen Amphitheatre
> rises up, was Nero's lake.
> Here where we admire baths—a rapid gift—
> a haughty estate had deprived the poor of dwellings.
> Where the Claudian portico unravels its spreading shade,
> was the furthest point of the palace's extremity.
> Rome has been restored to herself, and under your guardianship, Caesar,
> what used to be a master's plaything is now the people's. (*Spec.* 2.1–12)[44]

The work was completed under Titus. The amphitheater measures 615 by 510 feet on its two axes, with the arena floor measuring 246 by 144 feet (see fig. 10.25).[45] The seating capacity of its four tiers of bleachers, rising to a height of 150 feet, exceeded fifty thousand.[46] Seats were reserved by social class, with the senators in the lowest (and therefore best) seats, the equestrians ("knights") above them, and the plebs in the tiers above them. At the very top, the poorest and slaves enjoyed a distant view of the action. The emperor and special dignitaries like the Vestal Virgins enjoyed a special box in the center of one of the long sides—and the images of the gods occupied a similar box on

43. The more typical name arose as a result of the decision of the emperor Hadrian to relocate Nero's Colossus (which had been reworked in line with more traditional images of the sun god Helios after Nero's suicide) to the plaza beside the Flavian Amphitheater to make room for his Temple of Venus and Roma. The Colossus stood there throughout the rest of the Roman period and lingered long in the memory of the people, eventually giving its name to the amphitheater.

44. Translation from Roman, "Martial and the City," 93.

45. Connolly and Dodge, *Ancient City*, 192, 202; Claridge, *Rome*, 312.

46. Connolly and Dodge, *Ancient City*, 197; Claridge, *Rome*, 314.

Figure 10.25. The Flavian Amphitheater exterior (left) and interior (right). Note the network of tunnels beneath the arena that allowed for staging of events, dramatic entrances of men and beasts, and other effects.

the opposite side.[47] The arena would later come to be equipped with an extensive series of tunnels, lifts, and trap doors that allowed different points of entry for different combatants, beasts, or machinery; it may even have once had the capacity to be flooded for the re-creation of naval battles. It made provision, in other words, for the best special effects available in the first and second centuries. An inscription indicates that the project was funded largely from the spoils of the Jewish War, including the proceeds from the sale of tens of thousands of Jewish prisoners of war as slaves.[48]

Figure 10.26. The brick substructure of the rounded, domed end of one of the large halls of Titus's bath complex on the Oppian/Esquiline Hill.

A large gladiatorial training school, the Ludus Magnus, stood east of the Colosseum. An underground tunnel gave combatants access to the arena.[49] Titus also constructed a new bath complex just northeast of the Colosseum (see fig. 10.26), a substantial complex covering an area about two-thirds the area of the Colosseum itself, as a public benefaction—notably extending his father's policy of returning to popular use land that the last Julio-Claudian emperor had appropriated—and doing so, once again, by providing a highly functional

47. Claridge, *Rome*, 314.
48. Connolly and Dodge, *Ancient City*, 192; Claridge, *Rome*, 314.
49. Claridge, *Rome*, 319.

Figure 10.27. A denarius of Titus showing the facade of the restored Capitolium on the reverse with the cult images of Juno, Jupiter, and Minerva visible in the interior.

Used by permission of Classical Numismatic Group, LLC (auction 88, lot 1298).

public building (see the testimony of Martial, *Spec.* 2.5–8).[50]

Vespasian also gave attention to restoring the Temple of Jupiter Capitolinus, so named for its placement atop the Capitoline Hill to the west of the Roman Forum (see fig. 10.27). Jupiter was worshiped here alongside Juno and Minerva. This was the Roman cult par excellence; many Roman colonies would also build a temple to the Capitoline trio as a mark of their pious alignment with the mother city. This temple had been destroyed in a fire that occurred in connection with the riots in the capital in the months leading up to Vitellius's capture and death. Representations on coins and carved reliefs variously show the temple with a facade of four or six columns. Excavations have shown that the front of the temple had three parallel rows of six columns. This may have been reduced to four columns in some representations for simplicity and balance (the four columns creating three equal spaces for doors or cult statues).[51] Vespasian's plan for funding the project involved having the Jewish population of the empire continue to pay their temple tax after the destruction of the Jerusalem temple as always. The funds, however, would no longer be used in connection with the activity and support of the Jerusalem temple, and certainly not for its restoration, but would instead be handed over for the restoration and maintenance of the Temple of Jupiter (Josephus, *J.W.* 7.218; Dio Cassius, *Hist. rom.* 46.7.2). Thus the tribute that was regarded by Jews universally as due the God of Israel was now to be rendered to Caesar and the principal Roman deities. It is possible that one of the reasons John, the author of Revelation, spoke such strong words against his fellow Jews—calling the Jewish bodies in Smyrna and Philadelphia, at least, a "synagogue of Satan" (Rev. 2:9; 3:9)—is that he detested the fact that they would buy toleration from Rome at the cost of giving the money due God for God's worship over to the emperors for the support of their demonic, idolatrous religion.

50. Dumser, "Urban Topography," 147.

51. In addition to figure 10.27, one can compare a denarius from the Republican period (75 BC) minted under M. Volteius, showing the facade of the temple with four columns and three pairs of closed bronze doors for each of the three sacred areas (*cellae*) of the divine trio (see www.cngcoins.com/Coin.aspx?CoinID=186976) and a sesterce minted under Vespasian showing the restored temple with six columns and the three cult images (see www.cngcoins.com/Coin.aspx?CoinID=66125).

Figure 10.28. The Temple of Saturn (on the left) and the remaining three columns and partial architrave of the Temple of the Deified Vespasian and Titus (on the right).

During his short reign (AD 79–81), Titus began the construction of a new temple to be dedicated to his deified father, Vespasian, and to be located between the ancient Temple of Saturn and the Temple of Concordia. After Titus's early death, his younger brother and successor Domitian, the last emperor of the Flavian dynasty, oversaw the completion of the temple and its dedication jointly to Vespasian and Titus.[52] Even though it was squeezed into the space between existing temples, the Temple of the Deified Vespasian and Titus had a commanding location above the eastern part of the Roman Forum (see fig. 10.28). The architrave of the temple was decorated (at least in part) with the tools and sacred vestments of Roman priests, recalling the emperors' own role as Pontifex Maximus, or chief priest, of the Roman world.

The Flavian emperors also built palatial mansions for themselves. The excavated remains on the Palatine Hill particularly showcase the Domus Flavia, believed to have been built under Domitian and covering the whole of the central and eastern Palatine (see figs. 10.29, 10.30).[53] It was fabulous not only for

52. Claridge, *Rome*, 82. A small carving at the highest point of the underside of the vaulted archway of the Arch of Titus shows Titus being carried into the heavens on the back of an eagle, a standard image for *apotheōsis*, or deification.

53. See further, Connolly and Dodge, *Ancient City*, 218–25; Claridge, *Rome*, 127, 145–57.

Figure 10.29. The brick substructure of several of the buildings and halls comprising the Domus Flavia.

Figure 10.30. A particularly ornate fountain on the grounds of the Domus Flavia.

the scope of its living and meeting spaces but also for the extensiveness of its gardens and outdoor amenities, including an enclosed garden in the form of a small stadium or hippodrome that could accommodate private races (see fig. 10.31). The Domus Flavia also overlooked the Circus Maximus, the most famous racetrack in Rome, which sat immediately south of the Palatine. Domitian took advantage of this by creating a lavish, private garden terrace—a kind of perpetual, private box seating for the imperial family. The spread of the imperial palaces throughout the first century incidentally obliterated or overbuilt the entirety of what was an elite residential neighborhood during the late Republic.

Figure 10.31. The garden stadium of the Domus Flavia.

The wealth, luxury, and ostentation embodied in the public spaces of Rome and the semiprivate homes of its rulers were the prizes of conquest and political intimidation. They were spoils rather than wages or rewards. The temples dedicated to its deified, deceased rulers were the ultimate attempts to legitimate Rome's imperialism not just as the will of the traditional gods but as the achievement of the new imperial "gods." The more prophetic-minded among the early Christians were highly critical of Rome's imperial practices. As John the Seer contemplated these and other facets of Rome's hegemony over the circle of lands around the Mediterranean—most notably the violence to which the empire resorted as its final argument—he could not believe that the God of Israel, the God of the prophets, would allow such a regime to continue long. The ruins of Rome are a constant reminder not only of Rome's greatness but also of the fact that no empire forged by human beings endures. History proved the epithet "Eternal" Rome (see fig. 10.32) to be a lie, now no more than tourist propaganda, vindicating John's summons to look to the kingdom of God and of his Christ if one ever hopes to find a truly stable homeland.

Figure 10.32. A gold aureus minted under Hadrian with the goddess Roma on the reverse, a winged victory in her right hand offering a laurel wreath back to the goddess. The legend on the reverse reads *Roma Aeterna*, "Eternal Rome."

11

READING REVELATION IN ROMAN ASIA

We began our tour of Roman Asia and sites related to the composition, content, and initial reception of John's Revelation with the conviction that immersing ourselves in the lived spaces and experiences of the Christians addressed by John would help us read Revelation alongside them. We sought thereby to open our minds and imaginations to *their* experience of hearing Revelation read in their assemblies and to its function as an "unveiling"—the meaning of the Greek word *apokalypsis* that opens the book (Rev. 1:1)—of specific relevance to them. John believed himself to have been instructed to send his book specifically to *these* congregations and presented it to them as an *open* book, one that he had been commanded *not* to seal up for some future time and audience (22:10). It seems appropriate to conclude our tour, then, with a brief exploration of how Christians living in Roman Asia, perhaps specifically in Ephesus and Pergamum as the sites whose early Roman environment has been most thoroughly exposed by archaeology, would have been equipped to process the contents of Revelation. We will also explore how doing so would have oriented them to the realities around them, such as the ideologies and practices (some of which prominently functioned to sustain those ideologies) that they regularly encountered.[1] What connections would we have made if we were part of those audiences?

1. For further exploration, see Friesen, *Imperial Cults*, 135–217; Howard-Brook and Gwyther, *Unveiling Empire*; deSilva, *Discovering Revelation*.

We would not have missed the explicit political claims that John makes on Jesus's behalf from the very outset. We hear John declare Jesus to be the "ruler of the kings of the earth" and his followers to constitute a "kingdom" for the one God that Jesus has been forging from "every tribe and language and people and nation" (Rev. 1:5–6; 5:9). We might be uncomfortable hearing such claims spoken aloud, even in a private house, since the vast majority of people around us would identify the emperor Domitian as the one who holds such dominion and would acknowledge Rome's empire as extending over "every tribe and people and language and nation" (13:7), even as visual marvels like the reliefs in the Sebasteion in Aphrodisias proclaim. But here, "honor and power" are ascribed to Jesus "into the ages of ages" (1:6). Domitian is answerable to Jesus; Jesus's kingdom will outlast Rome's.

John takes us by surprise as he summons us to envision, before we are three minutes into the recital of his book, Jesus returning on the clouds of heaven in such a manner that everyone will witness the event—and be driven to mourn as they find themselves entirely caught off guard, being held accountable to a figure they despised, if they even knew anything about him at all. From the outset, we are made mindful of the coming day that will bring all the pretensions of human "kingdoms," including those of Rome, to an abrupt end.

Throughout Revelation, John will press upon our minds the fact that *this* encounter is the principal crisis facing humankind (it returns in Rev. 6:12–17; 14:14–20; 19:11–21; 20:11–15). This is what John would have us keep in the forefront of our consciousness as we consider how to respond to all of the more quotidian crises that loom before us and our fellow Christ-followers in the other cities—whether growing tensions with local Jewish communities, the adverse consequences of our neighbors' disapproval and hostility, or the challenges of simply providing for a family in the midst of such social pressures. What response to this immediate challenge in the here and now will become a cause for approval rather than censure—or outright condemnation!—in the then and there of Christ's return?

We are not prepared for the awesome appearance of the glorified Christ, for even John presents *himself* as wholly unprepared for what he sees (Rev. 1:12–18). By their ingenuity and at great expense, local craftsmen working with marble, alabaster, and ivory represented the emperors of the Flavian house in their new temple as glimmering, larger-than-life beings, but the glory of the living Christ shows all of this effort for what it is—a contrived imitation of the real thing. When John speaks prophetic oracles to each congregation on behalf of *this* figure, we begin to fathom that these words carry far greater force, promise greater reward, and pose direr threat than any imperial edicts delivered by the heralds of those lesser rulers.

As John invites us more fully into his visionary experience, he raises our eyes to a space above and beyond the cities where our attention is typically focused. He lifts our eyes even beyond Rome (which the imperial temples and shrines in our cities present as the center of our world) and beyond the jurisdiction of the emperor—the *autokratōr*, the divine agent that rules the "whole earth," as he is referred to in so many inscriptions. We are drawn rather to the spaces beyond the visible earth and heavens where the one and only living God, the *Pantokratōr*, the "All-Powerful," reigns from *his* throne (Rev. 4:1–2; see fig. 11.1). Angels and archangels and all the company of heaven know and honor the true center of the cosmos. They proclaim the honor due God as the one "who made all things," by whose "will they came into being and were made" (4:11). As the scene widens before our eyes, we see "every created being in heaven and on earth and under the earth and in the sea" acclaiming God and his regent, Jesus: "To the One seated upon the throne and to the Lamb belong blessing and honor and glory and power into the ages of ages" (5:13).

Figure 11.1. The carved throne of a priestess of Ceres (Demeter), the goddess of the wheat harvest.

Author photo, courtesy of the Louvre, France.

Figure 11.2. Apollo, adorned with a wreath (*stephanos*), holding a seven-stringed harp (*kithara*) and libation bowl (*phialē*). Each of the twenty-four elders has these three accoutrements as well (Rev. 4:10; 5:8).

This vision changes our perspective as we sit gathered in one of the few homes owned by Christ-followers that is large enough to accommodate our assembly. We regularly see the vast majority of our neighbors gathering piously around *other* centers to offer their worship—whether to the traditional gods or to their imperial agents. We are reminded during every public festival or major holy day that we are a small minority deviating from the path followed confidently by so many—a path we, for the most part, formerly followed ourselves. But John shows us a much larger cosmic majority with whose practice we have aligned ourselves. We are not the deviants after all!

As John's visions proceed, he leads us to look at many landmarks in our city and the activities that take place in and around them quite differently as well. The majority around us are taking the worship that is due the one and only God, their maker and the creator of all that sustains their lives (Rev. 4:11), and throwing it away on "demons and idols of gold and silver and bronze and stone and wood, which can neither see nor hear nor walk about" (9:20). Our many neighbors are the ones looking in the wrong directions around a false center, aligned with "demons," the associates of Satan, the archenemy of God and of the cosmic order (see 13:4). They also continue to fail to honor the one God by continuing to live heedless of God's commandments, not turning away from "their murders or their sorceries or their fornication or their thefts" (9:21).

After the scene in God's court beyond the visible material creation is set (Rev. 4:1–11), the action that follows reminds us who has genuine authority in the present age by virtue of having authority to bring it to its close. Jesus—the "Lamb"—has won this unique authority by means of his singular achievement of redeeming a multitude of people for God's kingdom at the cost of his own life (notably, not through shedding the blood of others through conquest!). He alone can step into the space created by the angel's challenge (5:2) to take in hand the divine mandate for the conquest of the powers of this age and the establishment of God's eternal reign over the contested territory of "the kingdom of this world" (5:9–10; 11:15). The inability of any being to step into that space to take the scroll, save for the Lamb, communicates a great deal about the limits even on the emperors' power, living or dead and divinized! Indeed, the absence of Rome's deified emperors from John's vision of heaven may be significant in a context in which others would speak about their presence there. John *will* find a place for the Olympian gods and the emperors in his cosmos, of course, but not in any place that resembles their vaunted heaven.

Heavenly scenes of acclamation of the Creator and the Redeemer give way to the dramatic action of the book, a narrative account of how the

Figure 11.3. A Roman-period balance (cf. Rev. 6:5–6).
Author photo, courtesy of the Bergama Museum, Türkiye.

forces of God and the Lamb break into and overrun the spaces of our city, the province, and the empire as a whole. It is a relentless narrative of a future in which everything that is out of alignment with the true center of the cosmos is either brought back into alignment or else eliminated, if it persists in supporting the rebellion in which Satan has enmeshed the inhabitants of the earth. In John's visionary unveiling of this future, real power belongs to God and to the Lamb, not to the powers of this age. John will not keep us in suspense about this: Already by the breaking of the sixth seal we see the end of the story and the powerlessness and abject terror of all the "great ones" that strut about upon the stage of history for their brief hour. Seals, trumpets, and bowls offer a pervasive portrayal of a world standing under the threat of God's imminent judgment, not a world enjoying the favor of "the gods" as the public discourse would have us believe.

As John's visions unfold, we are reminded of all the causes that have provoked the "wrath" of God and the Lamb (Rev. 6:16–17). By this point, John has drawn attention to one important cause that he will continue to

Figure 11.5. A pair of bronze incense shovels from the early Roman period (cf. Rev. 8:3, 5).
Author photo, courtesy of the Israel Museum, Jerusalem.

Figure 11.4. A fragmentary, first-century AD relief of a scene from a gymnasium. An athlete holds a large palm branch, a symbol of his victory in a recent contest (cf. Rev. 7:9).
Author photo, courtesy of the British Museum, England.

underscore: the murder of God's faithful ones, whose blood cries out for vindication (6:9–11; 16:5–7; 17:6; 18:24; 19:2). Near the end of the sequence of trumpets, he will draw attention to a second: the perseverance of the majority of earth's inhabitants in the idolatrous worship everywhere in evidence in our own and neighboring cities (9:20–21) and, as a corollary, their stubborn refusal to give honor to the God to whom worship is in fact due (14:6–7; 16:9, 11). The scene of abject terror on the day of the Lord (6:12–17) gives way to a vision of the Church Triumphant, the "innumerable multitude" drawn from every nation, language, and people group gathered in worship before God and the Lamb and sheltered by them for eternity (7:9–17; see fig. 11.4). The vast scope of the Lamb's redemption and the kingdom into which we have been inducted again infuses the twenty of us gathered in a Christ-follower's house with boldness.

The seven trumpets sound and reveal what happens when God begins to take back his gifts (in creation) and to withdraw his protection (in restraining the demonic hordes) from the many who have proven ungrateful to the only God.[2] Rome boasts that it needs no walls, for the armies on its frontiers are

2. I draw this as an inference from the failure of the result *expected* to eventuate following these plagues—namely, the masses turning away from their idols and demons to honor *and* obey the one Creator God (Rev. 9:20–21).

its walls. But there are frontiers that Rome cannot guard. It has no protection against the demonic frontiers that could collapse at God's command. We hear the announcement that follows the sounding of the final trumpet as a proclamation of the end of Rome's empire that exposes the lie of its vaunted "eternal" destiny as the agent of the gods (Rev. 11:15). It is God and his Anointed—the crucified and risen Jesus—who will exercise truly *eternal* rule (so also 19:1–2, 6–7a). John has already shown us in his opening vision of the glorified Christ that Jesus is the Danielic "Son of Man" who will inherit the kingdoms of the world (Rev. 1:12–16; cf. Dan. 7:9–14) and share the rule with God's holy ones (Rev. 5:10; cf. Dan. 7:27).

The centerpiece of John's letter turns the public story about the emperors on its head as we hear John rewrite the stories about the origins and nature of Roman imperial rule (Rev. 12:1–13:18). We hear him recast the myth of Leto, Apollo, and Python, now aligning the imperial household with the monster rather than with the divine child.[3]

The emperors are not the provision of a benign providence for the good ordering of the human realm, as a proclamation concerning our calendar claimed a century ago and as the hymns offered to the emperors in their temples continue to promote. Rather, they emerge as an instrument of Satan as he continues in rebellion against God, seeking to draw as many of God's creatures as possible into that rebellion through the webs of deceit that he spins. He draws together the majority from "every tribe and people and language and nation" under the sway and the spell of Roma and its emperors (Rev. 13:7) to marvel at and worship them and the demonic forces that undergird their rule (13:4). Everywhere we travel in the eastern empire we see manifestations of the imperial cult. It has indeed proven its value as a vehicle for the legitimation of the emperors' rule and for the unification of the disparate people groups under its aegis (13:11–17). Part of the "unveiling" that Revelation offers concerns what participation in the imperial cult and the cults of the gods who uphold Roman rule really entails: It means worshiping Satan, "the ancient serpent," and worshiping his infernal tool for involving the world in his rebellion against God!

Augustus and his successors, moreover, were not the beginning of a golden age but the end of a corrupted age, part of the period of decline preceding God's renewal of all things. John's visions reveal this when the four beasts of Daniel 7 are merged together into the beast from the sea. The heads of

3. This is not unique to John's text. Seneca (*Octavia* 237–41) does the same in regard to Nero, and Dio Chrysostom (*Or.* 1.67–84) does the same in regard to Domitian. See Maier, *Apocalypse Recalled*, 243.

this empire are just another of the same that human beings have always experienced and that God's people have always had to endure—only worse, combining into itself all the bestial characteristics of its predecessors. What masquerades as piety, a virtue often associated with the emperors, particularly as "chief priest" (*Pontifex Maximus*) of the Roman world, is a slanderous affront to the one God and his heavenly court (Rev. 13:1, 5–6). All the labels applied to them in the inscriptions and hymns that flood our senses regularly—a god, son of a god, savior, lord—are in fact "slanderous names" stolen from God and his Anointed.

John doesn't downplay the beast's power but rather affirms the message of such visual rhetoric as we might encounter in Aphrodisias's Sebasteion as we see the array of peoples, lands, and nations conquered or otherwise absorbed into the beast's empire (Rev. 13:7). "Who can make war against him," indeed (13:4)? John doesn't let us forget, however, that the rhetoric of "peace" that is so prominent in expressions of the benefits of this empire merely masks the fact that empire has been created and continues to be maintained by violence, bloodshed, and war (6:9–11; 11:7; 13:7; 16:5–7; 17:6; 18:23–24). Our neighbors know this truth as well, of course. Even so highly placed a figure as the Roman senator and historian Tacitus could imagine a foreign chieftain warning his people: "To violence, rapine, and plunder they give the name 'government'; they make a desert and call it 'peace'" (*Agr.* 30, my trans.).

Satan conjures a second hench-beast—not one that we see emerging from afar, as from the sea, but one that emerges from the land in which we sit. In order to see what John is labeling a cult of an image of this beast that exercises unmatched military strength and rules over a multiethnic, multilingual empire, we need look no further than the provincial and local temples of the emperors and the activity that takes place in conjunction with their worship. John does not give enough detail here for us to know precisely what our minds should latch on to in our locality regarding this image of a second beast, but we know John is indicting *some* aspect of the local mechanisms that promote the imperial cult—like the *Koinon Asias*, for example, which is responsible for the much-celebrated provincial cult. We recognize "the indigenous collaboration" without which "imperialism cannot survive" (cf. Rev. 13:11–18).[4]

We witness the hosts of heaven and every creature worshiping God and the Lamb (Rev. 4:1–5:13). We see the great majority of earth dwellers worshiping the beast and the demonic power that upholds it (13:1–18). We hear an angel calling earth dwellers to worship God as is both right, since he is the source of all that is, and prudent, since "the hour of his judgment" arrives

4. Carey, "Book of Revelation," 166.

(14:6–7). John calls this summons an *euangelion*, often just "welcome news" but in some contexts a proclamation of an accession to power and a change in world rule. This seems like one of those times (11:15)!

Worship is where John draws the battle lines before us, in regard to which no retreat and no surrender seem to be possible, given what is at stake—namely, "keeping the commandments of God and holding fast to the testimony of Jesus" (Rev. 12:17) or "obeying God's commandments and keeping faith with Jesus" (14:12). The first and foremost of these commandments, of course, prohibits the worship of any god besides the one God (Exod. 20:2–6; Deut. 5:6–9)—a prohibition reinforced throughout the Jewish Scriptures, the extrabiblical tradition, and the New Testament writings.[5] How, where, and what we worship is the core of witness. Our choices here will determine whether we will bear witness to God and his Anointed in their uniqueness and their absolute claims on us or live out a divided witness that is, in the end, no witness at all. John acknowledges the very real costs of loyalty and witness (Rev. 2:8–11; 6:9–11; 11:3–13; 13:15–17; etc.) but also affirms the far greater rewards of the same (7:9–17; 14:1–5, 13; 15:1–4; 21:1–22:5)—and the far greater costs of breaking faith with God to align oneself with the pawns of God's enemy (6:12–17; 8:1–9:21; 14:9–11; 16:1–21; 19:19–21).

The Creator takes away what remains of the life-sustaining gifts of creation from the ungrateful, who merely confirm themselves in their ingratitude, and "Babylon" collapses into three parts (Rev. 16:19). John's boldness in the material that follows astounds us. We immediately connect a city that sits on seven hills and has "authority over the kings of the earth" (17:9, 18) with Rome, but the figure we see stands a world apart from the image of the goddess in the Temple of Roma and Augustus downtown or her portrayal on the reverse of so many coin issues. When John draws the veil from the goddess, he reveals her to be an insatiable prostitute, successfully seducing the world's elite and drawing them into partnerships that serve

Figure 11.6. A ritual libation bowl (*phialē*, cf. Rev. 16:1, 2, 3, etc.) from the Roman period, likely the second century AD. Author photo, courtesy of the Israel Museum, Jerusalem.

5. See deSilva, *Discovering Revelation*, 141.

her craving for wealth and luxury. Then he sets Roman imperialism beneath the lenses of the Hebrew prophets and their critiques of the practices of earlier seats of empire (particularly Tyre and historical Babylon in Isa. 13; 21; 23; Jer. 25:12–38; 50–51; Ezek. 26–28), further peeling away the veneer of the popularized images and mythology concerning Rome and her rule that surround us and showing these to be part of a grand deception that has succeeded in fooling the majority of our neighbors. And once again John is confirming for us that the rise of Rome was not the beginning of a new age for the world but rather another movement in the tired symphony of the present evil age. What had been true of empires past was equally, if not more, true of Rome's empire. And the judgment that had long since historically befallen these empires presses upon us an implicit argument from historical precedent: The same causes will bring down the same consequences where Rome is concerned.

As we listen to John's indictment, he reminds us again of Rome's violence, the means by which empire was forged and continues to be maintained, the final argument against dissenters against the imperial order, who call its legitimacy and its mechanisms of legitimation (like its propaganda of providence and peace) into question. Our brother Antipas was one. The many Christ-followers murdered by Nero in Rome were among them. More dissenters—"witnesses"—will follow.

John dwells at some length on Rome's parasitic economy, which siphons off the wealth, resources, and produce of its provinces empire-wide. Who prospers under this system? Those who facilitate Rome's parasitism through trade, shipping, and the like (Rev. 18:9–19). Perhaps the images of seduction and fornication become relevant here as those local authorities and elites who ought to have looked after the prosperity of the people in their own cities and villages are happy to facilitate their exploitation instead, as they have grown accustomed themselves to the benefits Roman rule has brought them. We might wish to object that Rome has also intervened financially on Asia's behalf when stricken by earthquakes or famines—the face of the Roman economy that both imperial and local elites loved to publicize—but we suspect John would tell us that Rome was simply giving emergency aid to a productive milk cow that it wanted to continue milking.

Dressing up the goddess Roma as a prostitute already communicated a great deal concerning the distance between the image Rome projected of itself and Rome's appearance in God's sight. John, however, takes further issue with Rome's self-aggrandizing ideology, admittedly embraced and reinforced quite willingly among provincials, especially the provincial elite. But our local leaders and neighbors claim for Rome what has never belonged to

Author photo, courtesy of the Louvre, France.

Figure 11.7. An *aulētēs*, a musician who plays the *aulos*, a pair of reed pipes (cf. the "flute" players whose song is silenced in Rev. 18:22). From a vase with Dionysiac scenes dated to the late first century BC, found in the area of Athens.

any worldly power—empire without limits in terms of space or time. The ideology captured in the speech of Revelation 18:7–8, modeled after speech placed on historic Babylon's lips in Isaiah 47:8 (again, the implicit argument from historical precedent), will be proven false (Rev. 18:2–3, 9–20). It is God alone who allots times and seasons to kingdoms (Dan. 2:21; 4:32), and history has never known a kingdom whose rise was not followed by its fall.

We are struck and, if truth be told, not a little put off by John's depiction of the dreadful and ironic fate that awaits *Roma*. The Romans loved to parade their images of the provinces as stripped and subjugated women (as in the reliefs of Claudius subduing Brittania or Nero subduing Armenia in the Sebasteion in Aphrodisias). John unveils an image of his own—*Roma*, stripped, devoured, consumed in a great conflagration (Rev. 17:16–17). The image of the goddess-qua-prostitute morphs into the image of a city going up in smoke (18:2–3, 9–20). The eschatology that John proclaims is a direct attack on the *absence* of eschatology in discourse about Rome wherever we might travel in Asia. Everything in these chapters motivates us to consider the angel's summons on God's behalf very carefully and to comply in every facet of our engagement: "Come out of her, my people, in order that you may not participate with her in her sins, in order that you may not receive a share in her plagues, for her sins have piled up as high as heaven, and God has called into remembrance her acts of injustice" (18:4–5). We have to face the sober fact that we cannot profit from a system forged and sustained in injustice without also participating in its punishment.

The scenes that follow give us further assurance that the Christ to whom we have committed ourselves is *indeed* "king of kings and lord of lords" (Rev. 17:14; 19:16), and the emperor is not, despite the authority he and his predecessors have exercised over all the lands around the Mediterranean—which the Romans simply call "Our Sea" (*Mare Nostrum*). The powerlessness of the "beast" before Christ at his coming at the head of the armies of heaven is on display in the effortlessness with which Christ disposes of these awe-inspiring entities, again boosting our confidence to align with Christ in the face of these powers (19:19–21). The reward of reigning together with Christ is promised to those who have lived as loyal witnesses in the "meanwhile" of our time (20:4–6).

One final scene at the hinge of the ages reaffirms the ultimate hierarchy of accountability (Rev. 20:11–15). It is no matter that the majority around us remain heedless of the God of Israel: The *Pantokratōr* does not require their consent. God's judgment of all whom God has made is a pervasive theme of the Jewish and Christian Scriptures (e.g., Pss. 96:10, 13; 98:9; Matt. 25:31–46; Rom. 2:5–11; 2 Cor. 5:9–10). This accountability and its eternal consequences are foundational tenets of the Christ cult (as in Heb. 6:2–3); if we disagreed, we would have already disassociated ourselves from this unpopular movement.

We are exhausted by this point. The work has played relentlessly upon not only our minds but also our emotions. But the last episodes of John's vision stir up a renewed energy within us. What John describes is what the dawning of a golden age truly looks like, as opposed to the "more of the same, but worse" that John had showed Roman imperial rule to be in Revelation 13 and 17–18. John's vision also shows the so-called golden age to have been, at best, merely gilt. Death, grief, lament, and pain—the coming of Augustus and his successors hadn't resolved any of these ongoing realities of human existence (and, in fact, aggravated all of these for a great many people). But when "the kingdom of this world has become the kingdom of our God and of his Anointed" (Rev. 11:15), the worm at the core of human existence will have been excised at last. The dimensions and grandeur of God's New Jerusalem stuns. If it were to land with its center over our city, its eastern wall would cover Rome and its western wall would reach the Euphrates River. Once again Rome's greatest pretensions pale before the grandeur of what the one true God can bring into being. The vision is interspersed with warnings about the kinds of behavior that leave one excluded from God's future. John's challenge to us could not be clearer: Live now here in Ephesus or Pergamum so as to be welcomed into the New Jerusalem rather than shut out.

Even secondhand experience of John's visions explains the glorified Christ's staunch opposition to the Christian teachers in our midst who have been pursuing compromise with our neighbors' expectations concerning the worship of gods other than the one God (Rev. 2:6, 14–15, 20–21). Our loyalty, obedience, and thereby *witness* cannot be compromised, no matter the cost. The refrain that we heard in those prophetic oracles—"to the one who conquers"—and the references throughout the visions to "those who conquered" strategically frame our situation as a contest or, perhaps more properly, a battle with indispensable goals to be achieved and antagonists to be accurately identified and resisted, which John's unveiling has allowed us to continue to do. Both the oracles and the visions have filled out the pictures of what "winning" and "losing" look like in the context of Roman Asia. Winning looks like uncompromised witness, even if it leads to death as it did for Antipas (2:13) and for many other loyal followers of Jesus (6:9–11; 17:6; 18:23–24; 19:2). Perhaps the most ominous disclosure in John's Revelation is that the tally of such witnesses is not yet complete and that the tensions leading to such obedience and loyalty unto death will increase significantly. But such obedience and loyalty unto death is also a participation in the heavenly armies' victory over Satan, the ancient serpent (12:10–12), and a victory that brings particular honors and rewards (20:4–6).

It is for the people in precisely this context that Revelation spread out the larger canopy of the spaces beyond everyday realities (the spaces of God's throne room and the spaces of the infernal regions) as well as the larger canopy of time beyond normal time (the dragon's ancient rebellion and God's forthcoming judgments on the powers that the dragon has mobilized and all who have given their allegiance to these powers), all to illumine the "here and now" of those audiences. And Revelation's interest in the past and the future was primarily about shaping John's audiences' allegiances and practices in their ongoing "present," the "meanwhile" that has now extended almost two millennia. Moving from the field of biblical studies to the field of church history, we know that John's word—alongside the word of many other voices—had its desired effect. Christ-followers throughout the empire chose to suffer execution rather than break faith with "the One who sits on the throne and the Lamb" (Rev. 5:13), and this witness would cause many to "fear God and give him glory . . . and worship the One who made heaven and earth and sea and springs of water" (14:7). Witness after the manner of the costly, self-giving sacrifice of the Lamb whom they followed would succeed in this regard where any outpouring of plagues would, according to John's unveiling, fail (9:20–21; 16:9, 11, 21).

BIBLIOGRAPHY

Arnold, Irene R. "Festivals of Ephesus." *American Journal of Archaeology* 76 (1972): 17–22.

Ascough, Richard S. "Greco-Roman Religions in Sardis and Smyrna." In Ascough, *Religious Rivalries*, 40–52.

———, ed. *Religious Rivalries and the Struggle for Success in Sardis and Smyrna.* Waterloo, ON: Wilfrid Laurier University Press, 2005.

Astin, A. E., F. W. Walbank, M. W. Frederiksen, and R. M. Ogilvie, eds. *Rome and the Mediterranean to 133 B.C.* 2nd ed. Vol. 8 of *The Cambridge Ancient History.* Cambridge: Cambridge University Press, 1989.

Aune, David E. *Revelation 1–5*. Word Biblical Commentary 52A. Dallas: Word Books, 1997.

———. *Revelation 6–16*. Word Biblical Commentary 52B. Nashville: Nelson, 1998.

Aurenhammer, Maria. "Sculptures of Gods and Heroes from Ephesus." In H. Koester, *Ephesos*, 251–80.

Bagnall, Roger S., Burak Yolaçan, Roberta Casagrande-Kim, Akin Ersoy, and Cumhur Tanriver, eds. *Graffiti from the Basilica in the Agora of Smyrna*. New York: New York University Press, 2016.

Balch, David L. "'A Woman Clothed with the Sun' and the 'Great Red Dragon' Seeking to 'Devour Her Child' (Rev 12:1, 4) in Roman Domestic Art." In *The New Testament and Early Christian Literature in Greco-Roman Context: Studies in Honor of David E. Aune*, edited by John Fotopoulos, 287–314. Leiden: Brill, 2006.

Bammer, Anton. "Recent Excavations at the Altar of Artemis in Ephesus." *Archaeology* 27 (1974): 202–5.

Bang, Peter Fibiger. "A Forum on Trade." In *The Cambridge Companion to the Roman Economy*, edited by Walter Scheidel, 296–303. Cambridge: Cambridge University Press, 2012.

Barclay, John M. G. *Jews in the Mediterranean Diaspora from Alexander to Trajan (323 BCE–117 CE)*. Berkeley: University of California Press, 1996.

Bauckham, Richard. *The Climax of Prophecy: Studies on the Book of Revelation*. London: T&T Clark, 1993.

Beale, Gregory K. *The Book of Revelation*. New International Greek Testament Commentary. Grand Rapids: Eerdmans, 1999.

Beitzel, Barry J., ed. *Lexham Geographic Commentary on Acts Through Revelation*. Bellingham, WA: Lexham, 2019.

Biguzzi, Giancarlo. "Ephesus, Its Artemision, Its Temple to the Flavian Emperors, and Idolatry in Revelation." *Novum Testamentum* 40 (1998): 276–90.

Birol, Hümeyra. "The Roman Temple on the Acropolis of Alaşehir (Philadelphia): The Study and Proposals related to Restitution and Conservation of the Existing Remains." Unpublished MA Thesis, Dokuz Eylül University, Türkiye.

Bowman, Alan K. "Provincial Administration and Taxation." In Bowman, Champlin, and Lintott, *Augustan Empire*, 344–70.

Bowman, Alan K., Edward Champlin, and Andrew Lintott, eds. *The Augustan Empire, 43 B.C.—A.D. 69*. 2nd ed. Vol. 10 of *The Cambridge Ancient History*. Cambridge: Cambridge University Press, 1996.

Bowman, Alan K., Peter Garnsey, and Dominic Rathbone, eds. *The High Empire, A.D. 70–192*. 2nd ed. Vol. 11 of *The Cambridge Ancient History*. Cambridge: Cambridge University Press, 2000.

Boxall, Ian. *Patmos in the Reception History of the Apocalypse*. New York: Oxford University Press, 2013.

———. "Reading the Apocalypse on the Island of Patmos." *Scripture Bulletin* 40 (2010): 22–33.

Broughton, T. Robert S. "Roman Asia." In vol. 4 of *An Economic Survey of Ancient Rome*, edited by Tenney Frank, 499–918. Baltimore: Johns Hopkins Press, 1938.

Burrell, Barbara. *Neokoroi: Greek Cities and Roman Emperors*. Boston: Brill, 2004.

Cadwallader, Alan H. "The Lust for Recognition and Influence: Laodikeia and the Quest for Neokorate Status." In *Revelation and Material Religion in the Roman East: Essays in Honor of Steven J. Friesen*, edited by Nathan Leach, Daniel Charles Smith, and Tony Keddie, 241–57. New York: Routledge, 2024.

Cahill, Nicholas D., ed. *Love for Lydia: A Sardis Anniversary Volume Presented to Crawford H. Greenewalt, Jr.* Cambridge, MA: Harvard University Press, 2008.

Carandini, Andrea, ed. *The Atlas of Ancient Rome: Biography and Portraits of the City*. 2 vols. Rev. ed. Princeton: Princeton University Press, 2017.

Carey, Greg. "The Book of Revelation as Counter-Imperial Script." In *In the Shadow of Empire: Reclaiming the Bible as a History of Faithful Resistance*, edited by Richard A. Horsley, 157–76. Louisville: Westminster John Knox, 2008.

———. *Rereading Revelation: Theology, Ethics, and Resistance*. Grand Rapids: Eerdmans, 2025.

Casson, Lionel. *Libraries in the Ancient World*. New Haven: Yale University Press, 2001.

Cicero. *Philippics*. Translated by Walter Ker. LCL. Cambridge, MA: Harvard University Press, 1957.

Cimok, Fatih. *Pergamum*. Istanbul: Turizm Yayınları, 1993.

Claridge, Amanda. *Rome: An Oxford Archaeological Guide*. 2nd ed. Oxford: Oxford University Press, 2010.

Collins, John J. "The Sibylline Oracles." In *The Old Testament Pseudepigrapha*, vol. 1, *Apocalyptic Literature and Testaments*, edited by J. H. Charlesworth, 317–472. Garden City, NJ: Doubleday, 1983.

Connolly, Peter, and Hazel Dodge. *The Ancient City: Life in Classical Athens and Rome*. Oxford: Oxford University Press, 1998.

Cooley, Alison E. *Res Gestae Divi Augusti: Text, Translation, and Commentary*. Cambridge: Cambridge University Press, 2009.

Cottier, M., M. Crawford, C. V. Crowther, J.-L. Ferrary, B. M. Levick, O. Salomies, and M. Wörrle, eds. *The Customs Law of Asia*. Oxford: Oxford University Press, 2009.

Coudry, Marianne, and François Kirbihler. "La lex Cornelia, une lex provinciae de Sylla pour l'Asie." In *Administrer les provinces de la République romaine*, edited by N. Barrandon and F. Kirbihler, 133–69. Rennes: Presses Universitaires, 2010.

Crook, J. A., Andrew Lintott, and Elizabeth Rawson, eds. *The Last Age of the Roman Republic, 146–43*. 2nd ed. Vol. 9 of *The Cambridge Ancient History*. Cambridge: Cambridge University Press, 1992.

Crouch, Dora. *Water Management in the Ancient Greek Cities*. Oxford: Oxford University Press, 1993.

Cuss, Dominique. *Imperial Cult and Honorary Terms in the New Testament*. Fribourg: University Press, 1974.

D'Andria, Francesco. *Hierapolis of Phyrgia: An Archaeological Guide*. Istanbul: Ege Yayınları, 2003.

———. "The Ploutonion of Hierapolis in Light of Recent Research (2013–17)." *Journal of Roman Archaeology* 31 (2018): 90–129.

Danker, Frederick W. *Benefactor: Epigraphic Study of a Graeco-Roman and New Testament Semantic Field*. St. Louis: Clayton House, 1982.

deSilva, David A. *Archaeology and the Ministry of Paul*. Grand Rapids: Baker Academic, 2025.

———. *Discovering Revelation: Content, Interpretation, Reception*. Grand Rapids: Eerdmans, 2021.

———. *Seeing Things John's Way: The Rhetoric of the Book of Revelation*. Louisville: Westminster John Knox, 2009.

———. *Unholy Allegiances: Heeding Revelation's Warning*. Peabody, MA: Hendrickson, 2013.

———. *A Week in the Life of Ephesus*. Downers Grove, IL: IVP Academic, 2020.

Dio Cassius. *Roman History*. Vol. 6, *Books 51–55*. Translated by Ernest Cary. LCL 83. Cambridge, MA: Harvard University Press, 1960.

Dumser, Elisha A. "The Urban Topography of Rome." In Erdkamp, *Cambridge Companion to Ancient Rome*, 131–50.

Dunn, James D. G. *The Acts of the Apostles*. London: Epworth, 1996.

Eck, Werner. "Provincial Administration and Finance." In Bowman, Garnsey, and Rathbone, *High Empire*, 266–92.

Edelstein, Emma J., and Ludwig Edelstein, trans. *Asclepius: A Collection and Interpretation of the Testimonies*. New York: Arno, 1975.

Edwards, James R. "The Rider on the White Horse, the Thigh Inscription, and Apollo: Revelation 19:16." *Journal of Biblical Literature* 137 (2018): 519–36.

Erdemgil, Selahattin, A. Evren, Ö. Özeren, et al. *The Terrace Houses in Ephesus*. Istanbul: Hitit Color, 1988.

Erdkamp, Paul, ed. *The Cambridge Companion to Ancient Rome*. Cambridge: Cambridge University Press, 2013.

———. "The Food Supply of the Capital." In Erdkamp, *Cambridge Companion to Ancient Rome*, 262–77.

Errington, R. M. "Rome Against Philip and Antiochus." In Astin, Walbank, Frederiksen, and Ogilvie, *Rome and the Mediterranean*, 244–89.

Fairchild, Mark R. *Christian Origins in Ephesus and Asia Minor*. Peabody, MA: Hendrickson, 2017.

Falconi, Marta. "Nero's Rotating Banquet Hall Unveiled in Rome." Phys.org, September 29, 2009. https://phys.org/news/2009-09-nero-rotating-banquet-hall-unveiled.html.

Fant, Clyde E., and Mitchell G. Reddish. *A Guide to Biblical Sites in Greece and Turkey*. Oxford: Oxford University Press, 2003.

Friesen, Steven. *Imperial Cults and the Apocalypse of John: Reading Revelation in the Ruins*. Oxford: Oxford University Press, 2001.

———. *Twice Neokoros: Ephesus, Asia and the Cult of the Flavian Imperial Family*. Leiden: Brill, 1993.

Galsterer, Hartmut. "Local and Provincial Institutions and Government." In Bowman, Garnsey, and Rathbone, *High Empire*, 344–60.

Gaston, Lloyd. "Jewish Communities in Sardis and Smyrna." In Ascough, *Religious Rivalries*, 17–24.

Grant, Frederick C. *Hellenistic Religions: The Age of Syncretism*. New York: Liberal Arts, 1957.

Graves, David. "What Is the Madder with Lydia's Purple? A Reexamination of the *Purpurarii* in Thyatira and Philippi." *Near East Archaeological Society Bulletin* 62 (2017): 64–91.

Griffin, Miriam. *Nero: End of a Dynasty*. London: Batsford, 1984.

Guidobaldi, Paola. *The Roman Forum*. Milan: Electa, 1997.

Guizzi, Francesco. "Greek and Latin Inscriptions of Laodikeia on the Lykos 2003–2018." In *15. Yılında Laodikeia (2003–2018)*, edited by Celal Şimşek, 165–80. Istanbul: Ege Yayınları, 2019.

Habicht, Christian. "New Evidence on the Province of Asia." *Journal of Roman Studies* 65 (1975): 64–91.

———. "The Seleucids and Their Rivals." In Astin, Walbank, Frederiksen, and Ogilvie, *Rome and the Mediterranean*, 324–87.

Hanfmann, George M. A., Louis Robert, and William E. Mierse. "The Hellenistic Period." In Hanfmann, Robert, and Mierse, *Sardis from Prehistoric Times to Roman Times*, 109–38.

———, eds. *Sardis from Prehistoric Times to Roman Times—Results of the Archaeological Exploration of Sardis, 1958–1975*. Cambridge, MA: Harvard University Press, 1983.

Hanfmann, George M. A., Pikret K. Yegül, and John S. Crawford. "The Roman and Late Antique Period." In Hanfmann, Robert, and Mierse, *Sardis from Prehistoric Times to Roman Times*, 139–67.

Harland, Philip A. *Associations, Synagogues, and Congregations: Claiming a Place in Ancient Mediterranean Society*. Minneapolis: Fortress, 2003.

———. "Honouring the Emperor or Assailing the Beast: Participation in Civic Life Among Associations (Jewish, Christian and Other) in Asia Minor and the Apocalypse of John." *Journal for the Study of the New Testament* 77 (2000): 99–121.

Harrison, James R. "The City of Rome from the Late Republic to the Julio-Claudian Period: An Epigraphic, Archaeological, and Numismatic Portrait." In Harrison and Welborn, *First Urban Churches* 6, 1–66.

———. "An Epigraphic Portrait of Ephesus and Its Villages." In Harrison and Welborn, *First Urban Churches* 3, 1–67.

Harrison, James R., and L. L. Welborn, eds. *The First Urban Churches 3: Ephesus*. Atlanta: SBL Press, 2018.

———. *The First Urban Churches 5: Colossae, Hierapolis, and Laodicea*. Atlanta: SBL Press, 2019.

———. *The First Urban Churches 6: Rome and Ostia*. Atlanta: SBL Press, 2021.

Hemer, Colin J. *The Letters to the Seven Churches of Asia in Their Local Setting*. Sheffield: JSOT Press, 1986. Repr., Grand Rapids: Eerdmans, 2001.

———. "The Sardis Letter and the Croesus Tradition." *New Testament Studies* 19 (1972–73): 94–97.

Henslin, Peter. "Augustus, Domitian and the So-Called Horologium Augusti." *Journal of Roman Studies* 97 (2007): 1–20.

Hind, John G. F. "Mithridates." In Crook, Lintott, and Rawson, *Last Age*, 129–64.

Horsley, G. H. R. "The Inscriptions of Ephesus and the New Testament." *Novum Testamentum* 24 (1992): 105–68.

———, ed. *New Documents Illustrating Early Christianity*. Vol. 1, *A Review of the Greek Inscriptions and Papyri Published in 1976*. Sydney: Macquarie University, 1981.

———, ed. *New Documents Illustrating Early Christianity*. Vol. 3, *A Review of the Greek Inscriptions and Papyri Published in 1978*. Sydney: Macquarie University, 1983.

———, ed. *New Documents Illustrating Early Christianity*. Vol. 4, *A Review of the Greek Inscriptions and Papyri Published in 1979*. Sydney: Macquarie University, 1987.

Howard-Brook, Wes, and Anthony Gwyther. *Unveiling Empire: Reading Revelation Then and Now*. New York: Orbis Books, 2001.

Josephus. *The Jewish War*. Vol. 3, *Books IV–VII*. Translated by Henry St. John Thackeray. LCL 210. Cambridge, MA: Harvard University Press, 1928.

———. *The Jewish War*. Translated by G. A. Williamson. Revised and with a new introduction, notes, and appendices, by E. Mary Smallwood. London: Penguin, 1981.

———. *Josephus in Ten Volumes*. Vol. 8, *Books XV–XVII*. Translated by Ralph Marcus. Cambridge, MA: Harvard University Press, 1963.

Judge, E. A. "Thanksgiving to the Benefactor of the World, Tiberius Caesar." In Llewelyn, *New Documents*, 9:22.

Kampmann, Ursula. "*Homonoia* Politics in Asia Minor: The Example of Pergamum." In H. Koester, *Pergamon*, 373–94.

Kästner, Volker. "The Architecture of the Great Altar of Pergamum." In H. Koester, *Pergamon*, 137–61.

Kearsley, R. A. "A Roman Road in Asia Minor." In Llewelyn, *New Documents*, 9:23–26.

Kekeç, Tevhit. *Pergamon*. Istanbul: Hitit Color, 1990.

Kerkeslager, Allen. "Apollo, Greco-Roman Prophecy, and the Rider on the White Horse in Rev 6:2." *Journal of Biblical Literature* 112 (1993): 116–21.

Knibbe, Dieter. "*Via Sacra Ephesiaca*: New Aspects of the Cult of Artemis Ephesia." In H. Koester, *Ephesos*, 151–56.

Knight, James. "Was Roma the Scarlet Harlot? The Worship of the Goddess Roma in Sardis and Smyrna." In Ascough, *Religious Rivalries*, 104–19.

Koester, Craig R. "The Message to Laodicea and the Problem of Its Local Context: A Study of the Imagery in Rev 3.14–22." *New Testament Studies* 49 (2003): 407–24.

———. *Revelation: A New Translation with Introduction and Commentary*. New Haven: Yale University Press, 2014.

Koester, Helmut, ed. *Ephesos: Metropolis of Asia; An Interdisciplinary Approach to Its Archaeology, Religion and Culture*. Valley Forge, PA: Trinity Press International, 1995.

———, ed. *Pergamon, Citadel of the Gods: Archaeological Record, Literary Description, and Religious Development*. Harrisburg, PA: Trinity Press International, 1998.

Kraybill, J. Nelson. *Apocalypse and Allegiance: Worship, Politics, and Devotion in the Book of Revelation*. Grand Rapids: Brazos, 2010.

———. *Imperial Cult and Commerce in John's Apocalypse*. Sheffield: Sheffield Academic, 1996.

Leon, Harry J. *The Jews of Ancient Rome*. Rev. ed. Peabody, MA: Hendrickson, 1995.

Levick, Barbara. "Greece and Asia Minor." In Bowman, Garnsey, and Rathbone, *High Empire*, 604–34.

———. "Greece (Including Crete and Cyprus) and Asia Minor from 43 B.C. to A.D. 69." In Bowman, Champlin, and Lintott, *Augustan Empire*, 641–75.

Lintott, Andrew. "The Roman Empire and Its Problems in the Late Second Century." In Crook, Lintott, and Rawson, *Last Age*, 16–39.

Llewelyn, S. R., ed. *New Documents Illustrating Early Christianity*. Vol. 9, *A Review of the Greek Inscriptions and Papyri Published in 1986–87*. Grand Rapids: Eerdmans, 2002.

Llewelyn, S. R., with R. A. Kearsley, eds. *New Documents Illustrating Early Christianity*. Vol. 6, *A Review of the Greek Inscriptions and Papyri Published in 1980–81*. Sydney: Macquarie University, 1991.

Magie, David. *Roman Rule in Asia Minor to the End of the Third Century After Christ*. 2 vols. Princeton: Princeton University Press, 1950.

Maier, Harry O. *Apocalypse Recalled: The Book of Revelation After Christendom*. Minneapolis: Fortress, 2002.

Malay, Hasan. *Greek and Latin Inscriptions in the Manisa Museum*. Vienna: Österreichische Akademie der Wissenschaften, 1994.

Marshall, Anthony J. "Flaccus and the Jews of Asia (Cicero *Pro Flacco* 28.67–69)." *Phoenix* 29 (1975): 139–54.

Mason, Steve. *A History of the Jewish War: A.D. 66–74*. Cambridge: Cambridge University Press, 2016.

Master, Daniel M., ed. *The Oxford Encyclopedia of the Bible and Archaeology*. 2 vols. New York: Oxford University Press, 2013.

Mayo, Philip L. *"Those Who Call Themselves Jews": The Church and Judaism in the Apocalypse of John*. Princeton Theological Monograph Series. Eugene, OR: Pickwick, 2006.

Melfi, Milena. "The Archaeology of the Aesclepieum of Pergamum." In *In Praise of Asclepius: Aelius Aristides, Selected Prose Hymns. Introduction, Text, Translation and Interpretative Essays*, edited by Donald A. Russell, Michael Trapp, and Heinz-Günther Nesselrath, 89–114. Tübingen: Mohr Siebeck, 2016.

Mitchell, Stephen. *The Celts in Anatolia and the Impact of Roman Rule*. Vol. 1 of *Anatolia: Land, Men, and Gods in Asia Minor*. Oxford: Clarendon, 1993.

Mitten, David G., and Aimée F. Scorziello. "Reappropriating Antiquity: Some Spolia from the Synagogue at Sardis." In Cahill, *Love for Lydia*, 135–46.

Muddiman, John. *The Epistle to the Ephesians*. Black's New Testament Commentary. Peabody, MA: Hendrickson, 2001.

Murphy-O'Connor, Jerome. *St. Paul's Ephesus: Texts and Archaeology*. Collegeville, MN: Liturgical Press, 2008.

Neufeld, Dietmar. "Christian Communities in Sardis and Smyrna." In Ascough, *Religious Rivalries*, 25–39.

Ogereau, J. "Customs Law of the Roman Province of Asia." In *New Documents Illustrating Early Christianity*. Vol. 10, *A Review of the Greek and Other Inscriptions and Papyri Published Between 1988 and 1992*, edited by S. R. Llewelyn and J. R. Harrison, 95–109. Grand Rapids: Eerdmans, 2012.

Oliver, James H. *The Ruling Power: A Study of the Roman Empire in the Second Century After Christ Through the Roman Oration of Aelius Aristides*. Transactions of the American Philosophical Society. New Series—volume 43, part 4. Philadelphia: American Philosophical Society, 1953.

Parker, Cyndi. "The Social and Geographical World of Laodicea." In Beitzel, *Lexham Geographic Commentary*, 684–96.

Pedley, John G. *Ancient Literary Sources on Sardis*. Cambridge, MA: Harvard University Press, 1972.

Pescarin, Sofia. *Rome: A Guide to the Eternal City*. New York: Barnes & Noble Books, 2000.

Pfeiffer, Charles F., and Howard F. Vos. *The Wycliffe Historical Geography of Bible Lands*. Chicago: Moody, 1967.

Picón, Carlos A., and Seán Hemingway, eds. *Pergamon and the Hellenistic Kingdoms of the Ancient World*. New York: The Metropolitan Museum of Art, 2016.

Pons, Mariona Vernet. "The Origin of the Name Sepharad: A New Interpretation." *Journal of Semitic Studies* 59 (2014): 297–313.

Price, S. R. F. *Rituals and Power: The Roman Imperial Cult in Asia Minor*. Cambridge: Cambridge University Press, 1984.

Radice, Betty. *The Letters of the Younger Pliny*. London: Penguin Books, 1963.

Ramsey, William. *The Letters to the Seven Churches*. Updated edition. Edited by Mark Wilson. Peabody, MA: Hendrickson, 1994.

Rapske, Brian. "Exiles, Islands, and the Identity and Perspective of John in Revelation." In *Christian Origins and Greco-Roman Culture: Social and Literary Context for the New Testament*, edited by Stanley E. Porter and Andrew W. Pitts, 311–46. Leiden: Brill, 2012.

Ratté, Christopher. "Reflections on the Urban Development of Hellenistic Sardis." In Cahill, *Love for Lydia*, 125–33.

Richardson, John. "The Administration of the Empire." In Crook, Lintott, and Rawson, *Last Age*, 564–98.

Roberts, Alexander, and James Donaldson, eds. *The Ante-Nicene Fathers*. Vol. 4. New York: Scribner's Sons, 1913.

Rogers, Guy MacLean. "An Ephesian Tale: Mystery Cults, Reverse Theological Engineering, and the Triumph of Christianity in Ephesus." In Harrison and Welborn, *First Urban Churches 3*, 69–91.

Roman, Luke. "Martial and the City of Rome." *Journal of Roman Studies* 100 (2010): 88–117.

Saffrey, H. D. "Relire L'Apocalypse à Patmos." *Revue Biblique* 82 (1975): 385–417.

Scherrer, Peter. "The City of Ephesos from the Roman Period to Late Antiquity." In H. Koester, *Ephesos*, 1–25.

———. *Ephesus: The New Guide*. Istanbul: Ege Yayınları, 2000.

Scherrer, Steven J. "Signs and Wonders in the Imperial Cult: A New Look at a Roman Religious Institution in the Light of Rev 13:13–15." *Journal of Biblical Literature* 103 (1984): 599–610.

Schnabel, Eckhard J. "Jewish Opposition to Christians in Asia Minor in the First Century." *Bulletin for Biblical Research* 18, no. 2 (2008): 233–70.

Seager, Andrew R. "The Architecture of the Dura and Sardis Synagogues." In *The Dura-Europos Synagogue: A Re-evaluation (1932–1992)*, edited by Joseph Gutman, 79–116. Atlanta: Scholars Press, 1992.

Seager, Andrew R., and A. Thomas Kraabel. "The Synagogue and the Jewish Community." In Hanfmann, Robert, and Mierse, *Sardis from Prehistoric Times to Roman Times*, 168–90.

Segala, Elisabetta, and Ida Sciortino. *Domus Aurea*. Milan: Electa, 1999.

Shaner, Katherine A. "Ephesus." In *The Oxford Encyclopedia of the Bible and Archaeology*, edited by Daniel Master, 370–81. Oxford: Oxford University Press, 2013.

Sherwin-White, Susan, and Amelie Kuhrt. *From Samarkhand to Sardis: A New Approach to the Seleucid Empire*. London: Duckworth, 1993.

Şimşek, Celal. *Ancient City Laodikeia*. Denizli: Denizli Metropolitan Municipality, 2015.

———. "Urban Planning of Laodikeia on the Lykos in the Light of New Evidence." In *Landscape and History in the Lykos Valley: Laodikeia and Hierapolis in Phrygia*, edited by Celal Şimşek and Francesco D'Andria, 1–52. Newcastle upon Tyne: Cambridge Scholars, 2017.

Smallwood, E. Mary. *The Jews Under Roman Rule: From Pompey to Diocletian*. 2nd ed. Leiden: Brill, 1981.

Smith, R. R. R. "The Imperial Reliefs from the Sebasteion at Aphrodisias." *Journal of Roman Studies* 77 (1987): 88–138.

"Stanford Digital Forma Urbis Romae Project." Accessed January 11, 2025. https://formaurbis.stanford.edu.

"Stanford Geospatial Model of the Roman World, The." Accessed January 11, 2025. https://orbis.stanford.edu.

Stewart Lester, Olivia. "Revealed History as Prophetic Rivalry: John's Apocalypse, the Sibylline Oracles, and the Prophecy of Apollo." *Early Christianity* 10 (2019): 461–80.

Storey, Glenn R. "Housing and Domestic Architecture." Erdkamp, *Cambridge Companion to Ancient Rome*, 151–68.

Strabo. *The Geography of Strabo*. Vol. 1. Translated by Horace Leonard Jones. Cambridge, MA: Harvard University Press, 1960.

———. *The Geography of Strabo*. Vol. 6. Translated by Horace Leonard Jones. Cambridge, MA: Harvard University Press, 1960.

Suetonius. *The Twelve Caesars*. Translated by Robert Graves. New York: Penguin Books, 1979.

Tacitus. *The Annals of Imperial Rome*. Translated by Michael Grant. New York: Penguin Books, 1996.

Thompson, Leonard L. *The Book of Revelation: Apocalypse and Empire*. Oxford: Oxford University Press, 1990.

Tibor, Grüll. *Patmiaka: Two Studies on Ancient Patmos*. Budapest: Eötvös-Füzetek, 1989.

Trebilco, Paul R. *The Early Christians in Ephesus from Paul to Ignatius*. Grand Rapids: Eerdmans, 2007.

———. *Jewish Communities in Asia Minor*. Cambridge: Cambridge University Press, 1991.

———. "The Jewish Community in Ephesus and Its Interaction with Christ-Believers in the First Century CE and Beyond." In Harrison and Welborn, *First Urban Churches 3*, 93–126.

Türkoğlu, Inci. "Philadelphia in Lydia." In *International Congress on Cultural Heritage and Tourism: Proceedings 19–21 May 2017*, edited by Necmi Uyanık, T. Arat, and C. Ç. Kilinç, 549–61. Konya: Nobel Bilim, 2017.

Uzunoğlu, Hüseyin, and Zerrin Aydin Tavukçu. "Some Inscriptions from Philadelphia." *Libri* 8 (2022): 159–66.

van Henten, Jan Willem. "Dragon Myth and Imperial Ideology in Revelation 12–13." In *Reality of Apocalypse: Rhetoric and Politics in the Book of Revelation*, edited by David L. Barr, 181–203. Atlanta: Society of Biblical Literature, 2006.

van Nijf, O. "The Social World of Tax Farmers and their Personnel." In Cottier, Crawford, Crowther, et al., *Customs Law of Asia*, 279–311.

Vos, Howard F. *Archaeology in Bible Lands*. Chicago: Moody, 1977.

Wainwright, Arthur. *Mysterious Apocalypse: Interpreting the Book of Revelation*. Nashville: Abingdon, 1993.

Walters, James C. "Egyptian Religions in Ephesos." In H. Koester, *Ephesos*, 281–309.

Weima, Jeffrey A. D. *The Sermons to the Seven Churches of Revelation: A Commentary and Guide*. Grand Rapids: Baker Academic, 2021.

Wettstein, Johann Jakob. *Novum Testamentum Graece*. 2 vols. Amsterdam: Officina Dommeriana, 1752.

White, L. Michael. "Urban Development and Social Change in Imperial Ephesus." In H. Koester, *Ephesos*, 27–79.

Wilson, Mark. *Biblical Turkey: A Guide to the Jewish and Christian Sites of Asia Minor*. Istanbul: Ege Yayınları, 2010.

———. "Did the Laodiceans Drink Lukewarm Water? A Hydrological Inquiry into the Temperature Metaphor of Revelation 3:15–16." *Lycus Journal* 8 (2023): 72–87.

———. "Neither Cold nor Hot but Lukewarm: Rethinking the Temperature Metaphor in Revelation 3:15–16." *Tyndale Bulletin* 76 (2025):1–29.

———. "The Social and Geographical World of Patmos." In Beitzel, *Lexham Geographic Commentary*, 619–28.

———. "The Social and Geographical World of Philadelphia." In Beitzel, *Lexham Geographic Commentary*, 674–83.

———. "The Social and Geographical World of Thyatira." In Beitzel, *Lexham Geographic Commentary*, 655–64.

Witherington, Ben, III. *Revelation*. New Cambridge Bible Commentary. Cambridge: Cambridge University Press, 2003.

Worth, Roland H. *The Seven Cities of the Apocalypse and Greco-Asian Culture*. New York: Paulist, 1999.

———. *The Seven Cities of the Apocalypse and Roman Culture*. New York: Paulist, 1999.

Wulf-Rheidt, Ulrike. "The Hellenistic and Roman Houses of Pergamon." In H. Koester, *Pergamon*, 299–330.

Yamauchi, Edwin. *The Archaeology of New Testament Cities in Asia Minor*. Grand Rapids: Baker, 1980.

Yarbro Collins, Adela. *The Combat Myth in the Book of Revelation*. Missoula: Scholars Press, 1976.

AUTHOR INDEX

Arnold, Irene R., 60n75, 61n76
Ascough, Richard S., 69n6, 128n27, 129n34, 130n36, 130n37
Aune, David E., 27n20, 32n6, 78n26, 111n53
Aurenhammer, Maria, 53n53

Balch, David L., 27n20
Bang, Peter Fibiger, 167n3
Barclay, John M. G., 10n45
Bauckham, Richard, 78n24, 182n36
Beale, Gregory K., 78n25
Biguzzi, Giancarlo, 15n58, 58n66, 59n69, 60n72, 60n73
Birol, Hümeyra, 144n17
Bowman, Alan K., 6n23, 7n30
Boxall, Ian, 20n4, 20n5, 21n10, 22n11, 26n18
Broughton, T. Robert S., 118n13
Burrell, Barbara, 55n58, 58n67, 59n70, 59n71, 61n77, 62n78, 62n79, 62n80, 71n11, 71n12, 71n13, 75n17, 86n6, 86n8, 87n14, 88n15, 89n16, 90n18, 90n19, 128n23, 128n27, 128n28, 129n29, 129n30, 151n11

Cadwallader, Alan H., 151n13, 151n14, 152, 152n15, 152n16, 152n17
Carey, Greg, 200n4
Casson, Lionel, 97n29
Cimok, Fatih, 98n30, 101n34
Claridge, Amanda, 167n4, 169n8, 170n9, 171n10, 172n12, 172n13, 172n14, 174n15, 174n16, 184n39, 186n42, 187n45, 187n46, 188n47, 188n48, 188n49, 190n52, 190n53
Collins, John J., 8n39
Connolly, Peter, 165n1, 167n4, 187n45, 187n46, 188n48, 190n53
Cooley, Alison E., 174n17, 174n18
Cottier, M., M., 46n35
Crawford, John S., 123n6, 124n8, 124n9, 125n13, 127n18, 132n42, 132n43
Crouch, Dora, 86n5
Cuss, Dominique, 27n21

D'Andria, Franceso, 163*n*b
Danker, Frederick W., 11n46, 11n47, 174n17
deSilva, David A., 8n3, 55n59, 59n71, 64n81, 111n54, 112n56, 112n57, 163*n*a, 169n6, 181n23, 193n1, 201n5
Dodge, Hazel, 165n1, 167n4, 187n45, 187n46, 188n48, 190n53
Dumser, Elisha A., 189n50
Dunn, James D. G., 78n27

Eck, Werner, 8n33
Edwards, James R., 26n19
Erdemgil, Selahattin, 41n25
Erdkamp, Paul, 167n2
Errington, R. M., 2n1, 2n2, 3n3, 3n4

Fairchild, Mark R., 31n4, 48n41, 49n42, 49n43, 79n23, 97n28, 99n31, 99n32, 111n51
Falconi, Marta, 175n22
Friesen, Steven, 8n32, 8n35, 11n46, 12n48, 12n49, 14, 14n54, 14n55, 15n59, 15n61, 16n62, 17n65, 33n15, 34n16, 37n20, 37n21, 37n22, 55n57, 55n59, 55n60, 56n61, 58n66, 59n69, 60n72, 60n73, 61n77, 64n81, 71, 71n11, 87n12, 88, 140n9, 149n9, 193n1

Galsterer, Hartmut, 5n20, 6n21
Gaston, Lloyd, 79n29, 133n46
Grant, Frederick C., 142n14
Graves, David, 117n8, 118n9
Griffin, Miriam, 178n28
Grüll, Tibor, 21n8, 22n12, 22n14
Guidobaldi, Paola, 169n8, 171n10
Guizzi, Francesco, 151n14, 152n15
Gwyther, Anthony, 193n1

Habicht, Christian, 3n5, 3n6, 96n26
Hanfmann, George M. A., 123n6, 124n8, 124n9, 125n12, 125n13, 127n18, 127n19, 127n20, 128n24, 129n33, 130n36, 130n37, 130n39, 130n40, 132n41, 132n42, 132n43, 133n47, 136
Harland, Philip A., 45n33, 118n11, 118n12, 118n15, 119n16
Harrison, James R., 43n28, 48n38
Hemer, Colin J., 21n10, 31n3, 31n5, 66n2, 69n8, 85n3, 85n4, 87n13, 118n13, 121n1, 125n15, 129n31, 136, 136n58, 141n12, 149n8, 157n25
Hemingway, Seán, 95n23
Hind, John G. F., 4n12, 4n13, 4n14, 4n15, 5n16
Horsley, G. H. R., 8n32, 48n40, 82n33, 129n34
Howard-Brook, Wes, 193n1

Judge, E. A., 124n10

Kampmann, Ursula, 111n52
Kearsley, R. A., 35n18, 117n17
Kekeç, Tevhit, 95n24, 95n25, 97n28, 98n30, 99n33, 104n38
Kerkeslager, Allen, 26n17
Knibbe, Dieter, 53n51
Knight, James, 71n9, 87n11, 128n25
Koester, Craig R., x, x*n*2, 20n6, 21n9, 32n6, 45n33, 68n4, 69n7, 78n26, 116n5, 118n13, 118n15, 128n24, 138n6, 141n10, 154n23, 157, 157n26, 158n27, 158n31, 158n33
Kraabel, A. Thomas, 133n46, 133n48
Kraybill, J. Nelson, 37n23, 47n37, 80n31
Kuhrt, Amelie, 127n17

Levick, Barbara, 7n28, 7n31, 8n34, 8n36, 8n38, 107n46
Lintott, Andrew, 3n7, 4n11
Llewelyn, S. R., 35n18

Magie, David, 6n25, 7n27, 7n30, 7n32, 8n37, 13n52, 117n7, 118n10, 124n11, 178n24
Maier, Harry O., 199n3
Marshall, Anthony J., 148n6
Mason, Steve, 180n32
Melfi, Milena, 106n40, 107n42, 107n43, 107n44, 107n45, 108n48, 108n49, 109n50
Mierse, William E., 125n12, 127n19, 127n20, 128n24, 129n33, 130n36, 130n37, 130n39, 130n40, 132n41, 133n47, 136
Mitchell, Stephen, 113n2
Mitten, David G., 129n32, 129n33, 134n50, 134n52
Muddiman, John, 149n8
Murphy-O'Connor, Jerome, 29n1, 32n7, 32n8, 32n11, 33n13, 33n14, 35n19, 38n24, 42n26, 43n27, 44n29, 44n30, 44n31, 45n34, 49n44, 52n47, 52n48, 52n50, 53n51, 54n54, 54n55

Oliver, James H., 12n50, 15n57, 168n5

Pescarin, Sofia, 172n14
Picón, Carlos A., 95n23
Price, S. R. F., 13n53, 33n15, 35n19, 37n21, 52n49, 56n62, 56n63, 59n69, 71n10, 71n12, 72n14, 86n9, 87n10, 89n16, 128n21, 128n22, 128n26, 149n9, 151n11

Ramsey, William, 141n12
Rapske, Brian, 19n3, 20n5, 20n6, 20n7
Ratté, Christopher, 123n4, 123n5, 125n14, 130n38
Richardson, John, 4n10, 5n17, 5n18, 5n19, 6n22
Robert, Louis, 125n12, 127n19, 127n20, 128n24, 129n33, 130n36, 130n37, 130n39, 130n40, 132n41, 133n47, 136
Rogers, Guy MacLean, 35n17, 50n45, 54n56
Roman, Luke, 178n27, 186n41, 187n44

Saffrey, H. D., 21n8, 22n13, 28n22
Scherrer, Peter, 37n21, 41n25, 44n31, 44n32, 60n74
Scherrer, Steven J., 104n39
Schnabel, Eckhard J., 9n42, 10n42
Sciortino, Ida, 174n19, 175n20, 177n23, 178n26
Scorziello, Aimée F., 129n32, 129n33, 134n50, 134n52
Seager, Andrew R., 133n46, 133n48, 134n51
Segala, Elisabetta, 174n19, 175n20, 177n23, 178n26
Shaner, Katherine A., 48n38, 56n64, 58n68
Sherwin-White, Susan, 127n17

Şimşek, Celal, 145n2, 145n3, 148n5, 151n10, 151n13, 152n18, 153n19, 154n20, 154n21, 154n22, 156n24, 160n35
Smallwood, E. Mary, 80n30
Smith, R. R. R., 15n59, 15n60, 16n62, 16n63, 18
Stewart Lester, Olivia, 25n16, 26n19

Tavukçu, Zerrin Aydin, 142n15
Thompson, Leonard L., 14n54, 19n1
Trebilco, Paul R., 9n40, 9n41, 10n44, 29n1, 29n2, 32n11, 32n12, 110*n*a, 110*n*b, 110*n*c, 121n3, 123n6, 124n7, 133n46, 133n47, 135n55, 135n56n, 136n57
Türkoğlu, Inci, 141n11, 144n17

Uzunoğlu, Hüseyin, 142n15

van Henten, Jan Willem, 27n20, 27n21
van Nijf, O., 4n9, 6n26, 46n36
Vos, Howard F., 95n22, 126n16

Wainwright, Arthur, ix*n*1
Walters, James C., 50n46
Weima, Jeffrey A. D., 157n25
Wettstein, Johann Jakob, ix, ix*n*1
White, L. Michael, 32n9
Wilson, Mark, 21n8, 28n23, 31n4, 32n8, 32n10, 33n13, 33n14, 33n15, 37n21, 43n28, 48n39, 48n41, 66n2, 68n3, 74n15, 74n16, 75n18, 86n5, 87n13, 95n20, 99n31, 102n36, 113n1, 115n4, 117, 120n17, 121n2, 121n3, 128n21, 132n44, 132n45, 134n49, 134n53, 138n1, 138n2, 138n6, 140n7, 148n7, 151n13, 154n23, 158n28, 158n29, 159n34, 160n36, 160n37, 161n38
Witherington, Ben, III, 28n25
Worth, Roland H., 3n8, 5n16, 6n24, 7n27, 7n29, 7n30, 45n33, 49n43, 53n52, 57n65, 83n2, 86n7, 90n17, 95n21, 97n27, 102n37, 104n38, 108n47, 112n56, 112n57, 118n14, 130n35, 138n3, 148n4
Wulf-Rheidt, Ulrike, 101n35

Yamauchi, Edwin, 141n13
Yarbro Collins, Adela, 26n19, 27n20
Yegül, Pikret K., 123n6, 124n8, 124n9, 125n13, 127n18, 132n42, 132n43

SCRIPTURE AND ANCIENT WRITINGS INDEX

Old Testament

Exodus

3:14 110
20:2–6 201
32:32–33 137

Numbers

25:1–2 119
25:1–3 112
31:15–16 112

Deuteronomy

5:6–9 201

Psalms

96:10 204
96:13 204
98:9 204
106:37 25n15, 80, 111

Isaiah

1:1 ix
13 202
21 202
23 202
47:8 203

Jeremiah

1:1–3 ix
25:12–38 202
50–51 202

Ezekiel

26–28 202

Daniel

2:21 203
2:28 x
4:32 203
7:9–14 199
7:27 199
8:26 x
12:4–9 x

Hosea

1:1 ix

Amos

1:1 ix

New Testament

Matthew

9:34 79
24:42 126
24:43–44 126
25:13 126
25:31–46 204

Mark

13:3–24 182n37
13:35 126
13:37 126

Luke

11:15 79
21:7–25 182n37
21:20–24 182

Acts

6:1–6 22
13 78n27
16:14–15 118
16:40 118
17:5–9 78
18:12–17 78
19:1–20:1 29
19:8–10 32
19:10 29, 79
19:21–41 48
19:26 29, 78, 79
19:35 61n77, 152
21:27–29 32
28:11 172

Romans

2:5–11 204
16:3–16 166

1 Corinthians

10:20–21 25n15, 80, 111

2 Corinthians

5:9–10 204

Colossians

1:7–8 29, 78, 112n55
4:12–13 29, 78, 112n55, 149

Hebrews

6:2–3 204

Revelation

1:1 x, 193
1:1–3 ix
1:4 ix
1:5–6 194
1:9 19, 19n2
1:11 ix, xi
1:12–18 194
2:1–3:22 xi
2:5 25
2:8–11 201
2:10 81
2:13 87, 111, 112, 205

2:14–15 112, 205
2:20 25
2:20–21 205
3:1–6 125
3:5 137
3:12 140, 141
3:15–16 156
3:17 159
4:1–2 195
4:1–11 196
4:1–5:13 200
4:10 195
4:11 195, 196
5:2 196
5:8 195
5:9 194
5:9–10 196
5:10 199
5:13 195, 205
6:1–2 26
6:3–8 26
6:9 19n2
6:9–11 200, 201, 203
6:12–17 194, 198, 201
6:16–17 197
7:9–17 109, 198, 201
8:1–9:21 201
9:1–3 163
9:1–12 26
9:20 25n15, 54, 109, 196
9:20–21 28, 111, 198, 198n2, 205
9:21 196
10:1–2 18
10:5–7 18
11:3–13 201
11:7 180, 200
11:15 13, 38, 196, 199, 201, 204
12:1–6 26
12:1–13:18 199
12:9 25, 27, 111
12:10–12 205
12:14 26
12:17 x, 201
12:17–13:18 27
13:1 184, 200
13:1–4 111
13:1–10 166
13:1–18 200, 204
13:3 15, 182
13:4 15, 17, 183, 196, 199
13:5–6 200
13:7 180, 194, 199, 200
13:7–8 15, 111
13:11–17 92, 199
13:11–18 15, 200
13:12 182
13:13–14 25
13:14 182
13:15 104
13:15–17 201
14:1–5 201
14:6–7 198, 201
14:7 63, 80, 205
14:9–11 201
14:12 x, 201
14:13 201
14:14–20 194
15:1–4 201
16:1 173
16:1–21 201
16:5–7 198, 200
16:9 198, 205
16:11 205
16:17–19:10 166
16:21 205
17:1–18:24 204
17:6 180, 198, 200, 203
17:9 165
17:10–11 180n33
17:14 204
17:16–17 203
17:18 47, 180
18:1–24 167
18:2–3 203
18:4–5 204
18:7–8 203
18:9–20 202, 203
18:11–13 168
18:11–20 47
18:12–13 47
18:15–19 47
18:23–24 200, 205
18:24 183, 198
19:1–2 199
19:2 198, 205
19:6–7 199
19:11–21 194
19:16 204
19:19–21 201, 204
20:1–3 163
20:1–10 27
20:3 25
20:4 19n2
20:4–6 204, 205
20:7–10 25
20:11–15 194, 204
21:1–22:5 201
22:1–2 107
22:10 x, 193
22:17 107

Old Testament Apocrypha and Pseudepigrapha

Baruch

4:7 25n15, 80, 111

4 Ezra

12:17–18 182

Dead Sea Scrolls

1QH 2.22 79
1QM 4.9 79

Classical Authors

Aelius Aristides

On Rome

9–10 15
10–13 167–68
108–9 12

Orationes

17.8 68
17.11 68
23.24 52
48.30 109

Aeschylus

Agammemnon

1080–86 26

Anonymous

Martyrdom of Polycarp

8.2 81
9.2–3 81
19.1 144

Sibylline Oracles

1.141–45 77
4.4–7 25
4.107–8 153
4.119–27 181n33
4.133–50 181n33
4.145–48 8
4.363–69 181n33
5.12–51 77
5.28–29 181n33
5.33–35 181n33

Antipater of Sidon

Greek Anthology

9.58 51

Appian

Civil Wars

5.1.9 42n26

Mithridatic Wars

12.4.22–23 88

Arrian

Anabasis

1.17.306 121

Caesar

Civil Wars

3.33 52
3.105 52

Cicero

Philippics

11.2.5 70

Pro Flacco

28.66–69 110
28.68 148

Dio Cassius

Historiae romanae

46.7.2 80, 189
48.24.1–2 42n26
51.20.6–7 35n19, 35n21
56.27.1–2 19n3
57 37n21
57.17.8 140n8
62.20.5 27n21
66.19.3 180n33

Dio Chrysostom

Orationes

1.67–84 199n3
21.10 181n33
31.54–55 52
34.48 111n52

Eusebius

Chronicon

2.154 149

Historia ecclesiastica

2.20 19n2

Galen

De cognoscendis curandi

9 123n6

Herodotus

Histories

1.47–91 121
1.94 121
5.53–54 32

Ignatius of Antioch

To the Ephesians

1.1–2 64
2.1 64
9.1 64

Irenaeus

Against Heresies

3.3.4 60n72
5.30.1–4 77n23

Josephus

Against Apion

239 32n11

Antiquities

12.147–53 9, 133
14.196–222 9n42
14.223–30 9
14.223–40 32n11
14.225–28 32
14.235 9, 133
14.247–55 110
14.256–64 9
14.259–61 133
14.262–64 32n11
14.301–17 32n11
15.89 42n26
16.27–65 32n11
16.162–65 10
16.167–68 32
16.167–73 10
16.171 133

Jewish War

4.618 12
4.657 182
6.420 183n38
7.158–62 186
7.218 189

Jerome

De viris illustribus

9 19n2

Juvenal

Satires

13.246 20

Livy

History of Rome

38.39.11 70

Martial

Epigrams

4.64.11 165

Spectacles

2 178
2.1–12 187
2.5–8 189

Minucius Felix

Octavius

6 15
23.5 54

Nicolaus of Damascus

Life of Augustus

1 13

Orosius

Adversus paganos

7.12 149

Ovid

Fasti

4.241–44 50

Tristia

1.4.69 165

Pausanias

Description of Greece

1.24.8 26
7.2.6–9 42
7.2.8–9 62n79
7.5.1–3 66

Philo

Flaccus

1.51 19n3
1.157 19n3
1.159 19n3

Plato

Republic

437D 158

Pliny the Elder

Natural History

4.23 21
5.29.105 145, 152n17
13.21.70 97
14.9.74 138n4
34.46 178
36.21.95–97 52

Pliny the Younger

Epistulae

10.96–97 81, 92–93

Plutarch

Antony

58.5 97n29

Marius

312–13 4

Quaestiones romanae

69 165

Polybius

The Histories

4.48.7 123n4
7.18.9 123n4
8.15–21 123n4

Polycarp of Smyrna

To the Philippians

11.3 79

Seneca

Octavia

237–41 199n3

Strabo

Geography

1.3.2 172n11
12.8.16 153
12.8.18 140, 140n8
13.4.1–2 85n3
13.4.8 140n8
13.4.11 138n4
13.4.14 157–58, 163
14.1.3 42
14.1.20 35
14.1.24 31, 44
14.1.37 66, 68
14.2.29 32

Suetonius

Divus Augustus

52 86

Nero

31 175
32 180n31
38 180
39 178
57.2 181n33

Tiberius

48.2 140

Tacitus

Agricola

30 200

Annales

2.47 124n9, 140
3.66–69 8n34, 71n11
3.69 19n3
4.13 19n3
4.15 71n11
4.30 19n3
4.37 86n6
4.55–56 69, 71, 125, 149
14.15 8n34
14.27 153
15.38–42 175
15.42–43 178, 179
15.44 175, 179
15.45 180
15.71 19n3

Historiae

2.8–9 180n33
5.13 183n38

Tertullian

De praescriptione haereticorum

36 19n2

Valerius Maximus

Memorable Deeds and Sayings

1.3.2 130n35
9.2.4 38

Varro

De lingua Latina

6.24 165

Virgil

Aeneid

1.236–37 14, 111
4.232 14, 111
6.784 165
6.792–93 12

Eclogues

4.10.2026 27n21

Georgics

6.784 165

Vitruvius

De architectura

3.2.7 52
8.3.14 153

Xenophon of Ephesus

Ephesian Tale

1.2–3 53n51x

SUBJECT INDEX

Acts of John, 24
agoras, civic, 8, 15, 33–34, 36, 37, 53, 56, 68, 72–76, 116, 156, 169–71, 186
agoras, commercial, 3, 43–45, 51, 68, 95, 104, 153–54
Alexander the Great, 2, 13, 66, 83, 121, 127
altars, 28, 37, 41, 50, 52, 58–59, 75, 85, 93–95, 100, 101, 106, 108, 110, 111, 115, 126, 172–73
amphitheaters, 57, 105, 187–88
Antiochus II, 145, 148
Antiochus III, 2–3, 9, 69, 85, 113, 123, 125, 132, 133, 138
Antipas, 112, 112n57, 202, 205
Antony, Mark, 6–7, 41, 42, 97n29, 169, 170–71, 173
Aphrodisias, 5, 15–18, 55–56, 58, 60, 171, 194, 203
Aphrodite, 15, 17, 28, 50, 141. *See also* Venus
Apollo, 22, 24–27, 105–6, 108, 115, 130, 141, 150, 195, 199
aqueducts, 34, 73, 157–58, 159, 175, 177
Artemis, 22–24, 26–27, 33, 34, 35–36, 37n21, 44, 51, 53–54, 61n77, 62n79, 75, 111, 115, 126–29, 141, 150
Asia, Roman province of
  history and administration, 1–8
  Jewish communities of (*see* Jewish communities)
associations, trade, 44–45, 117–19
athletic competitions, 14, 46, 49–50, 53, 60–61, 71, 87–88
Attalid kingdom. *See* Pergamum, kingdom of
Attalid kings, 3, 83, 98, 100, 106, 113, 138
Attalus I, 83, 85
Attalus II, 3, 85, 101, 138
Attalus III, 3, 85, 123
Augustus (Octavian), 6, 7–10, 11–13, 16–18, 27n21, 32, 33, 37–38, 42, 43, 46, 49, 52, 53, 55, 60, 86–88, 115, 128, 138, 140, 168–74, 199, 204

basilicas, 33, 36, 44, 75–76, 116, 133
baths, 34, 41, 42–43, 49, 60, 99, 101–3, 132–33, 155–56, 159–61, 163, 175, 177, 187, 188
bouleuteria, 36, 75, 135, 156. *See also* odeon

Caesar, Julius, 6–7, 9, 35, 37n21, 169–70
Caligula, 174
castellum aquae, 34, 159
churches, Christian, 64–65, 137, 144, 152, 162–63, 179
Claudius, 16, 17, 18, 44, 47, 54, 87, 125, 128, 174, 177, 203
Colossae, 29, 78, 112n55, 149, 153, 156
Cybele, 50, 51, 57, 69, 95, 129, 135, 141

Demeter, 34, 50, 75, 100, 130, 195
Didyma, 24–25, 31
Dionysus, 50, 69, 91, 99, 102, 129, 141
Domitian, 50, 55–61, 80, 87, 91, 107, 117, 140–41, 145, 149–50, 174, 181, 190–91, 194

earthquakes, 71n11, 74, 124–25, 127, 140, 149, 152, 163, 202
Epaphras, 29, 78–79, 112n55, 149
Ephesus
  geography and demographics, 29–32
  and imperial cult, 55–64
    Artemis Ephesia and Artemision, 31, 35, 42, 50–54
    Temple of Domitian, 55–59, 88, 140, 194
    Temple of Hadrian (Olympieion), 62–63, 65
    Temple of Rome and Augustus, 37–38, 201
  landmarks, 32–50

Eumenes I, 83, 100, 106
Eumenes II, 2, 3, 85, 94, 96–97, 101, 104, 106, 113
exile, 19–20, 21, 28

forum, sacred, 151–52
forums. *See* agoras, civic; agoras, commercial
freedmen, 43, 119, 145

games. *See* athletic competitions
governors, Roman, 5–8, 9, 10, 19–20, 81, 92, 110, 124, 148, 154, 158, 179
graffiti, 37, 76–77
gymnasia, 27–28, 49, 60, 68, 71, 88, 101–3, 107, 113, 130–33, 156, 198

Hadrian, 8, 62–63, 71–72, 90–91, 104, 152, 156, 160, 187n43
harbors, 21, 29, 31, 45–48, 66, 68, 145
Harpocrates, 51, 104, 152
harps, 195
Hestia, 34–35
Hierapolis, 29, 47, 78, 112n55, 149, 153, 156–58, 163–64
hymnodoi, 87
Hyrcanus II, 9, 10

Ignatius of Antioch, 64, 138n5
imperial cult, 8, 13–15, 37–38, 49–50, 55–64, 69–73, 81–82, 86–91, 110, 115–16, 127–29, 138, 140, 149–50, 152, 169–70, 184, 190
Isis, 50–51, 57, 104, 152
isopsephisms, 76–78

Jewish communities, 9–10, 32, 78, 113, 133–37, 138, 148–49
Jewish Revolt, 79–80, 179–88
Jezebel, 25, 119

Koinon Asias, 7, 11, 88, 174, 200

lamps, 64
Laodicea
  history and demographics, 145–50
  and imperial cult, 149–50, 152
  public structures, 152–56
  road network and layout, 145, 147–48
  temples and sacred areas, 150–51
  water system and baths, 156–61, 163
latrines, 42–43, 108
Leto, 26–27
libation bowls (*phialai*), 51, 100, 173, 195, 197, 201
libraries, 68, 97, 108
Livia Augusta, 33, 43, 49, 55, 71, 86n6, 88, 127
Lysimachus, 4, 31, 83

Miletus, 13, 21, 24, 60
Mithridates VI, 4–5, 38
monuments, funerary, 21, 38–39, 41–42

necropoleis (cemeteries), 148
neōkoros, 55n58, 59, 61, 63, 71, 86–91, 103, 116, 128, 132, 141, 150, 151–52
Nero, 15, 16, 27n21, 44, 46, 55n58, 77, 128, 174–81, 186–87, 199n3, 202, 203
Nicolaitans, 112, 119

odeon, 36, 99, 102

Patmos
  geography and demographics, 19–22
  temples of Artemis and Apollo, 22–25
Paul, 29, 48, 54, 78–79, 112n55, 118, 148–49, 166, 172n11
Paullus Fabius Maximus, 11
pax Augusta/Romana, 172
Pergamum, city of
  altar of Zeus and Athena Temple, 93–97
  Asclepion, 105–9, 111
  history, 83, 85–86
  and imperial cult, 55, 61–63, 86–91
  Jewish community, 110
  "Satan's throne," 87, 91, 111–12
  structures on lower acropolis, 98–105
  temple of Dionysus and theater, 98–99
  temple of Roma and Augustus, 12, 55, 86–88, 111, 115–16, 174, 201
  temple of Trajan and Zeus, 62, 85, 89–90, 116
Pergamum, kingdom of, 2–4, 83, 113, 121, 123, 138
Philadelphia
  archaeological and epigraphic record, 141–44
  history and demographics, 138, 140–41
  and imperial cult, 138, 140
Pliny the Younger, 81, 92–93
Polycarp of Smyrna, 79, 81, 144
Priene Calendar Inscription, 11–13, 17
prophecy, 24–26
publicans (*publicani*), 3–4, 6, 8, 46

Res gestae divi Augusti, 174
Revelation, interpretation of, ix–xi, 193–205
Roman imperial ideology, 10–18, 199–204
Rome
  Augustan construction and ideology, 168–74
  center of empire, 165–66
  city of seven hills, 165

economy, 167–68, 192
Flavian developments, 181–92
Neronian developments, 174–81
temple of *Divus Iulius*, 169–70, 172
temple of Jupiter Capitolinus, 80, 189
Royal Road, 32, 121

Sardis
and imperial cult, 124–25, 127–29
civic architecture, 130–33
history and demographics, 121, 123–26
synagogue, 133–37
temple of Artemis, 126–29, 137
Seleucid Empire, 2, 9, 69–70, 83, 85, 113, 121, 123, 145
Seleucus I, 2, 4, 113
Serapis (Sarapis), 50–51, 104, 152
Sextilius Pollio, 33, 34, 35, 39
shops, 38, 44, 76, 99, 136, 147
slaves, 43, 47–48, 53, 92, 183–84, 187, 188
Smyrna
archaeological record, 73–76
graffiti, 76–78
history and literary record, 66–73
and imperial cult, 55, 62, 69–73, 81–82
Jewish and Christian relations in, 78–81
stadia, 49, 74, 81, 105, 130–31, 142–43, 154–55, 191–92
synagogue of Satan, 79–80, 189

temples (general), 112, 115, 150, 154, 196, 199, 200
Antoninus Pius, 127–29
Aphrodite/Venus, 28, 170
Apollo, 24
Artemis (Ephesus), 31, 35, 42, 51–54
Artemis (Patmos), 22
Artemis (Sardis), 126–29, 137
Asclepius, 102, 105, 108
Athena, 95–97
Castor and Pollux, 171–72
Claudius, 176–77
Cybele, 69, 129
Demeter, 100–101
Dionysus, 99, 101
Domitian (Ephesus), 55–59, 88, 140, 194
Domitian (Laodicea), 149–50
Hadrian, 62–63, 65
Hera, 101, 129
Jerusalem, 9, 10, 32, 80, 110, 133, 148, 180, 183–86
Julius (Ephesus), 55
Julius (Rome), 169–70, 172
Jupiter (Rome), 80, 189
Peace, 186
Roma (Smyrna), 69, 71
Rome and Augustus (Aphrodisias), 15–18
Rome and Augustus (Ephesus), 37–38, 201
Rome and Augustus (Pergamum), 12, 55, 86–88, 111, 115–16, 174, 201
Serapis, 50, 104
Tiberius, 71, 88
Trajan, 62, 85, 89–90, 116
Vespasian and Titus, 190
Zeus, 69, 93–95, 111, 127, 143–44, 151–52
temple tax, 79–80, 110, 189
theaters
Ephesus, 37, 48–49
Laodicea, 154–55
Pergamum, 93, 98–99, 105, 108–9
Philadelphia, 143
Sardis, 130–31
Smyrna, 68, 73–74
Thyatira, 115
theologoi, 59
Thyatira
archaeological record, 113–17, 120
history and demographics, 113
and imperial cult, 115–16
and trade guilds, 117–19
Tiberius, 15, 33, 55, 71, 86n6, 88, 124–25, 127, 128, 140, 149, 175, 179
Titus, 49–50, 56, 57, 59, 80, 116–17, 154, 183–85, 187–88, 190
tombs, 39, 42, 47, 108, 174. *See also* monuments; *necropoleis*
town houses, 39–41
trade, 7, 18, 21, 23, 31–32, 47–48, 66, 118, 121, 145, 153–54, 202
Trajan, 8, 62, 81, 85, 89–90, 92–93, 116, 154, 160, 177

Venus, 14, 17, 170–71, 187n43. *See also* Aphrodite
Vespasian, 8, 12, 49, 56, 57, 59n69, 80, 87, 115, 117, 128, 140, 165, 181–82, 186–87, 189–90

wreaths, 11, 16, 81–82, 87, 184, 192, 195

Zeus, 12, 26, 51, 62, 69, 72, 75, 80, 85, 89–90, 93–96, 108–9, 111, 127–29, 134, 141, 143, 145, 151–52

"This is an excellent resource. It takes readers on a visual tour of the places in which Revelation was written and first read, and it immerses them in the cultural context and issues the book addresses. For those wanting a vivid sense of Revelation's setting or who plan to visit the sites themselves, this is an indispensable guide."

—**Craig R. Koester**, Luther Seminary (emeritus)

"This volume complements deSilva's earlier volumes on the archaeology of the world of Jesus and the ministry of Paul. Readers follow the geographical contours of Revelation from the province of Asia to Patmos and each of the seven churches in order. The book concludes, perhaps surprisingly, by traveling to Rome, unnamed but ever-present in John's Apocalypse. Over two hundred photographs and maps amply illustrate the volume, particularly the archaeological remains at each site. DeSilva's guide immerses you in the visual world of John's first audience."

—**Mark Wilson**, director, Asia Minor Research Center, Antalya, Türkiye

"For over two decades deSilva has contributed significantly to the study of John's Apocalypse. This volume is yet another stellar and invaluable guide for reading Revelation. He expertly grounds Revelation in the real-world, first-century context of Asia Minor. Having visited the seven cities of Revelation for nearly two decades, I can confidently say that deSilva masterfully guides readers through the cities and world of Revelation. The color pictures, maps, and explanations make this volume pop and come to life."

—**Alan S. Bandy**, New Orleans Baptist Theological Seminary

"In *Archaeology and the Revelation of John*, the material world of Roman Asia Minor is coherently deciphered to illuminate this apocalyptic text. DeSilva operates like a seasoned tour guide. Even the geographic outline from Patmos to Rome simulates a realistic 'tour experience' designed to interpret the real-world claims of this vital text. Highly recommended!"

—**Ronald Herms**, director, Institute for the Study of Christian Origins (Tübingen)

"This book opens up the seven cities of Revelation's Roman imperial and Jewish contexts. Full-color photos and site plans illustrate this 'grounded' reading of Revelation, exploring landscapes of Türkiye and the island of Patmos. The chapter on recently excavated Laodicea is especially helpful, as is the chapter on Smyrna."

—**Barbara Rossing**, author of *The Rapture Exposed: The Message of Hope in the Book of Revelation*

"An indispensable companion for readers interested in the history and meaning of John's Apocalypse. Complete with color pictures and the latest historical scholarship, here is a much-welcomed update to the works of Ramsay and Hemer."

—**Jason Borges**, Asia Minor Research Center, Antalya, Türkiye

"This great book offers a compelling exploration of John's Revelation through the lens of archaeology, bringing ancient contexts vividly to life. By weaving together historical evidence and thoughtful interpretation, deSilva deepens the reader's understanding of one of the Bible's most complex texts. Both scholarly and accessible, this book invites readers to see Revelation not as a mystery but as a message rooted in real places, cultures, and discoveries."

—**Cenk Eronat**, vice president, TUTKU Educational Travel

ARCHAEOLOGY AND THE NEW TESTAMENT

Archaeology and the Ministry of Paul

Archaeology and the World of Jesus

Archaeology and the Revelation of John